Dough Magic!

D0689932

Dough Magic!

Turn Refrigerated Dough into
Hundreds of Tasty Family Favorites!

BY THE PILLSBURY EDITORS

Clarkson Potter/Publishers
New York

ALSO BY PILLSBURY®

Pillsbury: Best Chicken Cookbook
Pillsbury: Best Cookies Cookbook
Pillsbury: Best Muffins & Quick Breads Cookbook
Pillsbury: Best of the Bake-Off® Cookbook
Pillsbury: Fast and Healthy® Cookbook
Pillsbury: Best Desserts
Pillsbury: The Best of Classic® Cookbooks
Pillsbury: One-Dish Meals Cookbook
Pillsbury: Complete Cookbook
Pillsbury: 30-Minute Meals
Pillsbury Doughboy™: Family Pleasing Recipes
Pillsbury: Appetizers
Pillsbury Doughboy™: Slow Cooker Recipes

For more great recipes, visit www.pillsbury.com.

Front cover photograph: Grands!® Strawberry Shortcakes,
   page 268
Back cover photographs (from top to bottom): Individual
   Chicken Pot Pies, page 227; Mexican Beef 'n Bean
   Pizza, page 163; Easy Crescent Dogs™, page 141;
   Cinnamon-Pecan Pull Apart, page 99
Frontis photograph: Individual Chicken Pot Pies, page 227

Copyright © 2003 by General Mills, Inc.,
Minneapolis, Minnesota

All rights reserved. No part of this book may be reproduced
or transmitted in any form or by any means, electronic or
mechanical, including photocopying, recording, or by any
information storage and retrieval system, without permis-
sion in writing from the publisher.

Published by Clarkson Potter/Publishers,
New York, New York.
Member of the Crown Publishing Group,
a division of Random House, Inc.
www.randomhouse.com

The trademarks referred to herein are trademarks of
The Pillsbury Company or its affiliates.

CLARKSON N. POTTER is a trademark and POTTER and
colophon are registered trademarks of Random House, Inc.

Printed in China

Library of Congress Cataloging-in-Publication Data
Pillsbury: dough magic! : turn refrigerated dough into
hundreds of tasty family favorites! / The Pillsbury Editors
   p.   cm.
Includes index
1. Baking.   I. Pillsbury Company.
   TX769 .P523   2003
   641.8'15—dc21   2003004753

ISBN 0-609-60863-0

10 9 8 7 6 5 4 3 2 1

First edition

CREDITS
GENERAL MILLS, INC.
Director, Book and Electronic Publishing: Kim Walter
Manager, Book Publishing: Lois Tlusty
Editor: Kelly Kilen
Recipe Development and Testing: Pillsbury Test Kitchens
Photography: General Mills Photo Studios
   and Image Center

CLARKSON POTTER/PUBLISHERS
THE CROWN PUBLISHING GROUP
President: Jenny Frost
Senior Vice President/Publisher: Lauren Shakely
Vice President/Executive Editor/Director of Cookbook
Program: Pam Krauss
Editorial Assistant: Adina Steiman
Creative Director: Marysarah Quinn
Designer: Caitlin Daniels Israel
Managing Editor: Amy Boorstein
Associate Managing Editor: Mark McCauslin
Senior Production Editor: Sibylle Kazeroid
Production Supervisor: Linnea Knollmueller
Director of Publicity: Leigh Ann Ambrosi

Contents

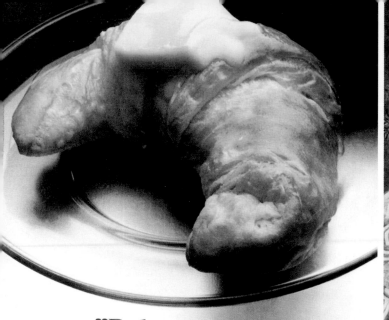

"Bake a good impression tonight."

Bake Pillsbury Crescent Rolls.
When the butter's still melting
on the roll, and the roll's melting
in your mouth, that's magic.

Bake the magic of Poppin' Fresh Dough.

Cookie Ideas Gal

Make them all with Pillsb
Refrigerated Holiday Cook

America's new way to bake (from

Pillsbury Holiday Cookie Kit

Holiday kit contains 2 packages
ated cookie dough—all mixed, ready to us
free stencil decorator and 25 cookie trimmin
Choose from four wonderful flavors: Butt
Nut, Toasted Coconut, Peanut or Sugar C

Pillsbury Slice 'n' Bake Cookies

Just slice, bake, decorate—get
dozen beautiful cookies from each kit.

So easy! For delicious Holiday Co
pretty as these—hurry...

Get Pillsbury's Holiday Cookie
AT YOUR GROCER'S DAI
where you find America's
most popular biscuits

NEW
Pillsb
REFRIGE
FOOD

♪ *Nothing says lovin' like something from*
the oven...and Pillsbury says it best!

(Available in Canada too!)

SCRATCH QUALITY. IT'S EASY AS...

PILLSBURY PIE CRUSTS

PILLSBURY
REFRIGERATED
PIE CRUST.

SIMPLY
UNFOLD,

FILL,

AND
BAKE.

NO ROOM FOR IMPROVEMENT

Grands! When your biscuits have 100% real buttermilk and Pillsbury's best fl
it's tough to make them any better. So we made them bigger. Pillsbur
Grands! Biscuits. Our biggest, fluffiest, most delicious biscuits ever.

Introduction: Dough—From Flour Barrel to Refrigerator

TOP LEFT: Warm crescent dinner rolls are never out of style—not in 1979 and not today.

TOP RIGHT: Cookie kits made holiday baking extra easy in 1960.

BOTTOM LEFT: In the '80s, you could definitely do "your own thing" by making pies the easy way.

BOTTOM RIGHT: One thing is for sure— in 1993, hungry appetites had more biscuit to love!

Long before the wizardry of "dough-in-a-can" came to supermarkets everywhere, The Pillsbury Company began with its roots in the flour milling business. In 1875, Pillsbury registered the familiar barrelhead with *"Pillsbury's BEST XXXX"* to indicate superior quality. As times changed throughout the nation, the need increased for new products like refrigerated dough to help meet the demands of busy homemakers. Thus, a new era of convenient, easy-to-use, homemade-tasting products was born.

In 1951, the biscuit and subsequent refrigerated dough revolution started when The Pillsbury Company purchased the Ballard and Ballard Company. Ballard's "Oven Ready Biscuits" offered a unique product that greatly simplified the way Americans baked. What made refrigerated biscuits so special? They were fast, easy, required no rolling or kneading and didn't leave a mess to clean up! You could just open the can, then bake and enjoy tender, delicious biscuits with "made-from-scratch" flavor. There are more than 2.5 billion refrigerated biscuits sold each year—now, that's a lot of lovin' from the oven!

Americans wanted more convenient products with a home-baked touch to share with their families. The jolly, giggling Doughboy™ made his television debut showcasing Crescent Dinner Rolls in 1965. The whimsical Doughboy™, himself a piece of dough, popped out of a can and came to life wearing a baker's hat and scarf. His commercials are famous for telling us "Nothin' Says Lovin' Like Something from the Oven," "Pillsbury Says It Best," "Mmm, Ahh, Ohh Poppin' Fresh™ Dough" and most recently, "My Heart to Yours." Look for the Doughboy Tip with many of the recipes.

Pillsbury has continued to meet the demand for more convenience by creating many wonderful and tasty refrigerated dough products. Cookies, pizza crust, pie crust and breadsticks are just some of the products in the lineup that help make our lives easier. Now in the new millennium, a line of frozen "ready-to-bake" dough products such as dinner rolls, sweet rolls and chocolate chip cookies has been introduced. These products are quickly becoming kitchen staples requested by family members again and again.

what everyone wants to know

Nothing beats a fresh, warm, delicious treat from the oven, and dough products like biscuits, breadsticks, crusty French loaf, pizza crust and crescent dinner rolls are the way to go. Here are answers to commonly asked questions about dough products to help you get the best-tasting recipes ever.

Q: How long can I store an unopened can of dough?

A: For the best quality, use refrigerated dough products before the "use-by" date on the package.

Q: Where should I store the dough?

A: Store refrigerated dough on a shelf in the refrigerator. Temperatures in the refrigerator crisper or in the door may be too warm or too cold. Keep dough refrigerated until you're ready to use it. Warm dough may be sticky and hard to handle.

Q: What if I forget to refrigerate the dough?

A: For food safety reasons, cans of refrigerated dough left unrefrigerated for more than 2 hours should be thrown away.

Q: Can I use some of the dough now and save some for later?

A: No, because opening the can activates the leavening that causes the dough to rise. However, once the can is open, the dough can be covered with plastic wrap and refrigerated for up to 2 hours before baking.

Chill out, slow down and simplify. But nobody said to skip dessert in the '90s!

Q: Can I freeze the unbaked dough?

A: No, freezing unbaked refrigerated dough may darken it and prevent it from rising during baking.

Q: Can I microwave the unbaked dough?

A: In general the answer to this is no because the uneven cooking pattern of a microwave prevents the dough from browning and may result in some underbaked portions of dough. However, there are a few instances where recipes have been specifically tested for the microwave and these are okay to use.

Q: Can I bake the dough in a toaster oven?

A: We recommend not using a toaster oven because the

America's new way to bake
(from Pillsbury)

3 TO 4 DOZEN PERFECT COOKIES FROM EVERY PACKAGE!   1. COOKIE PETAL SUNDAE CUPS

NEW! 3 cool dessert ideas from

Kissin' cousins of America's most popular biscuits ... *at your grocer's dairy case!*

small size often results in uneven heating and the dough may burn.

Q: Do I need to preheat the oven?

A: Yes, preheat the oven for 10 minutes or until the desired temperature is reached. This important step will help prevent the dough from baking unevenly.

Q: Can I freeze baked dough products?

A: Yes! For freshest flavor, wrap tightly and use within one month after freezing.

beautiful biscuits

Q: Can I make the biscuit dough flatter?

A: Yes, to flatten biscuits, pat them out by hand or roll them out with a rolling pin. For biscuit crusts or other recipes, slightly overlap the edges of the dough, pressing edges together to seal.

Q: Can I use the dough to top casseroles or fruit cobblers?

A: Yes, when topping casseroles or cobblers, place the biscuit dough on a hot filling to ensure the dough bakes completely. When baked on a filling, biscuits may be moist (but not doughy), even when completely done.

Q: Can I assemble my recipe ahead of time and bake it later?

A: Yes, recipes can be prepared up to 2 hours before baking. Cover the dish with plastic wrap and refrigerate. Remove plastic wrap before baking.

QUICK AND EASY FIX-UPS

For variety you may want to try adding one of these quick toppings before baking or add a simple spread after baking. All recipes make enough for 8 biscuits.

Before Baking Brush-Ons

Mix one of the following in a small bowl. Brush over biscuits and bake as directed on package.

GARLIC BRUSH-ON

1 tablespoon melted margarine, butter or olive oil
⅛ teaspoon garlic powder

HERB BRUSH-ON

1 tablespoon melted margarine, butter or olive oil
½ teaspoon dried basil, oregano, Italian seasoning or crushed rosemary leaves

ITALIAN BRUSH-ON

1 tablespoon melted margarine, butter or olive oil
1 tablespoon grated Parmesan cheese
¼ teaspoon dried Italian seasoning

Before Baking Sprinkles

Mix one of the following sprinkles in a small bowl. Sprinkle evenly over biscuits and bake as directed on package.

CRACKED PEPPER AND CHEESE SPRINKLE

¼ cup shredded mozzarella or Parmesan cheese
⅛ teaspoon cracked black pepper

PARSLEY-CHEDDAR SPRINKLE

¼ cup shredded Cheddar cheese
¼ teaspoon dried parsley flakes

CINNAMON AND SUGAR SPRINKLE

1 tablespoon sugar
⅛ teaspoon cinnamon

SEED SPRINKLE

1 teaspoon caraway seed or poppy seed
1 teaspoon sesame seed

creative crescents

Q: Where do I store crescent rolls in the refrigerator?

A: Crescents and other refrigerated dough products should be stored on a shelf in the main parts of the refrigerator. Temperatures in the refrigerator's door shelves or crisper may be too warm or too cold.

Q: Can I enlarge the unbaked dough pieces?

A: Yes, to enlarge dough rectangles or triangles, pat out by hand or roll out with a rolling pin.

Q: What is the best way to seal the unbaked dough seams and perforations?

A: The best way to seal the seams and perforations is by pressing the edges of dough together with fingertips. This prevents any filling from leaking out during baking.

Q: Can I use the dough to top casseroles or fruit cobblers?

A: Yes, when topping casseroles or cobblers, place the crescent dough on a hot filling to ensure the dough bakes completely.

Q: Can I assemble my recipe ahead of time and bake it later?

A: Yes, recipes can be prepared up to 2 hours before baking. Cover the dish with plastic wrap and refrigerate. Remove plastic wrap before baking.

EXTRA-SPECIAL CRESCENTS

Turn simple to extraordinary—make your crescent rolls extra-special by adding an extra-easy topping.

Brush With

BEFORE BAKING

- Beaten whole egg or egg white
- Caesar or Italian dressing
- Milk

AFTER BAKING

- Caesar or Italian dressing
- Honey
- Maple syrup
- Melted margarine or butter
- Olive oil

After Baking, Brush with Melted Margarine or Butter and Sprinkle With

- Cinnamon and sugar
- Coarse salt
- Cornmeal
- Crushed chips (corn chips, potato chips or tortilla chips)
- Crushed dried herbs
- Finely chopped fresh herbs
- Grated Parmesan cheese
- Finely chopped nuts
- Seasoned dry bread crumbs or crushed croutons
- Seeds (caraway, mustard, poppy or sesame)
- Seasoned powders (chili powder, garlic powder or onion powder)
- Seasoned salts (garlic salt, onion salt or seasoned salt)
- Taco seasoning

fabulous pies

Q: How long can I store an unopened box of pie crust?

A: For best quality, use before the "use-by" date on the package.

Q: Can I freeze the unbaked pie crust?

A: Yes, unbaked crusts can be frozen for up to 2 months if placed in the freezer before the "use-by" date.

Q: Can I use the crust in different size pans or use it to make other shapes?

A: Our pie crusts are designed for 8- or 9-inch pie pans and 10-inch tart pans, but they can also be used to make other same-size shapes. However, rolling the crusts larger or stretching them as you put them into the pan can cause shrinkage during baking.

Q: What type of pie pan do you recommend?

A: We recommend glass or dull metal pie pans. Shiny metal or disposable aluminum pans reflect heat and prevent the crust from browning. Dark pans may cause the crust to brown too much.

Easy as pie.   Ditto.   Same.

This 1991 ad shows that making pretty pies is really "as easy as pie."

Q: How can I prevent the pie crust from pulling away from the pan?

A: Press the crust firmly against the sides and bottom of the pie pan. By "anchoring" the crust to the pan, it won't pull away from the pan during baking.

Q: How can I prevent an unfilled crust from puffing up while it bakes?

A: Before baking an unfilled crust, generously prick the sides and bottom of crust with a fork. Pricking allows the steam to escape.

Q: How long should I cool pies before serving?

A: Cool dessert pies on a cooling rack at least 2 hours before cutting. Cool main dish pies and quiches 10 minutes before cutting.

Q: What is the best way to cut a pie after it's baked or prepared?

A: Cut the pie with a sharp, thin-bladed knife. When cutting meringue or ice cream pies, dip the knife in warm water to prevent sticking.

Q: How should I store my pie?

A: All pies containing eggs and dairy products must be stored in the refrigerator. All other pies can be stored at room temperature.

TERRIFIC TOP CRUSTS

Add a finishing touch to the top of two-crust pies by using one of the methods below before baking. Watch carefully while baking. If the crust is getting too brown, place a sheet of foil loosely on top of the pie to stop the browning.

- For a **Shiny Crust,** brush with milk.
- For a **Sugared Crust,** brush with water or milk and sprinkle with granulated sugar.
- For a **Glazed Crust,** brush with beaten whole egg or egg white.

For a baked two-crust pie, a **Sweet Glaze** can be added. Combine ½ cup powdered sugar and 2 to 3 teaspoons milk. Drizzle over completely cooled pie.

BAKE THE BEST PIE

Great pie crust should be golden brown, crisp with a brown undercrust, tender, flaky and cut nicely. Here are some solutions to common pie crust problems.

If This Happens	Try This
Unbaked pie crust cracks	Bring the crust to room temperature before using.
	Refrigerated crusts can be softened in the microwave. Follow the directions on the package.
	Do not microwave frozen crusts. The uneven heat of a microwave may melt some parts of the crust.
	Mend any cracks by wetting your fingers with cold water, pressing the edges of the crack together. Repairing cracks before baking reduces the chance of the crust cracking again during baking.
Crust edge gets too brown during baking	Cover the edge of the crust with strips of foil after the first 15 to 20 minutes of baking.
Bottom crust gets soggy	Use an oven temperature of 400°F. or above.
	Bake the pie on a preheated cookie sheet.
	For a two-crust pie, brush the bottom crust with a beaten egg white before filling.
	For a one-crust pie, bake the crust for 3 to 5 minutes before adding the filling.
	Cool the baked pie on a cooling rack.
Pie filling bubbles over the crust	Place a piece of foil on the lowest oven rack to catch the spills. This method is recommended for baking fruit and main dish pies.

pizza with pizzazz!

Q: Do I need to bake the crust before adding the toppings?

A: It is not necessary. However, prebaking the crust will result in a crisper crust. Bake the untopped crust at 400°F. for 7 minutes. Add toppings and continue baking for an additional 6 to 11 minutes.

Q: Can the pizza be baked on a baking stone or pizza stone?

A: The pizza crust may be baked on a stone that doesn't require preheating. Follow the directions that came with the stone for the correct baking time and temperature.

EASY HOMEMADE PIZZA

With Pillsbury® Refrigerated Pizza Crust, it's easy to make hot, delicious homemade pizza.

Choose Your Sauce	Add One or More Toppings
Barbecue sauce	Strips of deli roast beef or chicken
	Red onion rings
	Chopped green bell pepper
	Shredded Cheddar or Monterey Jack cheese
Alfredo sauce	Cooked, cubed chicken or shrimp
	Crisply cooked bacon
	Sliced green onions or olives
	Canned sliced mushrooms
	Shredded mozzarella or Parmesan cheese
Deli spinach dip	Quartered artichoke hearts
	Sliced water chestnuts
	Strips of red bell pepper
	Shredded Asiago, mozzarella or Parmesan cheese

cookie magic

In the '60s, America's "cool" new way to bake was to "slice and bake."

Pillsbury Slice'n Bake Cookies

MAKE THEM ALL! Create these 3 exciting cool desserts with any of Pillsbury's Slice'n Bake Cookies:
• Butterscotch Nut   • Crunchy Peanut
• Toasted Coconut   • Sugar Cookies
Fresh cookie dough all mixed, shaped, refrigerated. Just slice and bake!

Q: Can I use this dough in a cookie press?

A: No, our cookie dough is too firm to use in a cookie press.

Q: Is the raw cookie dough safe to eat?

A: Yes, our cookie dough is safe to eat because the eggs we use are dried and pasteurized. However, it was designed to be baked first, then eaten. We don't recommend the habit of eating any raw cookie dough because not all dough is made with pasteurized eggs or the dough may not have been refrigerated properly.

Q: When should I add decorations (sprinkles, colored sugar, etc.) to the cookies?

A: There are two ways to add decorations to your cookies. Sprinkle cookies with decorations before baking. Or spread your favorite frosting on cooled, baked cookies and decorate as desired.

Q: Can I add food color to the sugar cookie dough?

A: Yes, liquid or paste color can be used. Allow the dough to soften for up to 30 minutes at room temperature. Add 6 to 8 drops liquid color or dip end of toothpick into small amount of paste color and add to the dough; work it into the dough until the color is well blended. If more color is needed, add small amounts at a time. Shape the dough into a log; wrap tightly in plastic wrap. Refrigerate until firm, about 3 hours. Spoon, shape or roll the dough and bake as directed on the package.

Q: Can I add extra ingredients to the dough (candy, nuts, raisins, chocolate chips, coconut, etc.)?

A: Yes. First, break up the cookie dough in a large bowl. Then, add the desired ingredients and mix well. Drop the dough by teaspoonfuls onto ungreased cookie sheets. Bake as directed on the package.

Q: Can I roll the chocolate chip dough, or flavors other than the sugar cookie dough, and cut it with cookie cutters?

A: No, the chips, chunks or nuts would make rolling and cutting difficult. And, because of how these ingredients bake, the shapes might end up distorted.

Q: What is the best way to cut cookie dough so it doesn't crumble?

A: Slice the chilled dough with a serrated knife, sawing gently back and forth rather than pushing the knife through the dough. Give the roll of dough a slight turn after cutting each cookie to prevent the roll from flattening.

Q: Are there high altitude directions for your cookies?

A: No changes are necessary for baking our cookies at high altitude.

Q: Can I microwave the dough instead of baking the cookies in the oven?

A: No, the uneven cooking pattern of a microwave prevents the dough from browning and baking evenly.

Q: Can I bake these cookies in a toaster oven?

A: No, the uneven heating of a toaster oven may cause the cookies to burn.

Q: Can I bake these cookies in a convection oven?

A: Yes; follow the owner's manual guidelines that came with your oven.

Q: What type of cookie sheet do you recommend?

A: For best results, we recommend shiny aluminum cookie sheets for even baking and delicate browning. Dark finishes may cause cookies to brown more quickly whereas cookies baked on insulated pans will not brown as much on the bottom, making it more difficult to tell when cookies are done.

Q: What should I do if my cookies stick to the cookie sheet?

A: If the cookies cool too long or are difficult to remove, reheat the sheet of cookies in the oven for 1 minute, then immediately remove from the sheet.

Q: Which oven rack do I use?

A: Use the center rack of your oven for even baking.

Q: Do I need to preheat the oven?

A: Yes, preheat the oven for 10 minutes before baking. This important step helps the cookies bake evenly.

Q: How long can I store the unopened dough?

A: For best quality, use the cookie dough before the "use-by" date on the package.

Q: Can I use some of the dough now and save some for later?

A: Yes, rewrap the unused portion and refrigerate or freeze it for later use. Once opened, the dough should be used within 1 week.

Q: Can I freeze the unopened dough?

A: Our refrigerated cookie dough may be frozen for up to 2 months if frozen before the "use-by" date printed on the package. To thaw, place in the refrigerator overnight. Once opened, the dough should be used within 1 week.

GOOD AND EASY COOKIES

Get to the fun faster with Pillsbury® Refrigerated Cookies. Each easy-to-use soft roll of dough is ready for a little magic using one of three ways to get cookies in shape.

Start With

- 1 (20-oz.) pkg. Pillsbury® Refrigerated Sugar Cookies
- Colored decorator sugars or candy sprinkles, if desired
- Tinted frosting, decorating bag and tips, if desired
- Assorted candies or tinted coconut, if desired

ROLL AND CUT OUT

Generously sprinkle about ¼ cup flour onto work surface. Coat sides of dough with flour. Roll out dough to ⅛-inch thickness using additional flour as necessary to prevent sticking. Cut rolled dough into shapes with cookie cutters dipped in flour, keeping shapes very close together when cutting. Gently remove excess flour from cookies. Carefully remove any excess dough from around cookies. Shape excess dough into a ball, refrigerate until thoroughly chilled and reroll.

Gently lift cut-out cookies; place 2 inches apart on a cool, ungreased cookie sheet. Decorate later or sprinkle with colored decorator sugar or candy sprinkles.

Bake at 350°F. for 7 to 9 minutes or until light golden brown. Cool 1 minute; remove from cookie sheet with spatula. Cool completely, then decorate as desired.

SLICE AND SHAPE

Slice dough into ¼-inch slices to form shapes as shown at left. Handle dough as little as possible so that it doesn't become sticky. Place shapes 2 inches apart on a cool ungreased cookie sheet. Decorate later or sprinkle with colored decorator sugar or candy sprinkles.

Bake at 350°F. for 7 to 12 minutes or until light golden brown. Cool 1 minute; remove from cookie sheet with spatula. Cool completely, then decorate as desired.

SPOON AND SHAPE

Spoon dough from wrapper, then roll into balls or rolls to form shapes as shown at left. Handle dough as little as possible so that it doesn't become sticky. Place balls for shapes ¼ inch apart; place shapes 2 inches apart on a cool, ungreased cookie sheet.

Bake at 350°F. for 7 to 12 minutes or until light golden brown. Cool 1 minute; remove from cookie sheet with spatula. Cool completely, then decorate as desired.

best breadsticks!

Pillsbury® Refrigerated Breadsticks add a "wow" not only to spaghetti night but also to many other meal occasions. Here are just a few ideas for brushing, dipping or spreading Garlic, Parmesan or Soft Breadsticks after they're baked.

Add Some Flavor

BRUSH WITH

- Caesar or Italian salad dressing
- Olive oil
- Melted margarine or butter
- Honey (soft breadsticks)
- Maple syrup (soft breadsticks)

DIP IN

- Alfredo sauce
- Cheese fondue or cheese sauce
- Dips (onion, dill or spinach)
- Guacamole
- Marinara, pizza or spaghetti sauce
- Olive oil and shredded Parmesan cheese
- Ranch or blue cheese salad dressing
- Salsa

SPREAD WITH

- Flavored cream cheese
- Honey mustard
- Hummus
- Pesto
- Processed cheese spreads

easy french bread

Start with Pillsbury® Refrigerated Crusty French Loaf, then follow one of these easy recipes and get ready for rave reviews.

Crusty Garlic Bread

Heat oven to 350°F. Place dough, seam side down, on sprayed or greased cookie sheet. Slash top of dough as directed on package. In small bowl, combine 1 tablespoon melted margarine or butter and ¼ teaspoon garlic salt. Brush over dough. Bake at 350°F. for 26 to 30 minutes or until deep golden brown. Remove from cookie sheet and cool 5 minutes.

Parmesan Bread

Heat oven to 350°F. Place dough, seam side down, on sprayed or greased cookie sheet. Slash top of dough as directed on package. In small bowl, combine 2 tablespoons grated Parmesan cheese and ½ teaspoon crushed dried Italian seasoning. Brush top of dough with 1 tablespoon olive oil; sprinkle with cheese mixture. Bake at 350°F. for 28 to 33 minutes or until deep golden brown.

cinnamon roll creations

Q: What is the best type of pan to use for baking refrigerated sweet rolls?

A: For the best results, use a greased, round cake pan. If using a gray nonstick or dark pan, reduce the oven temperature by 25 degrees.

Something Special

When the occasion calls for something sweet and special, we've got you covered with Pillsbury® Refrigerated Cinnamon Rolls with Icing and three simple recipes.

Flutter-By Buns

Heat oven to 400°F. Separate one (12.4-oz.) can Pillsbury® Refrigerated Cinnamon Rolls with Icing into 8 rolls. Cut each roll in half crosswise. Place 2 halves with rounded edges touching to form butterfly shape on greased cookie sheet; flatten slightly. Bake at 400°F. for 11 to 17 minutes or until golden brown.

"Try my new Pillsbury Swirls."

"The prettiest hot rolls that ever came to dinner."

"Poppin' Fresh," the Pillsbury Dough Boy, has a fondness for fresh, hot, home-baked dinner rolls.

But (being notoriously softhearted) he doesn't think they should be a lot of bother for you.

That's why he's so tickled over his new Swirls.

All you do is: (1) Pop open the Poppin' Fresh Dough. (2) Bake.

You get eight light, tender, golden, flaky, perfectly lovely, swirly-peaked rolls. In minutes. Fresh and hot from the oven.

The Dough Boy isn't one for making outlandish claims. But he says new Swirls make fresh home baking prettier and easier than ever.

Being a Dough Boy, he ought to know.

SWIRLS 8 QUICK DINNER ROLLS

Poppin' Fresh Dough. In the dairy case.

Even the Doughboy thought these Swirls were "groovy" in 1966. The new shape made dinner rolls prettier and easier than ever.

Remove stems from 16 stemmed maraschino cherries. At top of each "butterfly" where "antennae" would be, make 2 small holes with toothpick; insert 2 cherry stems into each roll. Remove lid from icing, microwave on HIGH for 10 to 15 seconds or until of drizzling consistency. Drizzle icing over rolls; decorate with cherries. Serve warm. Makes 8 rolls.

Teddy Bear Rolls

Heat oven to 350°F. Separate 1 (1 lb. 1.5-oz.) can Pillsbury® Refrigerated Cinnamon Rolls with Icing into 5 rolls. Place 4 rolls in center of greased 9-inch square pan, sides lightly touching. Unroll remaining dough; cut into 8 pieces. Bend each piece into U-shape to form ear. On edge of each roll, press 2 "ears" on side facing corners of pan; tuck dough ends under and pinch to attach. Bake at 350°F. for 25 to 29 minutes or until golden brown. Carefully remove from pan; cool on wire rack. Separate into 4 rolls.

Reserve 1 tablespoon icing. Spread remaining icing over each hot roll. For each roll, arrange 2 raisins for eyes and 1 small heart-shaped candy in center for nose. Combine reserved 1 tablespoon icing, powdered sugar and 10 drops red food color; mix well. Spoon icing into small resealable food storage plastic bag; seal bag. Cut tiny hole in one bottom corner of bag. Pipe icing to complete nose and mouth and into center of each ear. Makes 4 rolls.

Cinnamon Roll Wreath

Heat oven to 375°F. Separate 1 (12.4-oz.) can Pillsbury® Refrigerated Cinnamon Rolls with Icing into 8 rolls; place in a circle, sides touching, on ungreased large cookie sheet to form wreath. Bake for 12 to 14 minutes or until golden brown.

Meanwhile, add green food color to icing; blend well. Carefully remove warm wreath from cookie sheet; place on serving plate or tray. Cool slightly. Spread green icing over wreath. Decorate each roll with 3 candied cherry halves. Makes 8 servings.

frozen rolls and biscuits

Q: I accidentally put my bag of frozen rolls in the refrigerator—what should I do?

A: Frozen sweet rolls stored in the refrigerator for more than 24 hours should be thrown away because they will stick together and may not rise.

Q: Which oven rack do I use?

A: Use the center rack of your oven for even baking.

QUICK FIX-UPS

Have warm-from-the-oven baked treats on your table in a flash! Bake the desired number of Pillsbury® Home Baked Classics™ Frozen Biscuits, Dinner Rolls or Sweet Rolls, then add a final flourish.

Biscuits and Dinner Rolls

BRUSH WITH

- Honey
- Maple Syrup
- Melted margarine or butter
- Olive oil

BRUSH WITH OLIVE OIL, MELTED MARGARINE OR BUTTER AND SPRINKLE WITH

- Chopped fresh or crushed dried herbs
- Garlic powder or garlic salt
- Grated Parmesan cheese
- Seeds (caraway, mustard, poppy or sesame)

Sweet Rolls

SPRINKLE WITH

- Candy sprinkles
- Chocolate shot
- Chopped nuts
- Coconut
- Miniature chocolate chips

Index of Recipes by Product

Doughboy Recommends

chapter 1
Inviting
Appetizers
and Snacks

CRESCENT-WRAPPED BRIE, page 62

taco crescent stars

PREP TIME: 40 minutes
YIELD: 12 appetizers

12 paper baking cups

1 (8-oz.) can Pillsbury®
Refrigerated Crescent Dinner Rolls

¼ lb. lean ground beef

1 tablespoon taco seasoning mix
(from 1.25-oz. pkg.)

1 tablespoon cream cheese

1 tablespoon water

1½ oz. (⅓ cup) shredded
Cheddar-Monterey Jack
cheese blend

¼ cup crushed tortilla chips

½ cup chunky-style salsa

⅓ cup sour cream

1 tablespoon chopped
green onions

1. Heat oven to 375°F. Flatten paper baking cups; lightly spray with nonstick cooking spray. Separate dough into 4 rectangles. Firmly press perforations to seal. Press each to form 6x4-inch rectangle.

2. Cut each rectangle into 3 smaller rectangles. With tip of sharp knife, cut small triangle from short sides of each rectangle. Place rectangle on sprayed paper baking cup. Place triangles on either side of rectangle. Press dough together to seal, forming 6-point star. Place each in ungreased muffin cup. Bake at 375°F. for 11 to 13 minutes or until golden brown.

3. Meanwhile, brown ground beef in small skillet over medium-high heat for 3 to 4 minutes or until thoroughly cooked, stirring frequently. Drain. Add taco seasoning mix, cream cheese and water; mix well. Cook and stir over low heat until thoroughly heated and cream cheese is melted.

4. Remove crescent stars from oven. Fill each star with scant tablespoon beef mixture. Top each with cheese and tortilla chips. Cover with foil. Return to oven; bake an additional 4 to 6 minutes or until cheese is melted.

5. To serve, remove from baking cups. Top each with 1 teaspoon salsa, 1 teaspoon sour cream and green onions. Serve warm.

NUTRITION INFORMATION PER SERVING: **Serving Size:** 1 Appetizer; Calories 130; Calories from Fat 70 **% Daily Value:** Total Fat 8g 12%; Saturated Fat 3g 15%; Cholesterol 15mg 5%; Sodium 330mg 14%; Total Carbohydrate 10g 3%; Dietary Fiber 0g 0%; Sugars 2g; Protein 4g; Vitamin A 4%; Vitamin C 0%; Calcium 4%; Iron 4% **Dietary Exchanges:** ½ Starch, ½ Medium-Fat Meat, 1 Fat **OR** ½ Carbohydrate, ½ Medium-Fat Meat, 1 Fat **Carbohydrate Choices:** ½

doughboy tip

Add a five-star finish to these spicy snacks by topping with shredded lettuce, sliced ripe olives, chopped tomato and mild or hot chopped chiles.

castle burger bites

PREP TIME: 25 minutes (Ready in 45 minutes)
YIELD: 48 appetizers

BUNS

1 (11-oz.) can Pillsbury®
Refrigerated Breadsticks

FILLING

1 egg

3 tablespoons dried minced onion

2 tablespoons milk

1 tablespoon Worcestershire sauce

½ teaspoon salt

⅛ teaspoon pepper

½ cup unseasoned dry
bread crumbs

1 lb. lean ground beef

1. Heat oven to 375°F. Separate dough into 12 breadsticks; cut each into 4 pieces. Place on ungreased cookie sheet.

2. Bake at 375°F. for 10 to 12 minutes or until lightly browned. Immediately remove from cookie sheet; place on wire racks. Cool 5 minutes or until slightly cooled. Split each in half, keeping tops and bottoms together to form miniature buns.

3. Reduce oven temperature to 350°F. Beat egg in medium bowl. Add onion, milk, Worcestershire sauce, salt and pepper. Stir in bread crumbs. Add ground beef; mix well. Press beef mixture into thin layer in bottom of ungreased 13x9-inch pan.

4. Bake at 350°F. for 14 to 16 minutes or until thoroughly cooked.

5. To serve, cut cooked beef into 48 rectangles (8 strips crosswise and 6 strips lengthwise). Fill buns with miniature burgers. Serve immediately.

NUTRITION INFORMATION PER SERVING: **Serving Size:** 1 Appetizer; Calories 50; Calories from Fat 20 **% Daily Value:** Total Fat 2g 3%; Saturated Fat 1g 5%; Cholesterol 10mg 3%; Sodium 90mg 4%; Total Carbohydrate 4g 1%; Dietary Fiber 0g 0%; Sugars 1g; Protein 3g; Vitamin A 0%; Vitamin C 0%; Calcium 0%; Iron 2% **Dietary Exchanges:** ½ Starch OR ½ Carbohydrate **Carbohydrate Choices:** 0

doughboy tip

Create a crunchy topping by pressing sesame seed or poppy seed into the tops of some or all of the buns before baking. At serving time, set out dishes of ketchup and mustard for dipping the bite-sized burgers.

grands!® meatball pops

PREP TIME: 30 minutes
YIELD: 10 appetizers

1 (10.2-oz.) can (5 biscuits)
Pillsbury® Grands!® Refrigerated
Southern Style or
Buttermilk Biscuits

1⅓ oz. (⅓ cup) shredded
Monterey Jack or Cheddar cheese

10 refrigerated or frozen cooked
beef meatballs, thawed

¼ cup margarine or butter, melted

⅔ cup finely crushed seasoned
croutons

10 large appetizer picks or
lollipop sticks, if desired

1. Heat oven to 375°F. Line cookie sheet with parchment paper
   or spray with nonstick cooking spray. Separate dough into
   5 biscuits. With serrated knife, cut each biscuit in half horizontally to make 10 rounds. Press out each biscuit half to
   form 3-inch round.

2. Sprinkle each biscuit round with cheese to within ½ inch of
   edge. Top each with meatball. Bring up sides of dough over
   meatball; pinch edges to seal. Brush rounded tops and sides
   of dough with margarine; coat with croutons. Place seam
   side down on paper-lined cookie sheet.

3. Bake at 375°F. for 10 to 15 minutes or until golden brown.

4. To serve, place appetizer pick in each warm biscuit-wrapped
   meatball to form meatball pop.

NUTRITION INFORMATION PER SERVING: Serving Size: 1 Appetizer; Calories 275; Calories from Fat 145
% Daily Value: Total Fat 16g 25%; Saturated Fat 5g 25%; Cholesterol 35mg 12%; Sodium 690mg 29%;
Total Carbohydrate 22g 7%; Dietary Fiber 1g 4%; Sugars 5g; Protein 9g; Vitamin A 6%; Vitamin C 0%;
Calcium 6%; Iron 10% Dietary Exchanges: 1½ Starch, ½ High-Fat Meat, 2 Fat OR 1½ Carbohydrate,
½ High-Fat Meat, 2 Fat Carbohydrate Choices: 1½

doughboy tip
A fun way to serve these meatball
pops is with warm tomato pasta
sauce for dipping and grated
Parmesan or Romano cheese for
sprinkling on top.

mini picadillo empanadas

PREP TIME: 25 minutes (Ready in 50 minutes)
YIELD: 16 appetizers

½ lb. lean ground beef or turkey

1 cup chunky-style salsa

2 tablespoons raisins

20 pimiento-stuffed green olives, sliced (about ⅓ cup)

½ teaspoon cumin

⅛ teaspoon cinnamon

1 (16.3-oz.) can Pillsbury® Grands!® Refrigerated Buttermilk Biscuits

1. Heat oven to 350°F. Brown ground beef in large skillet over medium-high heat for 5 to 7 minutes or until thoroughly cooked, stirring frequently. Drain.

2. Add all remaining ingredients except biscuits. Bring to a boil. Reduce heat to medium; cook 3 to 4 minutes or until most of liquid has evaporated, stirring occasionally. Remove from heat.

3. Separate dough into 8 biscuits. With serrated knife, cut each biscuit in half horizontally to make 16 rounds. Press or roll each to form 4-inch round. Spoon 2 level measuring tablespoons beef mixture in center of each round. Fold dough over filling; press edges with fork to seal. Place on ungreased cookie sheets.

4. Bake at 350°F. for 15 to 20 minutes or until golden brown. Cool 5 minutes. Serve warm.

NUTRITION INFORMATION PER SERVING: Serving Size: 1 Appetizer; Calories 150; Calories from Fat 65 **% Daily Value:** Total Fat 7g 11%; Saturated Fat 2g 10%; Cholesterol 10mg 3%; Sodium 540mg 23%; Total Carbohydrate 16g 5%; Dietary Fiber 1g 4%; Sugars 5g; Protein 5g; Vitamin A 2%; Vitamin C 2%; Calcium 2%; Iron 6% **Dietary Exchanges:** 1 Starch, 1½ Fat **OR** 1 Carbohydrate, 1½ Fat **Carbohydrate Choices:** 1

doughboy tip

The ground meat filling can be prepared up to a day ahead and refrigerated in a microwave-safe container. Reheat the filling in the microwave oven before spooning the mixture onto the biscuit dough rounds.

crescent wellington spirals

PREP TIME: 20 minutes (Ready in 40 minutes)
YIELD: 16 appetizers

1 (8 oz.) can Pillsbury®
Refrigerated Crescent Dinner Rolls

5 oz. (1¼ cups) shredded
mozzarella cheese

36 thin slices pepperoni (2½ oz.)

1 (9-oz.) pkg. frozen spinach in a
pouch, thawed, drained

4 tablespoons sliced mushrooms
(from 4.5-oz. jar)

½ teaspoon garlic salt

1. Heat oven to 375°F. Spray large cookie sheet with nonstick cooking spray. Separate dough into 4 rectangles. Firmly press perforations to seal. Press each to form 6x4-inch rectangle.

2. Sprinkle each rectangle with heaping ¼ cup cheese to within 1 inch of one short side. Top cheese on each rectangle with 9 pepperoni slices, ¼ of the spinach, 1 tablespoon mushrooms and ⅛ teaspoon garlic salt.

3. Roll up each, starting at short side and rolling to untopped side. Cut each roll into 4 slices. Place slices cut side up on sprayed cookie sheet.

4. Bake at 375°F. for 13 to 18 minutes or until golden brown. Immediately remove from cookie sheet. Cool 2 minutes. Serve warm.

NUTRITION INFORMATION PER SERVING: Serving Size: 1 Appetizer; Calories 100; Calories from Fat 50 **% Daily Value:** Total Fat 6g 9%; Saturated Fat 2g 10%; Cholesterol 10mg 3%; Sodium 350mg 15%; Total Carbohydrate 7g 2%; Dietary Fiber 0g 0%; Sugars 1g; Protein 5g; Vitamin A 10%; Vitamin C 4%; Calcium 8%; Iron 4% **Dietary Exchanges:** ½ Starch, ½ Medium-Fat Meat, ½ Fat **OR** ½ Carbohydrate, ½ Medium-Fat Meat, ½ Fat **Carbohydrate Choices:** ½

doughboy tip

To dress up a platter of these snacks for a party, surround the edge of the plate with sprigs of curly leaf parsley or sweet basil.

flaky reuben slices

PREP TIME: 25 minutes
YIELD: 24 servings

ROLLS

1 (8-oz.) can Pillsbury®
Refrigerated Crescent Dinner Rolls

¼ lb. thinly sliced corned beef

2 oz. (½ cup) finely shredded
Swiss cheese

⅓ cup well-drained sauerkraut

DIPPING SAUCE

½ cup purchased Thousand Island
salad dressing

1 tablespoon milk

1. Heat oven to 375°F. Unroll dough into 2 long rectangles. Press each to form 12-inch-long rectangle; press perforations to seal.

2. Layer half of corned beef on each dough rectangle, cutting to fit if necessary. Top each with cheese and sauerkraut. Starting at long side, roll up each tightly; seal long edges. Place seam side down on ungreased cookie sheet; tuck edges under.

3. Bake at 375°F. for 12 to 14 minutes or until golden brown.

4. Meanwhile, in small bowl, combine dipping sauce ingredients; mix well.

5. To serve, cut warm rolls into 1-inch slices; place on serving platter. Serve with dipping sauce.

NUTRITION INFORMATION PER SERVING: **Serving Size:** ½₄ of Recipe; Calories 70; Calories from Fat 45 **% Daily Value:** Total Fat 5g 8%; Saturated Fat 1g 5%; Cholesterol 10mg 3%; Sodium 170mg 7%; Total Carbohydrate 5g 2%; Dietary Fiber 0g 0%; Sugars 1g; Protein 2g; Vitamin A 0%; Vitamin C 0%; Calcium 2% Iron 0% **Dietary Exchanges:** ½ Starch, 1 Fat **OR** ½ Carbohydrate, 1 Fat **Carbohydrate Choices:** 0

doughboy tip

Before adding the filling ingredients, scatter caraway seed onto the dough and press lightly with your fingertips or the back of a spoon.

stuffed crust pizza snacks

PREP TIME: 25 minutes (Ready in 50 minutes)
YIELD: 48 snacks

2 (10-oz.) cans Pillsbury®
Refrigerated Pizza Crust

8 oz. mozzarella cheese,
cut into 48 cubes

48 slices pepperoni (3 oz.)

¼ cup olive or vegetable oil

1½ teaspoons dried
Italian seasoning

2 tablespoons grated
Parmesan cheese

1. Heat oven to 400°F. Spray two 9-inch pie pans or one 13x9-inch pan with nonstick cooking spray. Remove dough from both cans; unroll. Starting at center, press out each dough rectangle to form 12x8-inch rectangle. Cut each rectangle into 24 squares.

2. Top each square with cheese cube and pepperoni slice. Wrap dough around filling to completely cover; firmly press edges to seal. Place seam side down with sides touching in sprayed pie pans.

3. In small bowl, combine oil and Italian seasoning; mix well. Drizzle over filled dough in pans. Sprinkle with Parmesan cheese.

4. Bake at 400°F. for 16 to 22 minutes or until golden brown. Serve warm.

NUTRITION INFORMATION PER SERVING: Serving Size: 1 Snack; Calories 65; Calories from Fat 25 **% Daily Value:** Total Fat 3g 5%; Saturated Fat 1g 5%; Cholesterol 5mg 2%; Sodium 150mg 6%; Total Carbohydrate 6g 2%; Dietary Fiber 0g 0%; Sugars 1g; Protein 3g; Vitamin A 0%; Vitamin C 0%; Calcium 4%; Iron 2% **Dietary Exchanges:** ½ Starch, ½ Fat OR ½ Carbohydrate, ½ Fat **Carbohydrate Choices:** ½

doughboy tip

Mozzarella cheese is fun because when you bite into these little snacks you get "cheese strings." Other cheeses, such as Monterey Jack or Cheddar, also make a tasty snack. Dip and dunk these super snacks in warm pizza sauce for an added treat.

italian ham appetizer squares

PREP TIME: 30 minutes
YIELD: 18 servings

1 (10.6-oz.) pkg. Pillsbury®
Refrigerated Garlic Breadsticks

6 thin slices cooked ham
(about 3 oz.)

6 thin slices provolone cheese
(about 4 oz.)

1 medium tomato, chopped

6 to 7 large ripe olives, sliced

½ cup chopped fresh basil

2 tablespoons purchased Italian
vinaigrette salad dressing

1. Heat oven to 375°F. Unroll dough; separate into 2 equal sections along center perforation. Place 1 inch apart in ungreased 15x10x1-inch baking pan or 13x9-inch (3-quart) glass baking dish. Press perforations to seal. Apply garlic spread from container evenly over each dough section.

2. Bake at 375°F. for 9 to 11 minutes or until light golden brown.

3. Remove partially baked crusts from oven. Top each crust with ham, cheese, tomato and olives. Return to oven; bake an additional 5 minutes or until cheese is melted and edges are golden brown.

4. To serve, cut each topped crust into 9 squares. Sprinkle with basil. Drizzle with salad dressing. Serve warm.

NUTRITION INFORMATION PER SERVING: **Serving Size:** ⅟₁₈ of Recipe; Calories 90; Calories from Fat 45 **% Daily Value:** Total Fat 5g 8%; Saturated Fat 2g 10%; Cholesterol 5mg 2%; Sodium 300mg 13%; Total Carbohydrate 8g 3%; Dietary Fiber 0g 0%; Sugars 1g; Protein 4g; Vitamin A 4%; Vitamin C 0%; Calcium 6%; Iron 4% **Dietary Exchanges:** ½ Starch, ½ Lean Meat, ½ Fat **OR** ½ Carbohydrate, ½ Lean Meat, ½ Fat **Carbohydrate Choices:** ½

doughboy tip

Fresh basil, a key ingredient in these squares, has incomparable flavor and fragrance, but it can wilt quickly in the refrigerator. Purchase it as close to the day you plan to serve it as possible. Then, trim the stems as you would with fresh flowers, and set the basil "bouquet" into a glass holding an inch or two of water. Cover the leaves with a plastic bag and store the basil in the refrigerator.

holiday herb crescent trees

PREP TIME: 1 hour
YIELD: 2 trees; 32 servings

2 (8-oz.) cans Pillsbury®
Refrigerated Crescent Dinner Rolls

¼ cup grated Parmesan cheese

1 teaspoon dried Italian seasoning

½ cup purchased chive
and onion potato topper
(from 12-oz. container)

30 slices cherry tomatoes
(about 8 to 10 tomatoes)

½ yellow bell pepper

Green onion curls
(see Doughboy Tip below)

1. Heat oven to 375°F. Unroll both cans of dough into 4 long rectangles. Firmly press perforations to seal. Sprinkle each rectangle with 1 tablespoon cheese and ¼ teaspoon Italian seasoning.

2. Starting at short sides, roll up dough to form 4 rolls. Cut each roll into 8 slices. Place slices cut side down on ungreased cookie sheets to form 2 trees. To form each tree, start by placing 1 slice for top; arrange 2 slices just below, with sides touching. Continue arranging rows of 3 slices, 4 slices and 5 slices. Use remaining slice for tree trunk. Refrigerate 1 tree.

3. Bake first tree at 375°F. for 11 to 13 minutes or until golden brown. Cool 1 minute; carefully loosen with spatula and slide onto wire rack to cool. Bake and cool second tree.

4. Place each tree on serving platter. Spoon potato topper into resealable food storage plastic bag; seal bag. Cut ¼-inch hole in bottom corner of bag. Pipe potato topper over trees. Place tomato slice on each pinwheel except top ones. From yellow bell pepper, cut 2 small stars using 1¼ to 1½-inch cutter; place 1 on top slice of each tree. Chop remaining bell pepper; sprinkle over trees. Top with onion curls. Refrigerate until serving time. To serve, pull apart pinwheels of tree.

NUTRITION INFORMATION PER SERVING: Serving Size: 1/32 of Recipe; Calories 60; Calories from Fat 35 % Daily Value: Total Fat 4g 6%; Saturated Fat 1g 5%; Cholesterol 0mg 0%; Sodium 135mg 6%; Total Carbohydrate 6g 2%; Dietary Fiber 0g 0%; Sugars 1g; Protein 1g; Vitamin A 0%; Vitamin C 4%; Calcium 6%; Iron 0% Dietary Exchanges: ½ Starch, ½ Fat OR ½ Carbohydrate, ½ Fat Carbohydrate Choices: ½

doughboy tip

Cut 1 green onion (with top) into 1-inch pieces. Cut pieces lengthwise into fine strips. Cover with ice water; let stand 10 minutes or until strips curl. Drain.

ham and cheese crescent snacks

PREP TIME: 15 minutes (Ready in 40 minutes)
YIELD: 24 snacks

1 (8-oz.) can Pillsbury®
Refrigerated Crescent Dinner Rolls

2 tablespoons margarine
or butter, softened

1 teaspoon prepared mustard

1 cup cubed cooked ham

⅓ cup chopped onion

⅓ cup chopped green bell pepper

4 oz. (1 cup) shredded Cheddar
or American cheese

1. Heat oven to 375°F. Unroll dough onto ungreased cookie sheet. Press or roll to form 13x9-inch rectangle; press perforations to seal. Pinch edges to form rim.

2. In small bowl, combine margarine and mustard; mix well. Spread mixture over crust. Sprinkle ham, onion, bell pepper and cheese over mixture.

3. Bake at 375°F. for 18 to 25 minutes or until edges are golden brown. Cut into squares. Serve warm. Store in refrigerator.

NUTRITION INFORMATION PER SERVING: Serving Size: ¹⁄₂₄ of Recipe; Calories 70; Calories from Fat 45 % Daily Value: Total Fat 5g 8%; Saturated Fat 2g 10%; Cholesterol 10mg 3%; Sodium 200mg 8%; Total Carbohydrate 4g 1%; Dietary Fiber 0g 0%; Sugars 1g; Protein 3g; Vitamin A 2%; Vitamin C 0%; Calcium 4%; Iron 0% Dietary Exchanges: ½ Starch, ½ High-Fat Meat OR ½ Carbohydrate, ½ High-Fat Meat Carbohydrate Choices: 0

doughboy tip

Once the topping for these party-ready appetizers has been spread over the dough, the cookie sheet can be covered with plastic wrap and refrigerated for up to 2 hours. When your guests arrive, or shortly before, bake as directed.

sausage snack wraps

PREP TIME: 30 minutes
YIELD: 48 snacks

2 (8-oz.) cans Pillsbury®
Refrigerated Crescent Dinner Rolls

48 cocktail-sized smoked link
sausages or hot dogs
(from 16-oz. pkg.)

1. Heat oven to 375°F. Separate both cans of dough into 16 triangles. Cut each triangle lengthwise into thirds. Place sausage on shortest side of each triangle. Roll up each, starting at short side of triangle and rolling to opposite point. Place on ungreased cookie sheets.

2. Bake at 375°F. for 12 to 15 minutes or until golden brown, switching position of cookie sheets halfway through baking. Serve warm.

NUTRITION INFORMATION PER SERVING: **Serving Size:** 1 Snack; Calories 60; Calories from Fat 35 **% Daily Value:** Total Fat 4g 6%; Saturated Fat 1g 5%; Cholesterol 5mg 2%; Sodium 160mg 7%; Total Carbohydrate 4g 1%; Dietary Fiber 0g 0%; Sugars 1g; Protein 2g; Vitamin A 0%; Vitamin C 0%; Calcium 0%; Iron 0% **Dietary Exchanges:** ½ Starch, ½ Fat OR ½ Carbohydrate, ½ Fat **Carbohydrate Choices:** 0

doughboy tip
Serve these mini dog-in-a-blanket snacks with ketchup, assorted mustards and pickle relish for dipping. If you wish, you can brush a little mustard onto the dough before rolling up the sausages for baking.

potato and bacon
mini pizzas

PREP TIME: 30 minutes (Ready in 45 minutes)
YIELD: 20 appetizers

20 (¼-inch-thick) slices red boiling potatoes (about 3 medium)

½ lb. thick-sliced smoky bacon

1 medium onion, sliced

1 (12-oz.) can Pillsbury® Golden Layers™ Refrigerated Flaky Biscuits

2 tablespoons Dijon mustard

½ cup sour cream

1 tablespoon chopped fresh parsley

1. Heat oven to 400°F. In medium saucepan, cook potato slices in boiling salted water over medium-high heat for 5 minutes. Drain.

2. Fry bacon in large skillet over medium-low heat until crisp. Drain on paper towels. Crumble bacon; set aside. In same skillet with bacon drippings, cook onion 5 to 7 minutes or until softened and separated into rings, stirring frequently.

3. Separate dough into 10 biscuits. Separate each biscuit into 2 layers; place biscuit rounds on ungreased large cookie sheet. Flatten each slightly. Spread each lightly with mustard. Top each dough round with onion and potato slice.

4. Bake at 400°F. for 9 to 15 minutes or until crusts are crisp and golden brown.

5. To serve, top each mini pizza with sour cream and crumbled bacon. Sprinkle with parsley. Serve warm.

NUTRITION INFORMATION PER SERVING: **Serving Size:** 1 Appetizer; Calories 100; Calories from Fat 45 **% Daily Value:** Total Fat 5g 8%; Saturated Fat 2g 10%; Cholesterol 5mg 2%; Sodium 330mg 14%; Total Carbohydrate 12g 4%; Dietary Fiber 1g 4%; Sugars 3g; Protein 3g; Vitamin A 0%; Vitamin C 0%; Calcium 0%; Iron 4% **Dietary Exchanges:** 1 Starch, ½ Fat OR 1 Carbohydrate, ½ Fat **Carbohydrate Choices:** 1

doughboy tip

These mini pizzas can be thrown together in an instant by cooking the potatoes and bacon up to 2 hours in advance. Cover and refrigerate separately until you're ready to assemble the pizzas.

spicy mexican quiche cups

PREP TIME: 30 minutes (Ready in 50 minutes)
YIELD: 22 appetizers

½ lb. bulk hot Italian sausage

2 oz. (½ cup) shredded Cheddar cheese

2 oz. (½ cup) shredded mozzarella cheese

½ cup chopped jalapeño chiles, seeds removed, if desired

6 eggs

6 tablespoons chunky-style salsa

1 (15-oz.) pkg. Pillsbury® Refrigerated Pie Crusts, softened as directed on package

1. Heat oven to 425°F. Brown sausage in medium skillet over medium heat until thoroughly cooked, stirring frequently. Drain. Set aside to cool.

2. In medium bowl, combine cheeses and chiles; mix well. Stir in cooled cooked sausage. Beat eggs thoroughly in another medium bowl. Stir in salsa.

3. Remove pie crusts from pouches. Unfold crusts; press out fold lines. With rolling pin, roll each crust to form 12-inch round. With 3½-inch round cutter, cut 22 rounds from crusts, rerolling scraps as necessary. Press each round into ungreased muffin cup or fluted tartlet pan.

4. Spoon 1 heaping tablespoon cheese mixture into each crust-lined cup. Top each with about 1 tablespoon egg mixture; divide any remaining egg mixture between cups.

5. Bake at 425°F. for 14 to 18 minutes or until filling is set. Serve warm.

NUTRITION INFORMATION PER SERVING: **Serving Size:** 1 Appetizer; Calories 140; Calories from Fat 80 **% Daily Value:** Total Fat 9g 14%; Saturated Fat 4g 20%; Cholesterol 70mg 23%; Sodium 250mg 10%; Total Carbohydrate 10g 3%; Dietary Fiber 0g 0%; Sugars 1g; Protein 5g; Vitamin A 4%; Vitamin C 0%; Calcium 6%; Iron 4% **Dietary Exchanges:** ½ Starch, ½ High-Fat Meat, 1 Fat **OR** ½ Carbohydrate, ½ High-Fat Meat, 1 Fat **Carbohydrate Choices:** ½

doughboy tip

Fresh cilantro, widely used in Latin American and Asian cooking, has a distinctive citrusy flavor that makes a pleasant, authentic garnish for these little Mexican quiches. Use sprigs to decorate the plate, or chop the cilantro and sprinkle over the top of each appetizer.

asiago, bacon and olive roll-ups

ROLL-UPS

5 slices bacon, cut into small pieces

2 oz. Asiago cheese, finely shredded (½ cup)

8 pitted medium-sized ripe olives, chopped

1 (8-oz.) can Pillsbury® Refrigerated Crescent Dinner Rolls

1 to 2 teaspoons purchased sun-dried tomato paste or Italian tomato paste

DIPPING SAUCE

¼ cup sour cream

¼ cup purchased ranch salad dressing

¼ teaspoon salt

PREP TIME: 20 minutes (Ready in 40 minutes)
YIELD: 16 appetizers

1. Heat oven to 350°F. Cook bacon until crisp. Drain on paper towel. In small bowl, combine bacon, cheese and olives; toss to mix.

2. Separate dough into 8 triangles; press out slightly. Cut each triangle in half lengthwise to make 16 triangles.

3. Spread thin layer of tomato paste on each triangle. Spoon 1½ teaspoons olive mixture on shortest side of each triangle; spread slightly. Roll up each, starting at shortest side of triangle and rolling to opposite point. Place point side down on ungreased cookie sheet.

4. Bake at 350°F. for 13 to 18 minutes or until golden brown.

5. Meanwhile, in small bowl, combine all dipping sauce ingredients; mix well. Place bowl of sour cream mixture in center of serving plate. Arrange warm roll-ups around bowl.

NUTRITION INFORMATION PER SERVING: **Serving Size:** 1 Appetizer; Calories 110; Calories from Fat 70 **% Daily Value:** Total Fat 8g 12%; Saturated Fat 2g 10%; Cholesterol 5mg 2%; Sodium 280mg 12%; Total Carbohydrate 6g 2%; Dietary Fiber 0g 0%; Sugars 1g; Protein 3g; Vitamin A 0%; Vitamin C 0%; Calcium 4%; Iron 2% **Dietary Exchanges:** ½ Starch, 1½ Fat OR ½ Carbohydrate, 1½ Fat **Carbohydrate Choices:** ½

doughboy tip
You'll be one step ahead if you make the sour cream dipping sauce a day in advance. Cover and refrigerate the dip until you're ready to serve these tasty snacks.

southwestern chicken biscuits

PREP TIME: 15 minutes (Ready in 35 minutes)
YIELD: 20 appetizers

2 (12-oz.) cans Pillsbury®
Golden Layers™ Refrigerated
Flaky Biscuits

1 (9-oz.) pkg. (2 cups) frozen
cooked Southwestern-seasoned
chicken breast strips,
thawed, diced

1 (4.5-oz.) can chopped
green chiles

4 oz. (1 cup) shredded
Monterey Jack cheese

1 cup chunky-style salsa

1 tablespoon instant minced onion

1. Heat oven to 400°F. Spray 20 muffin cups with nonstick cooking spray. Separate dough into 20 biscuits. Place 1 biscuit in each sprayed muffin cup; press in bottom and up sides of cup.

2. In medium bowl, combine all remaining ingredients; mix well. Spoon 2 tablespoons mixture into each biscuit-lined cup, gently pressing mixture with back of spoon.

3. Bake at 400°F. for 13 to 18 minutes or until edges are golden brown. Remove from muffin cups. Serve warm.

NUTRITION INFORMATION PER SERVING: Serving Size: 1 Appetizer; Calories 150; Calories from Fat 60 **% Daily Value:** Total Fat 7g 11%; Saturated Fat 2g 10%; Cholesterol 10mg 3%; Sodium 570mg 24%; Total Carbohydrate 15g 5%; Dietary Fiber 1g 4%; Sugars 2g; Protein 6g; Vitamin A 2%; Vitamin C 2%; Calcium 6%; Iron 6% **Dietary Exchanges:** 1 Starch, ½ Very Lean Meat, 1 Fat **OR** 1 Carbohydrate, ½ Very Lean Meat, 1 Fat **Carbohydrate Choices:** 1

doughboy tip

To whip up an easy accompaniment to this Southwestern starter, combine a can of black beans (rinsed and drained) with a can of whole kernel corn (drained) or leftover corn; toss with your favorite purchased vinaigrette. If you like, embellish this simple salad with finely chopped onion, chopped parsley, chopped red bell pepper and tomatoes.

curried chicken turnovers

PREP TIME: 15 minutes (Ready in 40 minutes)
YIELD: 14 appetizers

⅓ cup raisins

⅓ cup sour cream

¼ cup mango chutney

1¼ teaspoons curry powder

1 (5-oz.) can chunk chicken in water, drained

1 (15-oz.) pkg. Pillsbury® Refrigerated Pie Crusts, softened as directed on package

1. Heat oven to 400°F. In medium bowl, combine all ingredients except pie crusts; mix well.

2. Remove pie crusts from pouches. Unfold crusts; press out fold lines. With 3½-inch round cutter, cut 14 rounds from crusts.

3. Place about 1 tablespoon chicken mixture in center of each dough round. Brush edge of each round with water. Fold in half over filling; press edges with fork to seal. Place on ungreased cookie sheet.

4. Bake at 400°F. for 18 to 23 minutes or until light golden brown. Serve warm.

NUTRITION INFORMATION PER SERVING: **Serving Size:** 1 Appetizer; Calories 105; Calories from Fat 45 **% Daily Value:** Total Fat 5g 8%; Saturated Fat 3g 15%; Cholesterol 15mg 5%; Sodium 90mg 4%; Total Carbohydrate 12g 4%; Dietary Fiber 0g 0%; Sugars 0g; Protein 3g; Vitamin A 0%; Vitamin C 0%; Calcium 0%; Iron 0% **Dietary Exchanges:** 1 Starch, ½ Fat **OR** 1 Carbohydrate, ½ Fat **Carbohydrate Choices:** 1

doughboy tip

To make an easy dipping sauce for the chicken turnovers, mix ⅔ cup sour cream with ⅓ cup prepared mango chutney. Top it off with a dash of curry powder or chopped fresh cilantro.

pesto cheese 'n chicken bundle snacks

PREP TIME: 15 minutes (Ready in 40 minutes)
YIELD: 8 snacks

1 (8-oz.) can Pillsbury®
Refrigerated Crescent Dinner Rolls

⅓ cup light roasted garlic
cream cheese spread
(from 8-oz. container)

¼ cup purchased pesto

1 tablespoon jalapeño or
hot pepper jelly

½ cup Italian-style dry
bread crumbs

2 cups cubed cooked chicken

3 tablespoons crumbled
feta cheese

1 to 2 tablespoons water

1. Heat oven to 375°F. Separate dough into 4 rectangles. Firmly press perforations to seal. Cut each rectangle in half crosswise to make 8 pieces. Press each to form 4-inch square.

2. In medium bowl, combine cream cheese, pesto, jelly and 2 tablespoons of the bread crumbs; mix well. Stir in chicken and cheese.

3. Place ¼ cup chicken mixture in center of each square. Bring 4 corners of each square up over filling; twist firmly to seal. Brush top and bottom of each bundle with water; coat with remaining bread crumbs. Place on ungreased cookie sheet.

4. Bake at 375°F. for 14 to 22 minutes or until deep golden brown. Serve warm.

NUTRITION INFORMATION PER SERVING: **Serving Size:** 1 Snack; Calories 260; Calories from Fat 130 **% Daily Value:** Total Fat 14g 22%; Saturated Fat 4g 20%; Cholesterol 40mg 13%; Sodium 480mg 20%; Total Carbohydrate 19g 6%; Dietary Fiber 1g 4%; Sugars 4g; Protein 15g; Vitamin A 4%; Vitamin C 0%; Calcium 6%; Iron 8% **Dietary Exchanges:** 1 Starch, 2 Very Lean Meat, 2½ Fat **OR** 1 Carbohydrate, 2 Very Lean Meat, 2½ Fat **Carbohydrate Choices:** 1

doughboy tip

For the 2 cups of cubed cooked chicken called for in this recipe, cook ¾ pound boneless skinless chicken breast or open and drain two (5-ounce) cans of chunk chicken.

garlic herb and salmon empanadas

PREP TIME: 30 minutes (Ready in 50 minutes)
YIELD: 16 appetizers

1 (15-oz.) pkg. Pillsbury®
Refrigerated Pie Crusts, softened
as directed on package

6 oz. smoked salmon, flaked

1 (5.2-oz.) pkg. Boursin cheese
with garlic and herbs

1. Heat oven to 425°F. Line large cookie sheet with parchment paper or spray with nonstick cooking spray. Remove pie crusts from pouches. Unfold crusts; cut each into 4 wedges.

2. In small bowl, combine salmon and cheese; mix well. Spread about 2 tablespoons mixture evenly over half of each crust wedge to within ¼ inch of edges. Brush edges of crust with water. Fold untopped dough over filling, forming triangle; press edges to seal. Place on paper-lined cookie sheet.

3. Bake at 425°F. for 12 to 17 minutes or until golden brown. Remove from cookie sheet; place on wire rack. Cool 10 minutes.

4. To serve, cut each warm empanada in half, forming 2 triangles.

NUTRITION INFORMATION PER SERVING: **Serving Size:** 1 Appetizer; Calories 160; Calories from Fat 90 **% Daily Value:** Total Fat 10g 15%; Saturated Fat 5g 25%; Cholesterol 10mg 3%; Sodium 240mg 10%; Total Carbohydrate 13g 4%; Dietary Fiber 0g 0%; Sugars 1g; Protein 4g; Vitamin A 0%; Vitamin C 0%; Calcium 0%; Iron 0% **Dietary Exchanges:** 1 Starch, 2 Fat OR 1 Carbohydrate, 2 Fat **Carbohydrate Choices:** 1

doughboy tip

Serve these rich, smoky empanadas with a side of sour cream topped with chopped fresh chives or green onions.

crab-filled crescent snacks

PREP TIME: 25 minutes (Ready in 45 minutes)
YIELD: 32 snacks

1 (6-oz.) can crabmeat, rinsed, well drained

1 (3-oz.) pkg. cream cheese, softened

2 tablespoons sliced green onions

¼ teaspoon garlic salt

2 (8-oz.) cans Pillsbury® Refrigerated Crescent Dinner Rolls

1 egg yolk

1 tablespoon water

1 teaspoon sesame seed

1. Heat oven to 375°F. Spray large cookie sheet with nonstick cooking spray. In small bowl, combine crabmeat, cream cheese, green onions and garlic salt; mix well.

2. Separate both cans of dough into 16 triangles. Cut each triangle in half lengthwise to make 32 triangles.

3. Place 1 teaspoon crab mixture on center of each triangle about 1 inch from short side. Fold short ends of each triangle over filling; pinch sides to seal. Roll up. Place on sprayed cookie sheet.

4. In small bowl, combine egg yolk and water; mix well. Brush egg mixture over snacks. Sprinkle with sesame seed. Discard any remaining egg mixture.

5. Bake at 375°F. for 15 to 20 minutes or until golden brown. Serve warm.

NUTRITION INFORMATION PER SERVING: **Serving Size:** 1 Snack; Calories 65; Calories from Fat 25 **% Daily Value:** Total Fat 3g 5%; Saturated Fat 1g 5%; Cholesterol 15mg 5%; Sodium 200mg 8%; Total Carbohydrate 7g 2%; Dietary Fiber 0g 0%; Sugars 2g; Protein 2g; Vitamin A 0%; Vitamin C 0%; Calcium 0%; Iron 2% **Dietary Exchanges:** ½ Starch, ½ Fat **OR** ½ Carbohydrate, ½ Fat **Carbohydrate Choices:** ½

doughboy tip

Serve these crab snacks warm from the oven with a purchased sweet-and-sour sauce for dipping. A 9-ounce jar (about 1 cup) should be the right amount. Spoon the sauce into a decorative bowl for serving.

shrimp crescent bites

PREP TIME: 10 minutes (Ready in 45 minutes)
YIELD: 24 appetizers

1 (8-oz.) can Pillsbury®
Refrigerated Crescent Dinner Rolls

1½ teaspoons curry powder

⅓ cup flaked coconut

¼ cup apricot preserves

24 shelled deveined cooked
medium shrimp

24 sprigs fresh cilantro

1. Heat oven to 375°F. Unroll dough into 1 large rectangle. Gently press perforations to seal. Place curry powder in small strainer. Shake strainer to sprinkle dough evenly with curry powder. Sprinkle evenly with coconut.

2. Starting with long side, roll up dough jelly-roll fashion. With serrated knife, cut roll into 24 slices. Place cut side down on ungreased cookie sheet.

3. Bake at 375°F. for 13 to 15 minutes or until golden brown. Immediately remove from cookie sheet; place on wire rack. Cool 10 minutes or until completely cooled.

4. To serve, top each appetizer with ½ teaspoon apricot preserves and 1 shrimp. Garnish each appetizer with cilantro sprig.

NUTRITION INFORMATION PER SERVING: **Serving Size:** 1 Appetizer; Calories 55; Calories from Fat 20 **% Daily Value:** Total Fat 2g 3%; Saturated Fat 1g 5%; Cholesterol 10mg 3%; Sodium 130mg 5%; Total Carbohydrate 7g 2%; Dietary Fiber 0g 0%; Sugars 3g; Protein 2g; Vitamin A 2%; Vitamin C 0%; Calcium 0%; Iron 2% **Dietary Exchanges:** ½ Starch, ½ Fat **OR** ½ Carbohydrate, ½ Fat **Carbohydrate Choices:** ½

doughboy tip

These curry-coconut crescents can be baked up to several hours ahead, cooled and then wrapped in plastic wrap until needed. For the best texture and flavor, add the apricot preserves, shrimp and cilantro just before serving.

seafood appetizers

2 cups frozen cooked cocktail or salad shrimp

1 (8-oz.) can Pillsbury® Refrigerated Crescent Dinner Rolls

1 cup flaked imitation crabmeat (surimi), cut into small pieces

1 teaspoon seafood seasoning blend

1 teaspoon garlic powder

6 oz. (1½ cups) shredded Mexican cheese blend

1 teaspoon dried parsley flakes

1. Heat oven to 375°F. Thaw shrimp as directed on package. Drain well; press between paper towels to remove excess liquid. Cut shrimp into small pieces.

2. Unroll dough onto ungreased cookie sheet. Press to form 12x8-inch rectangle. Firmly press perforations to seal. Top dough with shrimp and all remaining ingredients.

3. Bake at 375°F. for 15 to 20 minutes or until crust is golden brown. Cut into squares. Serve warm.

NUTRITION INFORMATION PER SERVING: Serving Size: ¹⁄₂₄ of Recipe; Calories 80; Calories from Fat 35 % Daily Value: Total Fat 4g 6%; Saturated Fat 2g 10%; Cholesterol 30mg 10%; Sodium 210mg 9%; Total Carbohydrate 5g 2%; Dietary Fiber 0g 0%; Sugars 1g; Protein 5g; Vitamin A 2%; Vitamin C 0%; Calcium 6%; Iron 4% Dietary Exchanges: ½ Starch, ½ Very Lean Meat, ½ Fat OR ½ Carbohydrate, ½ Very Lean Meat, ½ Fat Carbohydrate Choices: 0

doughboy tip

Be sure to keep dough refrigerated until just before baking, as warm dough may be sticky and hard to handle. Fresh cooked or imitation lobster, cut into small pieces, can be used instead of crabmeat.

roasted red pepper and pesto pinwheels

PREP TIME: 15 minutes (Ready in 35 minutes)
YIELD: 16 appetizers

1 (8-oz.) can Pillsbury®
Refrigerated Crescent Dinner Rolls

⅓ cup purchased pesto

¼ cup chopped purchased
roasted red bell peppers
(from a jar)

1. Heat oven to 350°F. Unroll dough into 2 long rectangles. Firmly press perforations to seal. Spread rectangles with pesto to within ¼ inch of edges. Sprinkle with bell peppers.

2. Starting at short side, roll up each rectangle; pinch edges to seal. Cut each roll into 8 slices. Place cut side down on ungreased cookie sheet.

3. Bake at 350°F. for 13 to 17 minutes or until golden brown. Immediately remove from cookie sheet. Serve warm.

NUTRITION INFORMATION PER SERVING: Serving Size: 1 Appetizer; Calories 60; Calories from Fat 35 **% Daily Value:** Total Fat 4g 6%; Saturated Fat 1g 5%; Cholesterol 0mg 0%; Sodium 125mg 5%; Total Carbohydrate 6g 2%; Dietary Fiber 0g 0%; Sugars 1g; Protein 1g; Vitamin A 0%; Vitamin C 4%; Calcium 0%; Iron 0% **Dietary Exchanges:** ½ Starch, ½ Fat **OR** ½ Carbohydrate, ½ Fat **Carbohydrate Choices:** ½

doughboy tip

For a finishing touch, garnish each pinwheel with a small fresh basil leaf. If you grow your own basil, pinch off flowers as they form so the plant will continue to produce leaves. The flowers are edible, too, and taste like the leaves. If you have some, garnish the plate with them.

caramelized onion tartlets

1 (15-oz.) pkg. Pillsbury®
Refrigerated Pie Crusts, softened
as directed on package

2 tablespoons margarine or butter

¾ cup coarsely chopped red onion

2 eggs

½ cup sour cream

¼ teaspoon salt

⅛ teaspoon hot pepper sauce

3 oz. (¾ cup) finely shredded
Cheddar cheese

Additional chopped red onion,
if desired

PREP TIME: 30 minutes (Ready in 45 minutes)
YIELD: 24 appetizers

1. Heat oven to 400°F. Remove pie crusts from pouches. Unfold crusts; press out fold lines. With 3-inch round cutter or glass, cut 24 rounds from crusts, rerolling scraps as necessary. Press each round into ungreased miniature muffin cup.

2. Melt margarine in large skillet over medium-high heat. Add ¾ cup onion; cook 5 minutes, stirring occasionally. Reduce heat to medium; cook an additional 13 to 15 minutes or until onion is softened and golden brown, stirring occasionally. Remove from heat.

3. Beat eggs in medium bowl. Stir in sour cream, salt and hot pepper sauce. Stir in cooked onion and ¼ cup of the cheese. Spoon onion mixture into crust-lined cups. Sprinkle with remaining ½ cup cheese.

4. Bake at 400°F. for 10 to 15 minutes or until golden brown and set in center. Serve warm or at room temperature. Garnish with additional onion.

NUTRITION INFORMATION PER SERVING: Serving Size: 1 Appetizer; Calories 115; Calories from Fat 70 % Daily Value: Total Fat 8g 12%; Saturated Fat 4g 20%; Cholesterol 30mg 10%; Sodium 140mg 6%; Total Carbohydrate 9g 3%; Dietary Fiber 0g 0%; Sugars 1g; Protein 2g; Vitamin A 2%; Vitamin C 0%; Calcium 2%; Iron 0% Dietary Exchanges: ½ Starch, 1½ Fat OR ½ Carbohydrate, 1½ Fat Carbohydrate Choices: ½

doughboy tip

To make this recipe for a sit-down, eat-with-a-fork occasion, double the filling ingredients, except use 3 eggs. Prepare one pie crust in an 11x1-inch tart pan or a 9-inch pie plate. Add the filling and bake about 30 minutes or until set. Let the tart stand for 20 minutes before cutting into wedges.

crescent-wrapped brie **pictured on page 29**

PREP TIME: 20 minutes (Ready in 1 hour)
YIELD: 12 servings

1 (8-oz.) can Pillsbury®
Refrigerated Crescent Dinner Rolls

1 (8-oz.) round natural Brie cheese

1 egg, beaten

1. Heat oven to 350°F. Unroll dough; separate crosswise into 2 sections. Pat dough and firmly press perforations to seal, forming 2 squares. Place 1 square on ungreased cookie sheet. Place cheese on center of dough.

2. With small cookie or canapé cutter, cut 1 shape from each corner of remaining square; set cutouts aside.

3. Place remaining square on top of cheese round. Press dough evenly around cheese; fold bottom edges over top edges. Gently stretch dough evenly around cheese; press to seal completely. Brush with beaten egg. Top with cutouts; brush with additional beaten egg.

4. Bake at 350°F. for 20 to 24 minutes or until golden brown. Cool 15 minutes. Serve warm.

NUTRITION INFORMATION PER SERVING: **Serving Size:** ¹⁄₁₂ of Recipe; Calories 130; Calories from Fat 80 **% Daily Value:** Total Fat 9g 14%; Saturated Fat 4g 20%; Cholesterol 35mg 12%; Sodium 270mg 11%; Total Carbohydrate 7g 2%; Dietary Fiber 0g 0%; Sugars 1g; Protein 6g; Vitamin A 4%; Vitamin C 0%; Calcium 4%; Iron 4% **Dietary Exchanges:** ½ Starch, ½ High-Fat Meat, 1 Fat **OR** ½ Carbohydrate, ½ High-Fat Meat, 1 Fat **Carbohydrate Choices:** ½

doughboy tip

Serve this elegant, yet easy, appetizer with one or more of the following toppings: chutney, jalapeño jelly, fruit preserves or salsa.

red and green biscuit pull-apart

PREP TIME: 20 minutes (Ready in 35 minutes)
YIELD: 10 servings

¼ teaspoon garlic powder

¼ teaspoon salt, if desired

¼ teaspoon dried basil leaves, crushed

¼ teaspoon dried oregano leaves, crushed

1 (12-oz.) can Pillsbury® Golden Layers™ Refrigerated Flaky Biscuits

4½ teaspoons olive oil

¼ cup chopped green bell pepper

¼ cup chopped red bell pepper

1 oz. (¼ cup) shredded mozzarella cheese

2 tablespoons grated Romano or Parmesan cheese

1. Heat oven to 400°F. In small bowl, combine garlic powder, salt, basil and oregano; mix well.

2. Separate dough into 10 biscuits. Place 1 biscuit in center of ungreased cookie sheet. Arrange remaining biscuits in circle, edges slightly overlapping, around center biscuit. Gently press out to form 10-inch round.

3. Brush biscuits with oil. Top with bell peppers and cheeses. Sprinkle garlic powder mixture over top.

4. Bake at 400°F. for 12 to 15 minutes or until golden brown. To serve, pull apart warm biscuits.

NUTRITION INFORMATION PER SERVING: **Serving Size:** ¹⁄₁₀ of Recipe; Calories 120; Calories from Fat 60 **% Daily Value:** Total Fat 7g 11%; Saturated Fat 2g 10%; Cholesterol 3mg 1%; Sodium 390mg 16%; Total Carbohydrate 12g 4%; Dietary Fiber 0g 0%; Sugars 2g; Protein 3g; Vitamin A 4%; Vitamin C 8%; Calcium 4%; Iron 4% **Dietary Exchanges:** 1 Starch, 1 Fat OR 1 Carbohydrate, 1 Fat **Carbohydrate Choices:** 1

doughboy tip

This colorful holiday bread is great for a snack or to serve as a bread for supper or brunch. Double the spice mixture in this recipe and keep it on hand to season soups and stews or to sprinkle on cooked vegetables or buttered rolls and breads.

poinsettia brie with breadstick bites

PREP TIME: 45 minutes
YIELD: 8 servings

1 (8-oz.) round Brie cheese

1 (11-oz.) can Pillsbury® Refrigerated Breadsticks

2 tablespoons margarine or butter, melted

1 teaspoon sesame seed

½ teaspoon herbes de Provence

¼ teaspoon garlic powder

5 (1-inch) pieces roasted red bell peppers (from a jar)

1 teaspoon chopped yellow bell pepper

3 basil leaves

1. Heat oven to 375°F. Cut 15-inch piece of foil. Fold in half lengthwise; cut on fold to make 2 strips. Overlap 2 ends; fold together to make 29-inch strip. Fold lengthwise twice to make long strip 1½ inches wide. Overlap and fold remaining ends to form 8-inch diameter circle for collar. Spray inside of collar with nonstick cooking spray. Place on ungreased cookie sheet. Place cheese in center of collar.

2. Separate dough into 12 breadsticks. Cut each into 4 pieces; place in medium bowl. Drizzle dough with melted margarine. Sprinkle with sesame seed, herbes de Provence and garlic powder; toss to coat. Spoon breadstick pieces to fill space between cheese and foil collar on cookie sheet.

3. Bake at 375°F. for 15 minutes. Remove foil collar; bake an additional 5 to 10 minutes or until breadstick pieces are golden brown and cheese is soft.

4. Cut roasted pepper pieces into shapes to resemble poinsettia petals. Place in center of cheese. Sprinkle yellow bell pepper pieces in center of poinsettia. Place basil leaves around roasted pepper pieces to resemble leaves. Slide onto serving plate. Serve melted cheese with warm breadstick pieces.

NUTRITION INFORMATION PER SERVING: Serving Size: ⅛ of Recipe; Calories 230; Calories from Fat 120 **% Daily Value:** Total Fat 13g 20%; Saturated Fat 6g 30%; Cholesterol 30mg 10%; Sodium 500mg 21%; Total Carbohydrate 19g 6%; Dietary Fiber 1g 4%; Sugars 3g; Protein 9g; Vitamin A 10%; Vitamin C 10%; Calcium 6%; Iron 6% **Dietary Exchanges:** 1 Starch, 1 High-Fat Meat, 1 Fat OR 1 Carbohydrate, 1 High-Fat Meat, 1 Fat **Carbohydrate Choices:** 1

doughboy tip

Herbes de Provence is an herb blend that's popular in southern France. To substitute for the dried blend, you can improvise by mixing ⅛ teaspoon each of dried marjoram, thyme, summer savory, crushed rosemary and ground sage. If you prefer, just pick your favorite from the herbs listed above and sprinkle it onto the breadsticks.

green chile and cheese foldovers

PREP TIME: 20 minutes (Ready in 45 minutes)
YIELD: 16 appetizers

4 oz. (1 cup) finely shredded Muenster or Monterey Jack cheese

2 tablespoons finely chopped green onion tops

2 tablespoons finely chopped fresh cilantro or parsley

Dash salt

1 (4.5-oz.) can chopped green chiles, drained

1 (16.3-oz.) can Pillsbury® Grands!® Refrigerated Buttermilk Biscuits

1. Heat oven to 375°F. Spray large cookie sheet with nonstick cooking spray. In small bowl, combine cheese, green onions, cilantro, salt and green chiles; mix well.

2. Separate dough into 8 biscuits. With serrated knife, cut each biscuit in half horizontally to make 16 rounds. Press or roll each to form 3½-inch round. Place 1 tablespoon cheese mixture in center of each round. Fold dough over filling; press edges with fork to seal. Form each filled biscuit into crescent shape. Place on sprayed cookie sheet.

3. Bake at 375°F. for 11 to 16 minutes or until golden brown. Cool 5 minutes. Serve warm.

NUTRITION INFORMATION PER SERVING: Serving Size: 1 Appetizer; Calories 125; Calories from Fat 55 **% Daily Value:** Total Fat 6g 9%; Saturated Fat 2g 10%; Cholesterol 5mg 2%; Sodium 430mg 18%; Total Carbohydrate 14g 5%; Dietary Fiber 0g 0%; Sugars 4g; Protein 4g; Vitamin A 2%; Vitamin C 2%; Calcium 6%; Iron 4% **Dietary Exchanges:** 1 Starch, 1 Fat **OR** 1 Carbohydrate, 1 Fat **Carbohydrate Choices:** 1

doughboy tip
Make it a Mexican fiesta and arrange the warm appetizers on a pretty colorful plate. Set out bowls of refried beans, tomato salsa and guacamole to serve with the finished foldovers.

chile cheese puffs

PREP TIME: 20 minutes (Ready in 45 minutes)
YIELD: 32 servings

1 (11-oz.) can Pillsbury®
Refrigerated Breadsticks

2 eggs

8 oz. (2 cups) shredded
Cheddar cheese

¼ cup finely chopped onion

½ cup mayonnaise

¼ teaspoon salt

¼ teaspoon pepper

¼ teaspoon ground red pepper
(cayenne)

1 (4.5-oz.) can chopped green
chiles, drained

1. Heat oven to 375°F. Lightly grease 13x9-inch pan. Unroll dough into 1 long rectangle in greased pan. Starting at center, press out dough to edges of pan; press perforations to seal.

2. Beat eggs in medium bowl. Add all remaining ingredients; mix well. Spoon and spread mixture evenly over dough.

3. Bake at 375°F. for 17 to 22 minutes or until filling is set and edges are light golden brown. Cool 5 minutes. Cut into small squares. Serve warm.

NUTRITION INFORMATION PER SERVING: **Serving Size:** ½₂ of Recipe; Calories 90; Calories from Fat 50 **% Daily Value:** Total Fat 6g 9%; Saturated Fat 2g 10%; Cholesterol 25mg 8%; Sodium 170mg 7%; Total Carbohydrate 5g 2%; Dietary Fiber 0g 0%; Sugars 1g; Protein 3g; Vitamin A 2%; Vitamin C 0%; Calcium 6%; Iron 2% **Dietary Exchanges:** ½ Starch, 1 Fat **OR** ½ Carbohydrate, 1 Fat **Carbohydrate Choices:** 0

doughboy tip

Stir up a quick homemade salsa to serve with these cheese puff squares. To improvise, mix chopped fresh tomatoes, green chiles and finely chopped onion with some lime juice and a dash of ground cumin.

caraway breadstick twists

PREP TIME: 30 minutes
YIELD: 10 twists

1 (10.6-oz.) pkg. Pillsbury®
Refrigerated Garlic Breadsticks

1 teaspoon deli-style
brown mustard

2 oz. (½ cup) finely shredded
Swiss cheese

3 tablespoons finely
chopped onion

2 teaspoons finely chopped
fresh parsley

1 to 2 teaspoons caraway seed

1. Heat oven to 375°F. Spray cookie sheet with nonstick cooking spray. Unroll dough; separate into 2 equal sections along center perforation. Spread half of the garlic spread from container evenly over 1 dough section. Spread with mustard. Top with cheese, onion, parsley and caraway seed; press in firmly.

2. Place remaining dough section over topped dough; press edges to seal. Spread remaining garlic spread over top of dough.

3. With sharp knife, cut filled dough in half lengthwise; cut into pieces along perforations. Twist each dough strip 2 times, stretching slightly. Place 1 inch apart on sprayed cookie sheet. Firmly press down ends.

4. Bake at 375°F. for 10 to 15 minutes or until golden brown. Serve warm.

NUTRITION INFORMATION PER SERVING: **Serving Size:** 1 Twist; Calories 110; Calories from Fat 45 **% Daily Value:** Total Fat 5g 8%; Saturated Fat 2g 10%; Cholesterol 5mg 2%; Sodium 310mg 13%; Total Carbohydrate 13g 4%; Dietary Fiber 1g 4%; Sugars 2g; Protein 4g; Vitamin A 2%; Vitamin C 0%; Calcium 6%; Iron 4% **Dietary Exchanges:** 1 Starch, 1 Fat **OR** 1 Carbohydrate, 1 Fat **Carbohydrate Choices:** 1

doughboy tip

Serve these savory twists warm from the oven with spicy mustard for dipping.

sun-dried tomato crescents

PREP TIME: 30 minutes
YIELD: 8 crescents

1 (8-oz.) can Pillsbury®
Refrigerated Crescent Dinner Rolls

8 teaspoons purchased sun-dried
tomato sauce and spread
(from 10-oz. jar)

4 teaspoons ricotta cheese

1 egg, beaten

½ to 1 teaspoon poppy seed

1. Heat oven to 375°F. Separate dough into 8 triangles. Place 1 teaspoon tomato sauce on shortest side of each triangle. Top each with ½ teaspoon ricotta cheese.

2. Roll up, starting at shortest side of triangle and rolling to opposite point. Place point side down on ungreased cookie sheet. Curve into crescent shape. Brush tops and sides with beaten egg. Sprinkle with poppy seed.

3. Bake at 375°F. for 10 to 13 minutes or until golden brown. Cool 5 minutes. Serve warm.

NUTRITION INFORMATION PER SERVING: Serving Size: 1 Crescent; Calories 110; Calories from Fat 45 **% Daily Value:** Total Fat 5g 8%; Saturated Fat 1g 5%; Cholesterol 0mg 0%; Sodium 350mg 15%; Total Carbohydrate 14g 5%; Dietary Fiber 1g 4%; Sugars 4g; Protein 2g; Vitamin A 0%; Vitamin C 2%; Calcium 2%; Iron 4% **Dietary Exchanges:** 1 Starch, 1 Fat **OR** 1 Carbohydrate, 1 Fat **Carbohydrate Choices:** 1

doughboy tip

No poppy seed on hand? Sprinkle the dough with sesame seed, crushed fennel seed or coarse ground black pepper instead.

three-cheese crescent twirls

PREP TIME: 30 minutes
YIELD: 16 appetizers

2 oz. (½ cup) crumbled
blue cheese

1 oz. (¼ cup) shredded hot pepper
Monterey Jack cheese

2 tablespoons cream cheese,
softened

1 tablespoon mayonnaise

1 (8-oz.) can Pillsbury®
Refrigerated Crescent Dinner Rolls

2 teaspoons chopped fresh parsley

1. Heat oven to 375°F. Lightly spray cookie sheet with nonstick cooking spray. In small bowl, combine all cheeses and mayonnaise; mix until well blended and soft.

2. Separate dough into 2 long rectangles. Firmly press perforations to seal. Spread cheese mixture evenly over rectangles. Starting at short side, roll up each; pinch edges to seal. Cut each roll into 8 slices. Place cut side down on sprayed cookie sheet. Sprinkle with parsley.

3. Bake at 375°F. for 12 to 15 minutes or until golden brown. Immediately remove from cookie sheet. Cool 3 minutes. Serve warm.

NUTRITION INFORMATION PER SERVING: **Serving Size:** 1 Appetizer; Calories 80; Calories from Fat 45 **% Daily Value:** Total Fat 5g 8%; Saturated Fat 2g 10%; Cholesterol 5mg 2%; Sodium 240mg 10%; Total Carbohydrate 7g 2%; Dietary Fiber 0g 0%; Sugars 2g; Protein 2g; Vitamin A 2%; Vitamin C 0%; Calcium 4%; Iron 2% **Dietary Exchanges:** ½ Starch, 1 Fat **OR** ½ Carbohydrate, 1 Fat **Carbohydrate Choices:** ½

doughboy tip

To jump-start preparation of these cheesy snacks, assemble the pinwheels up to 2 hours in advance and refrigerate them, covered, until baking time.

soft pesto pretzels

PREP TIME: 20 minutes (Ready in 40 minutes)
YIELD: 12 pretzels

1 (11-oz.) can Pillsbury®
Refrigerated Breadsticks

1 tablespoon purchased pesto

1 egg white

2 teaspoons grated
Parmesan-Romano cheese blend

1. Heat oven to 375°F. Line cookie sheet with parchment paper or use ungreased cookie sheet. Separate dough into 12 breadsticks. With finger, firmly press dough to make indentation lengthwise down center of each breadstick.

2. Spoon ¼ teaspoon pesto into each indentation. Fold dough lengthwise over pesto; press edges to seal.

3. Twist and stretch each breadstick to form 22-inch rope. Shape each rope into pretzel shape; 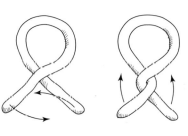 tuck ends under and press to seal. (See diagram.) Place on paper-lined cookie sheet. Beat egg white in small bowl until foamy. Brush over pretzels. Sprinkle with cheese.

4. Bake at 375°F. for 12 to 18 minutes or until golden brown. Serve warm.

NUTRITION INFORMATION PER SERVING: **Serving Size:** 1 Pretzel; Calories 80; Calories from Fat 20 **% Daily Value:** Total Fat 2g 3%; Saturated Fat 1g 5%; Cholesterol 0mg 0%; Sodium 210mg 9%; Total Carbohydrate 12g 4%; Dietary Fiber 0g 0%; Sugars 2g; Protein 2g; Vitamin A 0%; Vitamin C 0%; Calcium 0%; Iron 4% **Dietary Exchanges:** 1 Starch OR 1 Carbohydrate **Carbohydrate Choices:** 1

doughboy tip

Dip these soft and chewy pretzels into warm spaghetti sauce—yum! Add a crisp green salad and you'll have a lunch the kids will love.

goat cheese and sun-dried tomato bread bites

PREP TIME: 30 minutes (Ready in 50 minutes)
YIELD: 24 appetizers

1 (11-oz.) can Pillsbury®
Refrigerated Breadsticks

4 oz. (1 cup) crumbled chèvre
(goat) cheese with basil and garlic
or plain chèvre (goat) cheese

½ cup oil-packed sun-dried
tomatoes, drained,
coarsely chopped

1 egg

1 tablespoon water

Kosher or coarse salt, if desired

1. Heat oven to 375°F. Spray cookie sheet with nonstick cooking spray. Separate dough into 12 breadsticks; cut each in half crosswise to make 24 small breadsticks. Press each breadstick until 1½ inches wide.

2. With thumb, make indentation in center of each breadstick. Place 1 rounded teaspoon cheese in each indentation; top each with 1 teaspoon tomatoes. Roll up each jelly-roll fashion; place seam side down on sprayed cookie sheet.

3. In small bowl, combine egg and water; beat well. Lightly brush over tops of filled breadsticks. Sprinkle each with salt.

4. Bake at 375°F. for 12 to 17 minutes or until tops are light golden brown. Serve warm.

NUTRITION INFORMATION PER SERVING: Serving Size: 1 Appetizer; Calories 60; Calories from Fat 20 **% Daily Value:** Total Fat 2g 3%; Saturated Fat 1g 5%; Cholesterol 10mg 3%; Sodium 250mg 10%; Total Carbohydrate 7g 2%; Dietary Fiber 0g 0%; Sugars 1g; Protein 2g; Vitamin A 0%; Vitamin C 2%; Calcium 0%; Iron 2% **Dietary Exchanges:** ½ Starch, ½ Fat **OR** ½ Carbohydrate, ½ Fat **Carbohydrate Choices:** ½

doughboy tip

For a peppered-herb flavor, sprinkle the breadsticks before baking with coarse ground black pepper and dried basil leaves along with the salt.

frijole rollies

PREP TIME: 15 minutes (Ready in 35 minutes)
YIELD: 16 appetizers

1 (16-oz.) can refried beans

1 (1.25-oz.) pkg. taco
seasoning mix

2 (8-oz.) cans Pillsbury®
Refrigerated Crescent Dinner Rolls

4 oz. hot pepper Monterey Jack
cheese, cut into
2½x½x¼-inch strips

1. Heat oven to 375°F. Spray 2 cookie sheets with nonstick cooking spray. In medium bowl, combine refried beans and taco seasoning mix; mix well.

2. Separate dough into 16 triangles. Spread each with about 2 tablespoons bean mixture. Place cheese strip on shortest side of each triangle. Roll up, starting at shortest side, gently rolling dough around filling and rolling to opposite point. Place on sprayed cookie sheets.

3. Bake at 375°F. for 12 to 17 minutes or until golden brown, switching position of cookie sheets halfway through baking. Serve warm.

NUTRITION INFORMATION PER SERVING: Serving Size: 1 Appetizer; Calories 160; Calories from Fat 65 **% Daily Value:** Total Fat 7g 11%; Saturated Fat 3g 15%; Cholesterol 10mg 3%; Sodium 560mg 23%; Total Carbohydrate 19g 6%; Dietary Fiber 2g 8%; Sugars 5g; Protein 5g; Vitamin A 6%; Vitamin C 2%; Calcium 6%; Iron 6% **Dietary Exchanges:** 1 Starch, 1½ Fat **OR** 1 Carbohydrate, 1½ Fat **Carbohydrate Choices:** 1

doughboy tip
Chunky salsa, sour cream and guacamole are good dipping choices for these south-of-the-border appetizers.

goat cheese, marinara and pine nut braid

PREP TIME: 20 minutes (Ready in 55 minutes)
YIELD: 10 servings

1 (10.6-oz.) pkg. Pillsbury®
Refrigerated Garlic Breadsticks

½ cup purchased marinara sauce

1 oz. (¼ cup) crumbled chèvre
(goat) cheese

¼ cup grated Parmesan cheese or
finely shredded fresh
Parmesan cheese

¼ to ½ teaspoon dried rosemary
leaves, crushed

¼ cup pine nuts, toasted

2 tablespoons chopped fresh basil

1. Heat oven to 375°F. Spray cookie sheet with nonstick cooking spray. Unroll dough; separate into 2 equal sections along center perforation. Place dough sections next to each other on sprayed cookie sheet forming 10 parallel strips. Press to form 12x7-inch rectangle.

2. Spread marinara sauce lengthwise in 3-inch-wide strip down center of dough to within ½ inch of edges. Sprinkle chèvre cheese, 2 tablespoons of the Parmesan cheese, rosemary and pine nuts over sauce.

3. Cut dough on perforation lines up to filling. Fold strips of dough over filling, stretching slightly; press edges of dough together. Carefully spread garlic spread from container over dough. Sprinkle with remaining 2 tablespoons Parmesan cheese.

4. Bake at 375°F. for 17 to 22 minutes or until golden brown. Sprinkle with basil. Cool 10 minutes. Cut into crosswise slices. Serve warm.

NUTRITION INFORMATION PER SERVING: Serving Size: ¹⁄₁₀ of Recipe; Calories 140; Calories from Fat 60 **% Daily Value:** Total Fat 7g 11%; Saturated Fat 2g 10%; Cholesterol 5mg 2%; Sodium 390mg 16%; Total Carbohydrate 14g 5%; Dietary Fiber 1g 4%; Sugars 2g; Protein 5g; Vitamin A 4%; Vitamin C 0%; Calcium 8%; Iron 6% **Dietary Exchanges:** 1 Starch, 1½ Fat **OR** 1 Carbohydrate, 1½ Fat **Carbohydrate Choices:** 1

doughboy tip
Be sure to store chèvre (goat) cheese in the refrigerator, tightly wrapped in plastic and away from eggs, butter and other foods that might easily pick up other flavors.

cheesy twists

PREP TIME: 30 minutes
YIELD: 6 twists

¼ cup grated Parmesan cheese

½ teaspoon dried parsley flakes

¼ teaspoon garlic powder

Dash paprika

2 teaspoons margarine or
butter, melted

1 (8-oz.) can Pillsbury®
Refrigerated Crescent Dinner Rolls

1 egg white, beaten

2 teaspoons sesame seed

1. Heat oven to 375°F. In small bowl, combine cheese, parsley, garlic powder, paprika and margarine; mix well.

2. Unroll dough; separate crosswise into 2 equal sections along center perforations. Press perforations to seal. Spoon cheese mixture evenly over 1 dough section. Top with remaining dough section; press edges to seal. Cut into 6 strips. Twist strips; place on ungreased cookie sheet. Brush tops of strips lightly with egg white. Sprinkle with sesame seed.

3. Bake at 375°F. for 9 to 15 minutes or until golden brown. Serve warm.

NUTRITION INFORMATION PER SERVING: Serving Size: 1 Twist; Calories 175; Calories from Fat 80 **% Daily Value:** Total Fat 9g 14%; Saturated Fat 3g 15%; Cholesterol 5mg 2%; Sodium 560mg 23%; Total Carbohydrate 18g 6%; Dietary Fiber 1g 4%; Sugars 5g; Protein 5g; Vitamin A 2%; Vitamin C 0%; Calcium 6%; Iron 6% **Dietary Exchanges:** 1 Starch, 2 Fat **OR** 1 Carbohydrate, 2 Fat **Carbohydrate Choices:** 1

doughboy tip

Parmesan cheese, made from cow's milk, and pecorino Romano, made from sheep's milk, are both hard grating cheeses that are traditionally served with pasta. You can use either in this recipe.

savory biscuit monkey bread

PREP TIME: 15 minutes (Ready in 55 minutes)
YIELD: 10 servings

¼ cup margarine or butter, melted

½ teaspoon dry mustard

1 garlic clove, minced, or
¼ teaspoon garlic powder

1 (12-oz.) can (10 biscuits)
Pillsbury® Golden Layers™
Refrigerated Buttermilk Biscuits

1 (6-oz.) can (5 biscuits) Pillsbury®
Golden Layers™ Refrigerated
Buttermilk Biscuits

¼ cup grated Parmesan cheese

1. Heat oven to 400°F. In small bowl, combine margarine, dry mustard and garlic; mix well. Coat bottom of 8- or 9-inch round cake pan with 2 tablespoons of the margarine mixture.

2. Separate dough into 10 biscuits; cut each into quarters. Arrange biscuit pieces evenly in prepared pan. Drizzle reserved margarine mixture over biscuit pieces. Sprinkle with cheese.

3. Bake at 400°F. for 30 to 40 minutes or until golden brown. Invert bread onto wire rack; invert again onto serving plate. Serve warm.

NUTRITION INFORMATION PER SERVING: Serving Size: ⅟₁₀ of Recipe; Calories 235; Calories from Fat 115 **% Daily Value:** Total Fat 13g 20%; Saturated Fat 3g 15%; Cholesterol 0mg 0%; Sodium 710mg 30%; Total Carbohydrate 25g 8%; Dietary Fiber 1g 4%; Sugars 7g; Protein 5g; Vitamin A 4%; Vitamin C 0%; Calcium 4%; Iron 8% **Dietary Exchanges:** 1½ Starch, 2½ Fat **OR** 1½ Carbohydrate, 2½ Fat **Carbohydrate Choices:** ½

doughboy tip

This savory pull-apart bread goes well with soups and stews. To make a flavored butter to serve with the bread, blend ½ teaspoon dried basil or oregano leaves or another favorite herb into ¼ cup softened butter.

tomato-basil appetizer wedges

PREP TIME: 20 minutes (Ready in 1 hour 10 minutes)
YIELD: 12 servings

1 Pillsbury® Refrigerated Pie Crust (from 15-oz. pkg.), softened as directed on package

½ cup Italian-style dry bread crumbs

⅓ cup chopped fresh basil

¼ cup grated Romano cheese

¼ teaspoon salt

¼ teaspoon freshly ground black pepper

1 cup ricotta cheese

3 tablespoons extra-virgin or regular olive oil

3 Italian plum tomatoes, seeded, diced

1. Heat oven to 400°F. Remove crust from pouch; unfold crust. Place on ungreased cookie sheet; press out fold lines. With rolling pin, roll to form 12-inch round.

2. In medium bowl, combine bread crumbs, basil, Romano cheese, salt, pepper, ricotta cheese and oil; mix well. Stir in tomatoes. Spoon and spread over crust to within 3 inches of edge. Fold edge of crust 3 inches over filling; crimp crust slightly.

3. Bake at 400°F. for 25 to 35 minutes or until golden brown. Cool 15 minutes. Cut into wedges. Serve warm or cool.

NUTRITION INFORMATION PER SERVING: **Serving Size:** ¹/₁₂ of Recipe; Calories 175; Calories from Fat 100 **% Daily Value:** Total Fat 11g 17%; Saturated Fat 4g 20%; Cholesterol 11mg 4%; Sodium 230mg 10%; Total Carbohydrate 14g 5%; Dietary Fiber 0g 0%; Sugars 2g; Protein 5g; Vitamin A 6%; Vitamin C 2%; Calcium 10%; Iron 2% **Dietary Exchanges:** 1 Starch, 2 Fat **OR** 1 Carbohydrate, 2 Fat **Carbohydrate Choices:** 1

doughboy tip

Add a fresh finish to these appetizers by garnishing each serving with a thin slice of fresh plum tomato and shredded fresh basil.

southwestern flatbread

PREP TIME: 20 minutes (Ready in 40 minutes)
YIELD: 20 servings

2 teaspoons olive oil

1 (11-oz.) can Pillsbury®
Refrigerated Crusty French Loaf

½ cup roasted salted shelled
sunflower seeds

1 teaspoon Mexican chili powder

½ to 1 teaspoon coarse salt

1. Heat oven to 375°F. Brush large cookie sheet with 1 teaspoon of the oil. Unroll dough onto oiled cookie sheet. With rolling pin, roll out to form 17x14-inch rectangle. Drizzle dough with remaining 1 teaspoon oil; brush to spread.

2. In small bowl, combine sunflower seeds and chili powder; mix well. Sprinkle over dough. Firmly roll rolling pin over dough, pressing in seeds. (Break any air bubbles that form.) Sprinkle dough with salt.

3. Bake at 375°F. for 12 to 16 minutes or until golden brown. Remove from cookie sheet; place on wire rack. Cool 10 minutes. Tear or cut into pieces. Serve warm.

NUTRITION INFORMATION PER SERVING: Serving Size: ¹⁄₂₀ of Recipe; Calories 60; Calories from Fat 25 **% Daily Value:** Total Fat 3g 5%; Saturated Fat 0g 0%; Cholesterol 0mg 0%; Sodium 220mg 9%; Total Carbohydrate 7g 2%; Dietary Fiber 1g 4%; Sugars 1g; Protein 2g; Vitamin A 0%; Vitamin C 0%; Calcium 0%; Iron 4% **Dietary Exchanges:** ½ Starch, ½ Fat OR ½ Carbohydrate, ½ Fat **Carbohydrate Choices:** ½

doughboy tip

Serve this zesty flatbread with soup, stew or hearty chili—it's perfect for mopping up all the savory juices. You might want to use pine nuts instead of sunflower seeds for a slightly different flavor.

quick 'n easy herb flatbread

PREP TIME: 25 minutes
YIELD: 9 servings

1 (10-oz.) can Pillsbury®
Refrigerated Pizza Crust

1 tablespoon olive or vegetable oil

½ to 1 teaspoon dried basil leaves

½ to 1 teaspoon dried rosemary
leaves, crushed

½ teaspoon minced garlic

⅛ teaspoon salt

1 small tomato

1 oz. (¼ cup) shredded fresh
Parmesan cheese

1. Heat oven to 425°F. Spray cookie sheet with nonstick cooking spray. Unroll dough; place on sprayed cookie sheet. Starting at center, press out dough to form 12x8-inch rectangle.

2. In small bowl, combine oil, basil, rosemary and garlic; mix well. Brush over dough. Sprinkle with salt.

3. Chop tomato; place in shallow bowl. With back of spoon, crush tomato. Spread tomato over dough.

4. Bake at 425°F. for 5 to 9 minutes or until edges are light golden brown. Sprinkle with cheese. Bake an additional 2 to 3 minutes or until cheese is melted and edges are golden brown. Cut into squares. Serve warm.

NUTRITION INFORMATION PER SERVING: Serving Size: ⅑ of Recipe; Calories 100; Calories from Fat 25 **% Daily Value:** Total Fat 3g 5%; Saturated Fat 1g 5%; Cholesterol 2mg 1%; Sodium 290mg 12%; Total Carbohydrate 15g 5%; Dietary Fiber 1g 4%; Sugars 2g; Protein 4g; Vitamin A 0%; Vitamin C 0%; Calcium 4%; Iron 6% **Dietary Exchanges:** 1 Starch, ½ Fat OR 1 Carbohydrate, ½ Fat **Carbohydrate Choices:** 1

doughboy tip

Personalize this flatbread with a sprinkling of chopped green or red bell pepper or sliced ripe olives.

breadstick focaccia

PREP TIME: 15 minutes (Ready in 40 minutes)
YIELD: 6 servings

1 (11-oz.) can Pillsbury®
Refrigerated Breadsticks

1 teaspoon olive oil

2 teaspoons chopped fresh
rosemary

½ teaspoon coarse salt

1 tablespoon slivered pitted
ripe olives

6 thin red bell pepper strips

1. Heat oven to 375°F. Separate dough into 12 breadsticks. Starting at center of ungreased cookie sheet, coil strips loosely into a spiral, pinching ends together securely as strips are added. Press down very firmly on tops of dough strips to form ½-inch-thick round of dough.

2. Drizzle dough with olive oil. Sprinkle rosemary, salt and olives over dough. Arrange bell pepper strips in spoke-fashion on top.

3. Bake at 375°F. for 20 to 25 minutes or until edges are deep golden brown. Cut into wedges. Serve warm.

NUTRITION INFORMATION PER SERVING: **Serving Size:** ⅙ of Recipe; Calories 145; Calories from Fat 25 **% Daily Value:** Total Fat 3g 5%; Saturated Fat 1g 5%; Cholesterol 0mg 0%; Sodium 580mg 24%; Total Carbohydrate 25g 8%; Dietary Fiber 0g 0%; Sugars 3g; Protein 4g; Vitamin A 2%; Vitamin C 4%; Calcium 0%; Iron 8% **Dietary Exchanges:** 1½ Starch, ½ Fat OR 1½ Carbohydrate, ½ Fat **Carbohydrate Choices:** 1½

doughboy tip

Fresh rosemary resembles thick pine needles on woody branches. To cook with the rosemary, strip the needles off of the stems and chop the needles into small bits. Discard the woody stems.

Doughboy Recommends

chapter 2
Grand Weekend Brunches

EASY CHERRY-ALMOND COFFEE CAKE, page 94

pumpkin-pecan braid

PREP TIME: 20 minutes (Ready in 50 minutes)
YIELD: 6 servings

COFFEE CAKE

¾ cup canned pumpkin

⅓ cup firmly packed brown sugar

1 teaspoon cinnamon

⅛ teaspoon ginger

⅛ teaspoon nutmeg

1 egg, separated

½ cup chopped pecans

1 (8-oz.) can Pillsbury®
Refrigerated Crescent Dinner Rolls

GLAZE

½ cup powdered sugar

2 to 3 teaspoons milk

GARNISH

1 tablespoon chopped pecans

1. Heat oven to 350°F. Spray cookie sheet with nonstick cooking spray. In medium bowl, combine pumpkin, brown sugar, cinnamon, ginger, nutmeg and egg yolk; blend well. Stir in ½ cup pecans.

2. Unroll dough onto sprayed cookie sheet. Firmly press edges and perforations to seal. Press to form 13x7-inch rectangle. Spread filling lengthwise in 3½-inch-wide strip down center of dough to within 1 inch of ends.

3. With scissors or sharp knife, make cuts 1 inch apart on long sides of dough rectangle just to edge of filling. Fold strips at an angle across filling, overlapping ends and alternating from side to side. Beat egg white in small bowl until foamy; brush over dough.

4. Bake at 350°F. for 20 to 30 minutes or until deep golden brown. Immediately remove from cookie sheet; place on serving platter.

5. In small bowl, blend glaze ingredients until smooth, adding enough milk for desired drizzling consistency. Drizzle over warm coffee cake. Sprinkle with 1 tablespoon pecans. Serve warm.

NUTRITION INFORMATION PER SERVING: **Serving Size:** ⅙ of Recipe; Calories 330; Calories from Fat 150 **% Daily Value:** Total Fat 17g 26%; Saturated Fat 3g 15%; Cholesterol 35mg 12%; Sodium 300mg 13%; Total Carbohydrate 38g 13%; Dietary Fiber 3g 12%; Sugars 23g; Protein 5g; Vitamin A 140%; Vitamin C 0%; Calcium 4%; Iron 10% **Dietary Exchanges:** 2 Starch, ½ Fruit, 3 Fat **OR** 2½ Carbohydrate, 3 Fat **Carbohydrate Choices:** 2½

doughboy tip

Because you are adding your own spices to this home-baked bread, be sure to use plain canned pumpkin rather than pumpkin pie filling, which has already been sweetened and spiced.

poppy seed swirl loaf

PREP TIME: 15 minutes (Ready in 1 hour 25 minutes)
YIELD: 12 servings

BREAD

½ cup poppy seed filling
(from 12½-oz. can)

2 teaspoons grated lemon peel

1 (11-oz.) can Pillsbury®
Refrigerated Crusty French Loaf

⅓ cup golden raisins

FROSTING

⅓ cup powdered sugar

1 to 2 teaspoons water

1. Heat oven to 350°F. Grease cookie sheet. In small bowl, combine poppy seed filling and lemon peel; mix well.

2. Unroll dough onto floured surface, forming 13x12-inch rectangle. Drop poppy seed mixture by small teaspoonfuls over dough to within ½ inch of edges; gently spread being careful not to stretch dough. Sprinkle with raisins. Starting with one long side, loosely roll up dough; pinch edges to seal. Place seam side down on greased cookie sheet.

3. Bake at 350°F. for 28 to 35 minutes or until bread is deep golden brown and sounds hollow when tapped with finger. Cool 30 minutes.

4. In small bowl, blend frosting ingredients until smooth, adding enough water for desired spreading consistency. Spread frosting over top of cooled bread. Let stand 5 minutes or until set. Cut into crosswise slices. Serve warm.

NUTRITION INFORMATION PER SERVING: Serving Size: 1⁄12 of Recipe; Calories 130; Calories from Fat 20 **% Daily Value:** Total Fat 2g 3%; Saturated Fat 0g 0%; Cholesterol 0mg 0%; Sodium 160mg 7%; Total Carbohydrate 24g 8%; Dietary Fiber 2g 8%; Sugars 12g; Protein 3g; Vitamin A 0%; Vitamin C 0%; Calcium 6%; Iron 6% **Dietary Exchanges:** 1 Starch, ½ Fruit, ½ Fat **OR** 1½ Carbohydrate, ½ Fat **Carbohydrate Choices:** 1½

doughboy tip

If you like lemon, you'll love this swirled loaf. For extra lemon flavor, use lemon juice instead of water for the frosting and stir in a little extra grated lemon peel. To serve, slice the bread, then arrange the slices on a pretty platter garnished with long, twisted curls of lemon peel.

crescent caramel swirl

PREP TIME: 20 minutes (Ready in 55 minutes)
YIELD: 12 servings

½ cup butter
(do not use margarine)

½ cup chopped nuts

¾ cup firmly packed brown sugar

1 tablespoon water

2 (8-oz.) cans Pillsbury®
Refrigerated Crescent Dinner Rolls

1. Heat oven to 350°F. Melt butter in small saucepan. Coat bottom and sides of 12-cup fluted tube pan with 2 tablespoons of the melted butter; sprinkle pan with 3 tablespoons of the nuts. Add remaining nuts, brown sugar and water to remaining melted butter. Bring to a boil, stirring occasionally. Boil 1 minute, stirring constantly.

2. Remove dough from both cans; do not unroll. Cut each long roll into 8 slices. Arrange 8 slices, cut side down, in nut-lined pan; separate layers of each pinwheel slightly. Spoon half of brown sugar mixture over dough. Place remaining 8 dough slices alternately over bottom layer. Spoon remaining brown sugar mixture over slices.

3. Bake at 350°F. for 23 to 33 minutes or until deep golden brown. Cool 3 minutes. Invert onto serving platter or waxed paper. Serve warm.

NUTRITION INFORMATION PER SERVING: **Serving Size:** 1/12 of Recipe; Calories 290; Calories from Fat 160 **% Daily Value:** Total Fat 18g 28%; Saturated Fat 7g 35%; Cholesterol 20mg 7%; Sodium 370mg 15%; Total Carbohydrate 29g 10%; Dietary Fiber 1g 4%; Sugars 16g; Protein 3g; Vitamin A 6%; Vitamin C 0%; Calcium 2%; Iron 6% **Dietary Exchanges:** 1 Starch, 1 Fruit, 3½ Fat **OR** 2 Carbohydrate, 3½ Fat **Carbohydrate Choices:** 2

doughboy tip

Don't be tempted to substitute margarine for the butter in this sticky-bun-style treat. Besides giving the dish a rich, caramel flavor, butter makes a coffee cake that also holds together better than one made with margarine.

cream cheese-raspberry coffee cake

PREP TIME: 30 minutes (Ready in 1 hour)
YIELD: 12 servings

COFFEE CAKE

2 (8-oz.) cans Pillsbury®
Refrigerated Crescent Dinner Rolls

1 teaspoon sugar

FILLING

1 (8-oz.) pkg. cream cheese,
softened

¼ cup sugar

2 teaspoons grated orange peel

1 teaspoon vanilla

1 egg

1 pint (2 cups) fresh raspberries

GLAZE

½ cup powdered sugar

1 tablespoon margarine
or butter, softened

2 teaspoons orange juice

doughboy tip

Fresh raspberries are delicate and extremely perishable, so plan to use them within a day or two of when you buy them. When you're at the market, choose sweet-smelling berries that are firm and fresh with no signs of mold. Be sure to store these fragile gems in a moisture-proof container in the refrigerator.

1. Heat oven to 350°F. Spray large cookie sheet or 14-inch pizza pan with nonstick cooking spray. Separate both cans of dough into 16 triangles. Reserve 4 triangles for topping. On sprayed cookie sheet, arrange 12 triangles in circle with points toward center, leaving 3-inch hole in center. Press dough to form 14-inch ring; press seams together to seal. Fold outer and center edges up ¼ inch.

2. In medium bowl, combine all filling ingredients except raspberries; mix well. Gently stir in raspberries. (Mixture will be thin.) Spoon filling over dough.

3. With scissors or pizza cutter, cut each reserved triangle lengthwise into thirds. Place 1 teaspoon sugar on work surface. Press each dough strip into sugar. Arrange sugared dough strips, sugar side up, evenly in spoke-fashion over filling. Press ends to seal at center and outer edges.

4. Bake at 350°F. for 25 to 30 minutes or until golden brown. Cool 10 minutes.

5. In small bowl, combine all glaze ingredients; stir until smooth. Drizzle over warm coffee cake. Serve warm.

NUTRITION INFORMATION PER SERVING: **Serving Size:** 1/12 of Recipe; Calories 270; Calories from Fat 125 **% Daily Value:** Total Fat 14g 22%; Saturated Fat 6g 30%; Cholesterol 40mg 13%; Sodium 530mg 22%; Total Carbohydrate 31g 10%; Dietary Fiber 2g 8%; Sugars 17g; Protein 5g; Vitamin A 8%; Vitamin C 4%; Calcium 2%; Iron 8% **Dietary Exchanges:** 1 Starch, 1 Fruit, 3 Fat **OR** 2 Carbohydrate, 3 Fat **Carbohydrate Choices:** 2

monkey bread

PREP TIME: 25 minutes (Ready in 1 hour 5 minutes)
YIELD: 12 servings

½ cup sugar

1 teaspoon cinnamon

2 (16.3-oz.) cans Pillsbury®
Grands!® Refrigerated
Buttermilk Biscuits

½ cup raisins, if desired

1 cup firmly packed brown sugar

¾ cup margarine or butter, melted

1. Heat oven to 350°F. Lightly grease 12-cup fluted tube pan. In food storage plastic bag, combine sugar and cinnamon.

2. Separate dough into 16 biscuits; cut each into quarters. Place dough pieces in bag; shake to coat. Arrange pieces in bottom of greased pan. Arrange raisins among biscuit pieces.

3. In small bowl, combine brown sugar and margarine; mix well. Pour over biscuit pieces.

4. Bake at 350°F. for 33 to 37 minutes or until golden brown and biscuits are no longer doughy in center. Cool in pan for 10 minutes. Invert onto serving plate. Serve warm. Pull apart for serving.

NUTRITION INFORMATION PER SERVING: Serving Size: ½ of Recipe; Calories 605; Calories from Fat 245 **% Daily Value:** Total Fat 27g 42%; Saturated Fat 6g 30%; Cholesterol 0mg 0%; Sodium 1,280mg 53%; Total Carbohydrate 82g 27%; Dietary Fiber 2g 8%; Sugars 50g; Protein 7g; Vitamin A 14%; Vitamin C 0%; Calcium 4%; Iron 16% **Dietary Exchanges:** 3 Starch, 3 Fruit, 4 Fat **OR** 6 Carbohydrate, 4 Fat **Carbohydrate Choices:** 5½

doughboy tip

To punch up the crunch in this anytime sweet treat, stir in about ½ cup chopped walnuts or pecans along with the raisins.

country apple coffee cake

PREP TIME: 20 minutes (Ready in 1 hour 10 minutes)
YIELD: 8 servings

COFFEE CAKE

2 tablespoons margarine
or butter, softened

1½ cups chopped peeled apples

1 (12-oz.) can Pillsbury® Golden
Layers™ Refrigerated
Flaky Biscuits

⅓ cup firmly packed brown sugar

¼ teaspoon cinnamon

⅓ cup light corn syrup

1½ teaspoons whiskey,
if desired

1 egg

½ cup pecan halves or pieces

GLAZE

⅓ cup powdered sugar

¼ teaspoon vanilla

1 to 2 teaspoons milk

1. Heat oven to 350°F. Using 1 tablespoon of the margarine, generously grease 9-inch round cake pan or 8-inch square pan. Spread 1 cup of the apples in greased pan.

2. Separate dough into 10 biscuits; cut each into quarters. Arrange biscuit pieces, points up, over apples. Top with remaining ½ cup apples.

3. In small bowl, combine remaining 1 tablespoon margarine, brown sugar, cinnamon, corn syrup, whiskey and egg; beat 2 to 3 minutes or until sugar is partially dissolved. Stir in pecans. Spoon over biscuit pieces and apples.

4. Bake at 350°F. for 35 to 45 minutes or until deep golden brown. Cool 5 minutes. If desired, remove from pan.

5. In small bowl, blend all glaze ingredients until smooth, adding enough milk for desired drizzling consistency. Drizzle over warm cake. Serve warm or cool. Store in refrigerator.

NUTRITION INFORMATION PER SERVING: **Serving Size:** ⅛ of Recipe; Calories 330; Calories from Fat 130 **% Daily Value:** Total Fat 14g 22%; Saturated Fat 2g 10%; Cholesterol 25mg 8%; Sodium 510mg 21%; Total Carbohydrate 47g 16%; Dietary Fiber 2g 8%; Sugars 24g; Protein 4g; Vitamin A 4%; Vitamin C 0%; Calcium 2%; Iron 8% **Dietary Exchanges:** 1½ Starch, 1½ Fruit, 2½ Fat **OR** 3 Carbohydrate, 2½ Fat **Carbohydrate Choices:** 3

doughboy tip

For baking, choose apples that are tart enough to remain flavorful even after being cooked. Granny Smiths and McIntosh are excellent choices. Granny Smiths will retain more shape and texture than McIntosh apples, which will soften more.

easy cherry-almond coffee cake

pictured on page 85

pictured on page 85

PREP TIME: 10 minutes (Ready in 45 minutes)
YIELD: 6 servings

1 (12.4-oz.) can Pillsbury®
Refrigerated Cinnamon Rolls
with Icing

1½ cups cherry pie filling
(from 21-oz. can)

1 tablespoon slivered almonds

1. Heat oven to 375°F. Spray 9-inch round cake pan with nonstick cooking spray. Separate dough into 8 rolls; cut each roll into quarters. Place dough pieces rounded side down in sprayed pan. Spoon pie filling over rolls. Sprinkle with almonds.

2. Bake at 375°F. for 25 to 35 minutes or until deep golden brown. Cool 3 minutes. Invert onto cutting board or plate; invert again onto serving plate.

3. Remove lid from icing. Microwave on HIGH for 3 to 7 seconds. Stir icing; drizzle desired amount of icing over warm coffee cake. Serve warm.

NUTRITION INFORMATION PER SERVING: **Serving Size:** ⅙ of Recipe; Calories 260; Calories from Fat 70 **% Daily Value:** Total Fat 8g 12%; Saturated Fat 2g 10%; Cholesterol 0mg 0%; Sodium 470mg 20%; Total Carbohydrate 44g 15%; Dietary Fiber 1g 4%; Sugars 25g; Protein 3g; Vitamin A 0%; Vitamin C 2%; Calcium 2%; Iron 8% **Dietary Exchanges:** 1 Starch, 2 Fruit, 1½ Fat **OR** 3 Carbohydrate, 1½ Fat **Carbohydrate Choices:** 3

doughboy tip

Reinvent this easy, luscious treat with other pie fillings: Apple, peach or blueberry are all equally delicious choices. And instead of slivered almonds, you might like to sprinkling the pie filling with chopped pecans, walnuts or hazelnuts.

lemon-pecan sunburst coffee cake

PREP TIME: 25 minutes (Ready in 50 minutes)
YIELD: 8 servings

COFFEE CAKE

1 (16.3-oz.) can Pillsbury®
Grands!® Refrigerated Original
Flaky Layers Biscuits

¼ cup finely chopped pecans

¼ cup sugar

2 teaspoons grated lemon peel

2 tablespoons margarine
or butter, melted

GLAZE

½ cup powdered sugar

1½ oz. cream cheese
(from 3-oz. pkg.), softened

2½ to 3 teaspoons lemon juice

1. Heat oven to 375°F. Grease 9- or 8-inch round cake pan. Separate dough into 8 biscuits. Place 1 biscuit in center of greased pan. Cut remaining biscuits in half, forming 14 half circles. Arrange pieces around center biscuit, in sunburst pattern with cut sides facing same direction.

2. In small bowl, combine pecans, sugar and lemon peel; mix well. Brush margarine over top of biscuits. Sprinkle with pecan mixture.

3. Bake at 375°F. for 20 to 25 minutes or until golden brown.

4. In small bowl, blend all glaze ingredients until smooth, adding enough lemon juice for desired drizzling consistency. Drizzle glaze over warm coffee cake. Cool 10 minutes. Serve warm.

NUTRITION INFORMATION PER SERVING: **Serving Size:** ⅛ of Recipe; Calories 335; Calories from Fat 145 **% Daily Value:** Total Fat 16g 25%; Saturated Fat 4g 20%; Cholesterol 5mg 2%; Sodium 750mg 31%; Total Carbohydrate 42g 14%; Dietary Fiber 1g 4%; Sugars 22g; Protein 5g; Vitamin A 4%; Vitamin C 0%; Calcium 2%; Iron 8% **Dietary Exchanges:** 2 Starch, 1 Fruit, 3 Fat OR 3 Carbohydrate, 3 Fat **Carbohydrate Choices:** 3

doughboy tip

Although the lemon flavor in this brunch cake is delightful, the cake can also be made with orange peel and orange juice instead of the lemon. For an extra burst of flavor, sprinkle the finished glaze with grated lemon or orange peel.

chocolate chip-cinnamon roll coffee cake

PREP TIME: 10 minutes (Ready in 55 minutes)
YIELD: 16 servings

½ cup margarine or
butter, softened

2 (12.4-oz.) cans Pillsbury®
Refrigerated Cinnamon Rolls
with Icing

1 (3.4-oz.) pkg. vanilla pudding
and pie filling mix (not instant)

½ cup firmly packed brown sugar

¼ cup miniature semisweet
chocolate chips

1. Heat oven to 375°F. Using 1 tablespoon of the margarine, generously grease 12-cup fluted tube pan. Place remaining margarine in small microwave-safe bowl. Microwave on HIGH for 1 minute or until melted when stirred.

2. Separate both cans of dough into 16 rolls; cut each in half crosswise. Place half of roll pieces in greased pan. Sprinkle with half of the pudding mix and half of the brown sugar. Drizzle with half of the melted margarine. Repeat layering with remaining roll pieces, pudding mix, brown sugar and melted margarine. Sprinkle with chocolate chips.

3. Bake at 375°F. for 24 to 28 minutes or until rolls are deep golden brown and dough appears done when slightly pulled apart. Cool in pan 2 minutes. Invert onto serving platter. Cool 15 minutes.

4. Remove lid from icing. Microwave icing on HIGH for 10 to 15 seconds or until of drizzling consistency. Drizzle over warm coffee cake. Cut into wedges. Serve warm.

NUTRITION INFORMATION PER SERVING: Serving Size: ¹⁄₁₆ of Recipe; Calories 260; Calories from Fat 110 % Daily Value: Total Fat 12g 18%; Saturated Fat 3g 15%; Cholesterol 9mg 3%; Sodium 460mg 19%; Total Carbohydrate 35g 12%; Dietary Fiber 1g 4%; Sugars 19g; Protein 3g; Vitamin A 6%; Vitamin C 0%; Calcium 2%; Iron 6% Dietary Exchanges: 1 Starch, 1 Fruit, 2½ Fat OR 2 Carbohydrate, 2½ Fat Carbohydrate Choices: 2

doughboy tip

Melting or softening margarine or butter in the microwave is easy. Place it in a bowl that is microwave-safe and be sure to cover the dish with a piece of waxed paper to prevent spattering.

upside-down apple-walnut coffee cake

PREP TIME: 20 minutes (Ready in 1 hour)
YIELD: 8 servings

1½ cups chopped peeled apples

1 (12.4-oz.) can Pillsbury®
Refrigerated Cinnamon Rolls
with Icing

½ cup chopped walnuts

⅓ cup firmly packed brown sugar

2 tablespoons margarine
or butter, melted

2 tablespoons corn syrup

1. Heat oven to 350°F. Spray 9-inch glass pie pan with nonstick cooking spray. Spread 1 cup of the apples in sprayed pan.

2. Separate dough into 8 rolls; cut each into quarters. Place dough pieces in large bowl. Add remaining ½ cup apples and walnuts.

3. In small bowl, combine brown sugar, margarine and corn syrup; mix well. Add brown sugar mixture to dough mixture; toss gently to combine. Spoon mixture over apples in pan.

4. Bake at 350°F. for 28 to 38 minutes or until deep golden brown. Cool 5 minutes. Invert onto serving platter.

5. Remove lid from icing. Microwave icing on HIGH for 10 to 15 seconds or until of drizzling consistency. Drizzle over warm coffee cake. Serve warm.

NUTRITION INFORMATION PER SERVING: **Serving Size:** ⅛ of Recipe; Calories 290; Calories from Fat 115 **% Daily Value:** Total Fat 13g 20%; Saturated Fat 2g 10%; Cholesterol 10mg 3%; Sodium 400mg 17%; Total Carbohydrate 39g 13%; Dietary Fiber 2g 8%; Sugars 20g; Protein 4g; Vitamin A 4%; Vitamin C 0%; Calcium 2%; Iron 8% **Dietary Exchanges:** 1½ Starch, 1 Fruit, 2½ Fat **OR** 2½ Carbohydrate, 2½ Fat **Carbohydrate Choices:** 2½

doughboy tip

If you want to get a head start on making this recipe, chop the apples ahead of time, then cover them with cold water mixed with a teaspoon or two of lemon juice. This will help prevent the apples from turning brown. Drain the apples and pat dry just before using them in the recipe.

most requested recipe

cinnamon-pecan pull apart

PREP TIME: 20 minutes (Ready in 1 hour)
YIELD: 12 servings

¾ cup chopped pecans

⅔ cup firmly packed brown sugar

½ cup margarine or butter, melted

½ cup sour cream

1 teaspoon maple flavor or vanilla

2 (12.4-oz.) cans Pillsbury®
Refrigerated Cinnamon Rolls
with Icing

1. Heat oven to 350°F. Grease 12-cup fluted tube pan or one-piece 10-inch tube pan. In large bowl, combine all ingredients except cinnamon rolls; mix well.

2. Separate both cans of dough into 16 rolls; cut each into quarters. Add dough pieces to pecan mixture; toss gently to coat. Spoon roll mixture into greased pan.

3. Bake at 350°F. for 30 to 40 minutes or until deep golden brown. Cool 10 minutes. Invert onto serving plate. Spread with icing. Serve warm.

NUTRITION INFORMATION PER SERVING: Serving Size: ¹⁄₁₂ of Recipe; Calories 390; Calories from Fat 200 **% Daily Value:** Total Fat 22g 34%; Saturated Fat 5g 25%; Cholesterol 20mg 7%; Sodium 580mg 24%; Total Carbohydrate 42g 14%; Dietary Fiber 2g 8%; Sugars 21g; Protein 5g; Vitamin A 10%; Vitamin C 0%; Calcium 4%; Iron 10% **Dietary Exchanges:** 2 Starch, 1 Fruit, 4 Fat **OR** 3 Carbohydrate, 4 Fat **Carbohydrate Choices:** 3

doughboy tip

If you're a raisin lover, add about ½ cup raisins or golden raisins to the pecan mixture. To make the raisins plumper, cover them with hot water and soak for 10 minutes. Drain the raisins well before adding them to the other ingredients.

microwave caramel sticky buns

PREP TIME: 15 minutes
YIELD: 5 buns

TOPPING

¼ cup margarine or butter

½ cup firmly packed brown sugar

2 tablespoons light corn syrup

2 tablespoons whipping cream

BUNS

2 tablespoons margarine or butter

⅓ cup firmly packed brown sugar

½ teaspoon cinnamon

1 (10.2-oz.) can (5 biscuits) Pillsbury® Grands!® Refrigerated Buttermilk Biscuits

1. Place ¼ cup margarine in 9-inch microwave-safe pie pan. Microwave on HIGH for 40 to 60 seconds. Add all remaining topping ingredients; mix well. Microwave on HIGH for 1 minute; stir.

2. In shallow microwave-safe dish, melt 2 tablespoons margarine in microwave on HIGH for 20 to 30 seconds. In another shallow dish, combine ⅓ cup brown sugar and cinnamon; mix well.

3. Separate dough into 5 biscuits. Dip biscuits in melted margarine to coat all sides; dip in brown sugar mixture, coating well. Arrange biscuits in circle over topping in pie pan, leaving center open.

4. Microwave on HIGH for 4 to 6 minutes or until biscuits are no longer doughy in center. Cool 30 seconds; invert onto serving plate. Serve warm.

NUTRITION INFORMATION PER SERVING: **Serving Size:** ⅕ of Recipe; Calories 510; Calories from Fat 215 **% Daily Value:** Total Fat 24g 37%; Saturated Fat 8g 40%; Cholesterol 20mg 7%; Sodium 860mg 36%; Total Carbohydrate 70g 23%; Dietary Fiber 1g 4%; Sugars 47g; Protein 4g; Vitamin A 14%; Vitamin C 0%; Calcium 4%; Iron 12% **Dietary Exchanges:** 2 Starch, 2½ Fruit, 4½ Fat **OR** 4½ Carbohydrate, 4½ Fat **Carbohydrate Choices:** 4½

doughboy tip

Because these ooey, gooey rolls are cooked in the microwave, the cooking time is critical. Be sure to cook them just until they are no longer doughy, as the recipe directs. If they are microwaved for too long, they will become tough and the caramel might get hard.

nutty orange-butterscotch biscuits

PREP TIME: 10 minutes (Ready in 40 minutes)
YIELD: 6 biscuits

1 tablespoon margarine
or butter, softened

½ cup butterscotch caramel
ice cream topping

⅓ cup chopped pecans

2 teaspoons grated orange peel

6 Pillsbury® Home Baked
Classics™ Frozen Buttermilk
Biscuits (from 25-oz. pkg.)

1. Heat oven to 375°F. With 1 tablespoon margarine, generously grease bottom and sides of 9-inch round cake pan. Spread ice cream topping in greased pan. Sprinkle with pecans and orange peel. Place frozen biscuits over pecans and orange peel.

2. Bake at 375°F. for 25 to 28 minutes or until golden brown and biscuits are no longer doughy. Immediately invert on serving platter. Spread any topping remaining in pan over biscuits. Serve warm.

NUTRITION INFORMATION PER SERVING: **Serving Size:** ⅙ of Recipe; Calories 330; Calories from Fat 145 **% Daily Value:** Total Fat 16g 25%; Saturated Fat 3g 15%; Cholesterol 0mg 0%; Sodium 700mg 29%; Total Carbohydrate 41g 14%; Dietary Fiber 1g 4%; Sugars 17g; Protein 5g; Vitamin A 2%; Vitamin C 0%; Calcium 6%; Iron 6% **Dietary Exchanges:** 2 Starch, 1 Fruit, 2½ Fat **OR** 3 Carbohydrate, 2½ Fat **Carbohydrate Choices:** 3

doughboy tip

For a special occasion, garnish the serving platter with orange twists. To make the twists, cut a navel orange into thin slices. Make a slit in each slice from the edge to the center; twist the slice in opposite directions to make a semi-spiral.

lemon poppy seed puffs

PREP TIME: 30 minutes (Ready in 50 minutes)
YIELD: 8 puffs

1 (8-oz.) pkg. cream cheese, softened

1¼ cups sugar

2 teaspoons grated lemon peel

1 tablespoon lemon juice

2 tablespoons poppy seed

1 (16.3-oz.) can Pillsbury® Grands!® Refrigerated Buttermilk Biscuits

½ cup margarine or butter, melted

1. Heat oven to 375°F. In medium bowl, combine cream cheese, ½ cup of the sugar, 1 teaspoon of the lemon peel and lemon juice; mix well. In another medium bowl, combine remaining ¾ cup sugar, 1 teaspoon lemon peel and poppy seed; mix well.

2. Separate dough into 8 biscuits. Carefully split side of each biscuit halfway to form opening. Fill each opening with 2 rounded tablespoons cream cheese mixture. Press edges firmly to seal. Dip filled biscuits in melted margarine; coat with poppy seed mixture. Place in ungreased jumbo nonstick muffin cups.

3. Bake at 375°F. for 13 to 17 minutes or until puffed and golden brown. Cool 10 minutes. Run knife around edge of each biscuit to loosen; remove from muffin cups. Serve warm. Store in refrigerator.

NUTRITION INFORMATION PER SERVING: **Serving Size:** ⅛ of Recipe; Calories 545; Calories from Fat 280 **% Daily Value:** Total Fat 31g 48%; Saturated Fat 11g 55%; Cholesterol 30mg 10%; Sodium 910mg 38%; Total Carbohydrate 60g 20%; Dietary Fiber 1g 4%; Sugars 40g; Protein 7g; Vitamin A 20%; Vitamin C 0%; Calcium 6%; Iron 10% **Dietary Exchanges:** 2 Starch, 2 Fruit, 6 Fat **OR** 4 Carbohydrate, 6 Fat **Carbohydrate Choices:** 4

doughboy tip

These tender, lemony puffs are likely to disappear fast, but if you have any leftovers, store them in a resealable food-storage plastic bag in the refrigerator. To reheat the puffs, wrap them in foil and bake at 350° F. for 10 to 12 minutes or until heated through.

magic marshmallow crescent puffs

PREP TIME: 20 minutes (Ready in 35 minutes)
YIELD: 16 puffs

PUFFS

¼ cup sugar

2 tablespoons all-purpose flour

1 teaspoon cinnamon

2 (8-oz.) cans Pillsbury® Refrigerated Crescent Dinner Rolls

16 large marshmallows

¼ cup margarine or butter, melted

GLAZE

½ cup powdered sugar

½ teaspoon vanilla

2 to 3 teaspoons milk

1. Heat oven to 375°F. Spray 16 muffin cups with nonstick cooking spray. In small bowl, combine sugar, flour and cinnamon; mix well.

2. Separate dough into 16 triangles. Dip 1 marshmallow in margarine; roll in sugar mixture. Place marshmallow on shortest side of triangle. Roll up, starting at shortest side of triangle and rolling to opposite point. Completely cover marshmallow with dough; firmly pinch edges to seal. Dip 1 end in remaining margarine; place margarine side down in sprayed muffin cup. Repeat with remaining marshmallows.

3. Bake at 375°F. for 12 to 15 minutes or until golden brown. (Place foil or cookie sheet on rack below muffin cups to guard against spills.) Cool in pan 1 minute. Remove rolls from muffin cups; place on wire racks set over waxed paper.

4. In small bowl, blend all glaze ingredients until smooth, adding enough milk for desired drizzling consistency. Drizzle over warm rolls. Serve warm.

NUTRITION INFORMATION PER SERVING: **Serving Size:** 1 Puff; Calories 180; Calories from Fat 65 **% Daily Value:** Total Fat 7g 11%; Saturated Fat 2g 10%; Cholesterol 0mg 0%; Sodium 380mg 16%; Total Carbohydrate 27g 9%; Dietary Fiber 1g 4%; Sugars 15g; Protein 2g; Vitamin A 2%; Vitamin C 0%; Calcium 0%; Iron 4% **Dietary Exchanges:** 1 Starch, 1 Fruit, 1 Fat OR 2 Carbohydrate, 1 Fat **Carbohydrate Choices:** 2

doughboy tip

If there are kids on hand, jazz up the icing with rainbow sprinkles or their favorite candy decorations. For a more adult-style treat, sprinkle the puffs with finely chopped nuts. Either way you'll need about ¼ cup.

mocha-cream cheese crescents

PREP TIME: 15 minutes (Ready in 35 minutes)
YIELD: 8 crescents

ROLLS

¼ cup powdered sugar

4 oz. cream cheese, softened

1½ teaspoons coffee-flavored liqueur or cooled strong coffee

½ teaspoon vanilla

¼ cup finely chopped macadamia nuts

1 (8-oz.) can Pillsbury® Refrigerated Crescent Dinner Rolls

GLAZE

¼ cup semisweet chocolate chips

½ teaspoon shortening or oil

1. Heat oven to 350°F. Lightly grease cookie sheet. In small bowl, combine powdered sugar, cream cheese, liqueur and vanilla; blend well. Stir in macadamia nuts.

2. Separate dough into 8 triangles. Spoon 1 heaping tablespoon cream cheese mixture onto shortest side of each triangle. Loosely roll up, starting at shortest side and rolling to opposite point. Place point side down on greased cookie sheet. Curve into crescent shape.

3. Bake at 350°F. for 12 to 15 minutes or until golden brown. Cool 5 minutes.

4. Meanwhile, in small saucepan, melt glaze ingredients over low heat, stirring until smooth. Drizzle over warm rolls. Serve warm or cool. Store in refrigerator.

NUTRITION INFORMATION PER SERVING: Serving Size: 1 Crescent; Calories 220; Calories from Fat 140 **% Daily Value:** Total Fat 15g 23%; Saturated Fat 6g 30%; Cholesterol 15mg 5%; Sodium 260mg 11%; Total Carbohydrate 19g 6%; Dietary Fiber 1g 4%; Sugars 9g; Protein 3g; Vitamin A 4%; Vitamin C 0%; Calcium 2%; Iron 6% **Dietary Exchanges:** 1 Starch, 3 Fat OR 1 Carbohydrate, 3 Fat **Carbohydrate Choices:** 1

doughboy tip

Although the coffee-flavored liqueur gives these sweet rolls their characteristic mocha flavor, you can substitute another flavored liqueur such as amaretto (almond liqueur) or frangelico (hazelnut liqueur). Chopped nuts sprinkled over the crescents immediately after glazing add an appealing crunch.

citrus crescent swirls

PREP TIME: 15 minutes (Ready in 30 minutes)
YIELD: 24 swirls

½ cup firmly packed brown sugar

2 tablespoons margarine or butter

1 tablespoon grated orange peel

3 tablespoons orange juice

2 (8-oz.) cans Pillsbury®
Refrigerated Crescent Dinner Rolls

1. Heat oven to 375°F. Spray 12x½-inch pizza pan with non-stick cooking spray. In small saucepan, combine brown sugar, margarine, orange peel and juice; mix well. Cook over medium heat until bubbly, stirring constantly. Set aside.

2. Remove dough from each can, keeping dough in 1 piece; do not unroll. Cut each roll into 12 slices. Arrange slices cut side down in sprayed pan. Spoon brown sugar mixture evenly over slices.

3. Bake at 375°F. for 13 to 15 minutes or until golden brown. Remove rolls from pan with pancake turner. Serve warm.

NUTRITION INFORMATION PER SERVING: Serving Size: 1 Swirl; Calories 100; Calories from Fat 45 % Daily Value: Total Fat 5g 8%; Saturated Fat 1g 5%; Cholesterol 0mg 0%; Sodium 160mg 7%; Total Carbohydrate 12g 4%; Dietary Fiber 0g 0%; Sugars 6g; Protein 1g; Vitamin A 0%; Vitamin C 0%; Calcium 0%; Iron 2% Dietary Exchanges: ½ Starch, ½ Fruit, 1 Fat OR 1 Carbohydrate, 1 Fat Carbohydrate Choices: 1

doughboy tip

If you're expecting company and want to have these rolls ready to go, they can be made up to 4 hours ahead. Just prepare them as directed and cover with plastic wrap and refrigerate. When you're ready to bake them, remove the wrap and bake as directed.

most requested recipe
choose-a-glaze doughnuts

PREP TIME: 40 minutes
YIELD: 20 doughnuts and 20 holes

CHOCOLATE GLAZE

½ cup powdered sugar

1 tablespoon unsweetened cocoa

1 tablespoon margarine
or butter, melted

2 to 3 teaspoons milk

CITRUS GLAZE

½ cup powdered sugar

½ teaspoon grated lemon
or orange peel

2 to 3 teaspoons lemon
or orange juice

VANILLA GLAZE

½ cup powdered sugar

½ teaspoon vanilla

2 to 3 teaspoons milk

DOUGHNUTS

Oil for deep-frying

2 (7.5-oz.) cans Pillsbury®
Refrigerated Buttermilk Biscuits

1. In small bowl, blend desired glaze ingredients until smooth, adding enough liquid for desired glaze consistency. Cover; set aside.

2. Heat oil in deep fryer or heavy saucepan to 375°F.

3. Separate both cans of dough into 20 biscuits; cut hole in center of each. Fry biscuits and holes in hot oil for 1 to 1½ minutes on each side or until golden brown. Drain on paper towel.

4. Dip top of each doughnut into desired glaze. Serve warm.

NUTRITION INFORMATION PER SERVING: **Serving Size:** 1 Doughnut and 1 hole with chocolate glaze; Calories 130; Calories from Fat 70 **% Daily Value:** Total Fat 8g 12%; Saturated Fat 2g 10%; Cholesterol 0mg 0%; Sodium 260mg 11%; Total Carbohydrate 13g 4%; Dietary Fiber 0g 0%; Sugars 6g; Protein 2g; Vitamin A 0%; Vitamin C 0%; Calcium 0%; Iron 2% **Dietary Exchanges:** 1 Starch, 1½ Fat **OR** 1 Carbohydrate, 1½ Fat **Carbohydrate Choices:** 1

doughboy tip

Don't be afraid to deep-fry — it's easy! Just be sure to maintain the correct oil temperature so that the outside gets crisp and golden brown and the inside stays tender. One of the secrets of success is to fry the doughnuts in batches to keep from overcrowding the pan and causing a drop in the oil temperature.

ham and chile brunch pizza

PREP TIME: 30 minutes
YIELD: 6 servings

1 (10-oz.) can Pillsbury®
Refrigerated Pizza Crust

6 eggs

¼ teaspoon salt

⅛ teaspoon pepper

1 tablespoon margarine or butter

1 cup julienne-cut strips or
chopped cooked ham

1 (4.5-oz.) can chopped
green chiles

6 oz. (1½ cups) shredded
Monterey Jack cheese or hot
pepper Monterey Jack cheese

2 tablespoons chopped fresh
cilantro, if desired

1. Heat oven to 425°F. Grease 14-inch pizza pan. Unroll dough; place in greased pan. Starting at center, press out dough to edge of pan. Bake at 425°F. for 6 to 8 minutes or until crust begins to brown.

2. Meanwhile, in medium bowl, combine eggs, salt and pepper; beat well. Melt margarine in large skillet over medium heat. Add eggs; cook 1 to 2 minutes or until firm but still moist, stirring frequently.

3. Remove partially baked crust from oven. Spoon and spread eggs over crust. Top with ham, chiles and cheese.

4. Return to oven; bake an additional 8 to 12 minutes or until crust is deep golden brown. Sprinkle with cilantro. Cut into wedges.

NUTRITION INFORMATION PER SERVING: **Serving Size:** ⅙ of Recipe; Calories 355; Calories from Fat 171 **% Daily Value:** Total Fat 19g 29%; Saturated Fat 8g 40%; Cholesterol 250mg 83%; Sodium 1,121mg 47%; Total Carbohydrate 24g 8%; Dietary Fiber 1g 4%; Sugars 5g; Protein 22g; Vitamin A 16%; Vitamin C 6%; Calcium 24%; Iron 14% **Dietary Exchanges:** 1½ Starch, 3 Medium-Fat Meat **OR** 1½ Carbohydrate, 3 Medium-Fat Meat **Carbohydrate Choices:** 1½

doughboy tip

It will be easier to press the pizza dough into the pan if it's kept cold until you're ready to use it. If refrigerated dough gets too warm, it becomes sticky and hard to work with. If the dough should become sticky, just pop it back in the refrigerator for about 10 minutes.

italian frittata biscuits

PREP TIME: 15 minutes (Ready in 35 minutes)
YIELD: 8 servings

1 (16.3-oz.) can Pillsbury®
Grands!® Refrigerated
Buttermilk Biscuits

3 eggs

1¼ to 1½ teaspoons dried
Italian seasoning

½ cup diced cooked ham

4 oz. (1 cup) shredded 6-cheese
Italian blend

¼ cup roasted red bell peppers
(from a jar), drained, chopped

½ cup diced seeded Italian
plum tomatoes

2 tablespoons thinly sliced
fresh basil leaves

1. Heat oven to 375°F. Spray large cookie sheet with nonstick cooking spray. Separate dough into 8 biscuits. Place 3 inches apart on sprayed cookie sheet. Press out each biscuit to form 4-inch round with ¼-inch-high rim around outside edge.

2. Beat 1 of the eggs in small bowl. Brush over tops and sides of biscuits. Sprinkle with 1 teaspoon of the Italian seasoning.

3. In another small bowl, combine remaining 2 eggs and remaining ¼ to ½ teaspoon Italian seasoning; beat well. Spoon evenly into each biscuit. Top with ham, ½ cup of the cheese, roasted peppers, tomatoes, basil and remaining ½ cup cheese.

4. Bake at 375°F. for 15 to 20 minutes or until biscuits are golden brown and eggs are set.

NUTRITION INFORMATION PER SERVING: **Serving Size:** ⅛ of Recipe; Calories 290; Calories from Fat 125 **% Daily Value:** Total Fat 14g 22%; Saturated Fat 5g 25%; Cholesterol 90mg 30%; Sodium 920mg 38%; Total Carbohydrate 29g 10%; Dietary Fiber 1g 4%; Sugars 9g; Protein 12g; Vitamin A 12%; Vitamin C 10%; Calcium 12%; Iron 10% **Dietary Exchanges:** 2 Starch, 1 Medium-Fat Meat, 1 Fat **OR** 2 Carbohydrate, 1 Medium-Fat Meat, 1 Fat **Carbohydrate Choices:** 2

doughboy tip

This recipe is an inspiration for an Italian brunch! Serve the filled biscuits with an array of Italian olives, slices of fresh mozzarella cheese, sliced fresh pears topped with ricotta cheese and cappuccino.

most requested recipe

italian zucchini crescent pie

PREP TIME: 30 minutes (Ready in 55 minutes)
YIELD: 6 servings

2 tablespoons margarine or butter

4 cups thinly sliced zucchini

1 cup chopped onions

2 tablespoons dried parsley flakes

½ teaspoon salt

½ teaspoon pepper

¼ teaspoon garlic powder

¼ teaspoon dried basil leaves

¼ teaspoon dried oregano leaves

2 eggs, well beaten

8 oz. (2 cups) shredded Muenster or mozzarella cheese

1 (8-oz.) can Pillsbury® Refrigerated Crescent Dinner Rolls

2 teaspoons prepared mustard

1. Heat oven to 375°F. Melt margarine in 12-inch skillet over medium-high heat. Add zucchini and onions; cook 6 to 8 minutes or until tender, stirring occasionally. Stir in parsley flakes, salt, pepper, garlic powder, basil and oregano.

2. In large bowl, combine eggs and cheese; mix well. Add cooked vegetable mixture; stir gently to mix.

3. Separate dough into 8 triangles. Place in ungreased 10-inch pie pan, 12x8-inch (2-quart) glass baking dish or 11-inch quiche pan; press over bottom and up sides to form crust. Firmly press perforations to seal. Spread crust with mustard. Pour egg mixture evenly into crust-lined pan.

4. Bake at 375°F. for 18 to 22 minutes or until knife inserted near center comes out clean. If necessary, cover edge of crust with strips of foil during last 10 minutes of baking to prevent excessive browning. Let stand 10 minutes before serving.

NUTRITION INFORMATION PER SERVING: Serving Size: ⅙ of Recipe; Calories 370; Calories from Fat 230 **% Daily Value:** Total Fat 25g 38%; Saturated Fat 10g 50%; Cholesterol 105mg 35%; Sodium 790mg 33%; Total Carbohydrate 21g 7%; Dietary Fiber 2g 8%; Sugars 7g; Protein 15g; Vitamin A 20%; Vitamin C 10%; Calcium 30%; Iron 10% **Dietary Exchanges:** 1 Starch, 1 Vegetable, 1½ High-Fat Meat, 2½ Fat **OR** 1 Carbohydrate, 1 Vegetable, 1½ High-Fat Meat, 2½ Fat **Carbohydrate Choices:** 1½

doughboy tip

For a colorful finish, garnish each serving with crisscrosses of thin strips of roasted red bell pepper or red bell pepper rings.

canadian bacon and potato quiche

PREP TIME: 25 minutes (Ready in 1 hour 15 minutes)
YIELD: 8 servings

1 Pillsbury® Refrigerated Pie Crust (from 15-oz. pkg.), softened as directed on package

1 cup frozen diced hash-brown potatoes (from 30-oz. pkg.), thawed

1 cup cut (½-inch) fresh asparagus spears

1 cup diced Canadian bacon

6 oz. (1½ cups) shredded Havarti cheese

4 eggs

1 cup milk

½ teaspoon dried marjoram leaves

¼ teaspoon salt

1. Heat oven to 375°F. Prepare pie crust as directed on package for *one-crust baked shell* using 9-inch glass pie pan. Prick crust generously with fork. Bake at 375°F. for about 8 minutes or until light golden brown.

2. Remove partially baked crust from oven. Layer potatoes, asparagus, bacon and cheese in crust. In medium bowl, beat eggs, milk, marjoram and salt until well blended. Pour over mixture in crust.

3. Bake at 375°F. for 45 to 50 minutes or until knife inserted in center comes out clean. Let stand 5 minutes. Cut into wedges.

NUTRITION INFORMATION PER SERVING: **Serving Size:** ⅛ of Recipe; Calories 275; Calories from Fat 155 **% Daily Value:** Total Fat 17g 26%; Saturated Fat 7g 35%; Cholesterol 140mg 47%; Sodium 620mg 26%; Total Carbohydrate 16g 5%; Dietary Fiber 1g 4%; Sugars 0g; Protein 15g; Vitamin A 10%; Vitamin C 4%; Calcium 16%; Iron 6% **Dietary Exchanges:** 1 Skim Milk, 1 Vegetable, 1 High-Fat Meat, 1½ Fat **OR** 1 Carbohydrate, 1 Vegetable, 1 High-Fat Meat, 1½ Fat **Carbohydrate Choices:** 1

doughboy tip

The Danish Havarti cheese used in this recipe adds a mild, creamy flavor that is a nice complement to the asparagus and Canadian bacon. If you like, another cheese such as colby, mild Swiss or Monterey Jack can also be used.

sausage and egg biscuit bake

PREP TIME: 20 minutes (Ready in 1 hour 5 minutes)
YIELD: 8 servings

1 (16.3-oz.) can Pillsbury® Grands!® Refrigerated Buttermilk Biscuits

1 lb. bulk mild Italian sausage

1 tablespoon olive oil

1 medium onion, sliced

1 (8-oz.) pkg. (about 3 cups) sliced fresh mushrooms

1 red bell pepper, cut into julienne strips

3 teaspoons dried Italian seasoning

2 garlic cloves, minced

2 eggs

1 cup milk

4 oz. (1 cup) shredded mozzarella cheese

½ cup grated Parmesan cheese

1. Heat oven to 375°F. Grease 2½-quart baking dish. Bake biscuits as directed on can. Remove biscuits from cookie sheet; cool slightly. Reduce oven temperature to 350°F.

2. Meanwhile, crumble sausage into large skillet. Cook over medium-high heat until browned and no longer pink, stirring frequently. Remove from skillet; place on plate to cool slightly.

3. In same skillet, heat oil over medium heat until hot. Add onions; cook and stir until tender. Add mushrooms; cook and stir until mushrooms just begin to brown. Add bell pepper, Italian seasoning, garlic and cooked sausage; cook 3 minutes, stirring constantly.

4. Cut biscuits into quarters; place in large bowl. Add sausage mixture; mix well.

5. In medium bowl, beat eggs and milk until smooth. Pour over sausage mixture. Add mozzarella and Parmesan cheese; mix well. Spoon into greased baking dish.

6. Bake at 350°F. for 35 to 45 minutes or until firm.

NUTRITION INFORMATION PER SERVING: **Serving Size:** ⅛ of Recipe; Calories 470; Calories from Fat 245 **% Daily Value:** Total Fat 27g 42%; Saturated Fat 10g 50%; Cholesterol 100mg 33%; Sodium 1,300mg 54%; Total Carbohydrate 34g 11%; Dietary Fiber 2g 8%; Sugars 11g; Protein 22g; Vitamin A 6%; Vitamin C 12%; Calcium 26%; Iron 16% **Dietary Exchanges:** 2 Starch, 1 Vegetable, 2 High-Fat Meat, 2 Fat **OR** 2 Carbohydrate, 1 Vegetable, 2 High-Fat Meat, 2 Fat **Carbohydrate Choices:** 2

doughboy tip

It's easy to prepare fresh mushrooms. Just trim the stems and use a small brush or damp cloth to wipe away dirt and debris. It's best not to soak mushrooms, as they will absorb water like a sponge and then add excess moisture to your dish during cooking.

hash-brown potato and sausage pie

PREP TIME: 15 minutes (Ready in 1 hour)
YIELD: 6 servings

1 lb. bulk pork sausage

5 cups frozen shredded hash-brown potatoes

¼ cup chopped onion

8 oz. (2 cups) shredded Cheddar cheese

4 eggs

½ cup milk

1 Pillsbury® Refrigerated Pie Crust (from 15-oz. pkg.), softened as directed on package

1. Heat oven to 425°F. Spray 9-inch deep-dish glass pie pan with nonstick cooking spray. Cook sausage in large skillet over medium-high heat until thoroughly cooked, stirring frequently. Drain.

2. Add potatoes and onion to sausage in skillet; mix well. Cook 5 to 8 minutes or until potatoes are slightly soft, stirring occasionally. Remove from heat. Stir in cheese.

3. Beat eggs in large bowl. Add milk; blend well. Reserve 1 tablespoon egg mixture for topping. Add potato mixture to remaining egg mixture; mix well. Spoon potato-egg mixture into sprayed pie pan, keeping mixture away from edges.

4. Remove pie crust from pouch. Unfold crust; press out fold lines. Place over potato mixture, tucking edges of crust around potato mixture. Turn edges under and press to edge of pie pan. Cut several slits in crust for steam to escape. Brush with reserved tablespoon egg mixture.

5. Bake at 425°F. for 25 minutes. Cover top of pie with foil to prevent excessive browning. Bake an additional 15 to 20 minutes or until potatoes are tender and crust is deep golden brown. Cut into wedges.

NUTRITION INFORMATION PER SERVING: Serving Size: ⅙ of Recipe; Calories 640; Calories from Fat 335 **% Daily Value:** Total Fat 37g 57%; Saturated Fat 17g 85%; Cholesterol 220mg 73%; Sodium 930mg 39%; Total Carbohydrate 54g 18%; Dietary Fiber 3g 12%; Sugars 6g; Protein 26g; Vitamin A 12%; Vitamin C 10%; Calcium 26%; Iron 8% **Dietary Exchanges:** 3½ Starch, 2 High-Fat Meat, 3½ Fat **OR** 3½ Carbohydrate, 2 High-Fat Meat, 3½ Fat **Carbohydrate Choices:** 3½

doughboy tip

Top off wedges of this hearty pie with a spoonful of your favorite salsa. If you're planning on serving the pie for brunch, add a fresh fruit salad and a platter of miniature muffins. If it's a dinner choice, add a crisp mixed-greens salad and a basket of hearty rolls.

grands!® sausage gravy

PREP TIME: 20 minutes
YIELD: 8 servings

1 (16.3-oz.) can Pillsbury®
Grands!® Refrigerated
Buttermilk Biscuits

¾ lb. bulk pork sausage

⅓ cup all-purpose flour

½ teaspoon salt

¼ teaspoon coarse ground
black pepper

3 cups milk

1. Bake biscuits as directed on can.

2. Meanwhile, crumble sausage into large skillet. Cook over medium-high heat until browned and no longer pink, stirring frequently.

3. With wire whisk, stir flour, salt and pepper into sausage. Gradually stir in milk, cooking and stirring until mixture is bubbly and thickened.

4. Split warm biscuits; place on individual serving plates. Spoon sausage mixture over biscuits.

NUTRITION INFORMATION PER SERVING: **Serving Size:** ⅛ of Recipe; Calories 345; Calories from Fat 155 **% Daily Value:** Total Fat 17g 26%; Saturated Fat 5g 25%; Cholesterol 25mg 8%; Sodium 1,150mg 48%; Total Carbohydrate 36g 12%; Dietary Fiber 1g 4%; Sugars 13g; Protein 11g; Vitamin A 4%; Vitamin C 0%; Calcium 12%; Iron 10% **Dietary Exchanges:** 1½ Starch, 1 Low-Fat Milk, 3 Fat **OR** 2½ Carbohydrate, 3 Fat **Carbohydrate Choices:** 2½

doughboy tip

What an easy way to get to an old Southern favorite—yummy biscuits and gravy! And make it as flavorful as you like by using mild or spicy pork sausage. For a colorful garnish, sprinkle each serving with a mixture of chopped fresh parsley and chives.

hearty breakfast sandwiches

PREP TIME: 30 minutes
YIELD: 8 sandwiches

1 (16.3-oz.) can Pillsbury®
Grands!® Refrigerated
Buttermilk Biscuits

1 (12-oz.) pkg. (8 patties)
breakfast pork sausage patties

4 eggs

¼ teaspoon pepper

4 oz. (1 cup) shredded
mozzarella cheese

1. Heat oven to 350°F. Bake biscuits as directed on can. Keep warm.

2. Meanwhile, cook sausage patties as directed on package. Keep warm.

3. In small bowl, beat eggs and pepper until well blended. Spray medium skillet with nonstick cooking spray. Heat over medium heat until hot. Pour egg mixture into skillet. Reduce heat to low; cook until eggs are almost set but still moist, stirring occasionally from outside edge to center, allowing uncooked egg to flow to bottom of skillet.

4. Sprinkle cheese over eggs. Cover; remove from heat. Let stand 1 minute or until cheese is melted.

5. Split warm biscuits. Place 1 sausage patty on bottom half of each biscuit. Top each with eggs and top half of biscuit.

NUTRITION INFORMATION PER SERVING: Serving Size: 1 Sandwich; Calories 360; Calories from Fat 200 **% Daily Value:** Total Fat 22g 34%; Saturated Fat 8g 40%; Cholesterol 135mg 45%; Sodium 1,050mg 44%; Total Carbohydrate 25g 8%; Dietary Fiber 1g 4%; Sugars 5g; Protein 16g; Vitamin A 6%; Vitamin C 0%; Calcium 15%; Iron 10% **Dietary Exchanges:** 1½ Starch, 1½ High Fat Meat, 2 Fat **OR** 1½ Carbohydrate, 1½ High-Fat Meat, 2 Fat **Carbohydrate Choices:** 1½

doughboy tip

You can change the flavor of this easy handheld sandwich just by substituting a different cheese. You might want to try Cheddar, Swiss or a combination of colby and Monterey Jack cheeses. Add a little color and crunch by stirring ¼ cup chopped red or green bell pepper into the eggs before cooking.

grand weekend brunches   119

sausage-mushroom biscuit casserole

PREP TIME: 40 minutes (Ready in 1 hour 5 minutes)
YIELD: 12 servings

1 (12-oz.) pkg. pork sausage links

8 tablespoons margarine or butter

½ cup all-purpose flour

4 cups milk

1 (4.5-oz.) jar sliced mushrooms, drained

1 (2-oz.) jar real bacon pieces

¼ teaspoon pepper

12 eggs

1 (5-oz.) can (⅓ cup) evaporated milk

½ teaspoon salt

1 (12-oz.) can Pillsbury® Golden Layers™ Refrigerated Flaky Biscuits

1. Heat oven to 350°F. Lightly spray 13x9-inch (3-quart) glass baking dish with nonstick cooking spray. Crumble sausage into large saucepan; cook over medium-high heat until sausage is browned and thoroughly cooked, stirring frequently. Remove sausage from saucepan; drain. Set aside.

2. In same large saucepan, melt 6 tablespoons of the margarine. Add flour; stir with wire whisk until smooth. Cook over low heat for 1 minute, stirring constantly. Gradually stir in milk. Cook until bubbly and thickened, stirring constantly. Add cooked sausage, mushrooms, bacon and pepper; mix well. Set aside.

3. In large bowl, combine eggs, evaporated milk and salt; beat with wire whisk until well blended. Melt remaining 2 tablespoons margarine in large skillet over medium heat. Add egg mixture; cook until firm but still moist, stirring occasionally.

4. Pour ⅓ of sauce into sprayed baking dish. Top with half of egg mixture. Repeat layers. Top with remaining sauce.

5. Separate dough into 10 biscuits; cut each into quarters. Arrange biscuit pieces, points up, over sauce.

6. Bake at 350°F. for 20 to 25 minutes or until mixture is thoroughly heated and biscuits are golden brown.

NUTRITION INFORMATION PER SERVING: **Serving Size:** ¹⁄₁₂ of Recipe; Calories 390; Calories from Fat 225 **% Daily Value:** Total Fat 25g 38%; Saturated Fat 8g 40%; Cholesterol 240mg 80%; Sodium 1,010mg 42%; Total Carbohydrate 24g 8%; Dietary Fiber 1g 4%; Sugars 10g; Protein 17g; Vitamin A 16%; Vitamin C 0%; Calcium 16%; Iron 10% **Dietary Exchanges:** 1½ Starch, 2 High-Fat Meat, 1½ Fat **OR** 1½ Carbohydrate, 2 High-Fat Meat, 1½ Fat **Carbohydrate Choices:** 1½

doughboy tip

Don't confuse evaporated milk, which is called for in this recipe, with sweetened condensed milk. Evaporated milk has been processed to remove 60 percent of the water, producing a richer, thicker liquid. Sweetened condensed milk, on the other hand, has added sweeteners and a thick, caramel-like consistency and is used primarily for desserts.

cheesy smoked sausage breakfast cups

PREP TIME: 30 minutes
YIELD: 10 servings

1 (12-oz.) can Pillsbury® Golden Layers™ Refrigerated Buttermilk or Flaky Biscuits

4 eggs, beaten

4 oz. cocktail-sized smoked link sausages (about 13), cut into small pieces

2½ oz. (⅔ cup) finely shredded Cheddar cheese

1. Spray 10 muffin cups with nonstick cooking spray, or line cups with foil baking cups and spray with cooking spray.

2. Separate dough into 10 biscuits. Place 1 biscuit in each sprayed cup; firmly press in bottom and up sides.

3. Spray large nonstick skillet with cooking spray. Heat over medium heat until hot. Add eggs; cook until almost set but still moist, stirring occasionally. Stir in sausage pieces. Divide egg mixture evenly into biscuit-lined cups. Top each with 1 tablespoon cheese.

4. Bake at 400°F. for 11 to 13 minutes or until edges are light golden brown.

NUTRITION INFORMATION PER SERVING: Serving Size: ⅒ of Recipe; Calories 480; Calories from Fat 320 **% Daily Value:** Total Fat 35g 54%; Saturated Fat 19g 95%; Cholesterol 170mg 57%; Sodium 970mg 40%; Total Carbohydrate 15g 5%; Dietary Fiber 0g 0%; Sugars 3g; Protein 25g; Vitamin A 20%; Vitamin C 0%; Calcium 60%; Iron 10% **Dietary Exchanges:** 1 Starch, 3 High-Fat Meat, 2 Fat **OR** 1 Carbohydrate, 3 High-Fat Meat, 2 Fat **Carbohydrate Choices:** 1

doughboy tip

Add a splash of color to the finished cups by garnishing each serving with snipped fresh chives or diced roasted red peppers. Serve these tasty breakfast cups with a side of golden hashed brown potatoes and fresh seasonal fruit.

grands!® sunrise sandwiches

PREP TIME: 30 minutes
YIELD: 8 sandwiches

1 (16.3-oz.) can Pillsbury®
Grands!® Refrigerated
Buttermilk Biscuits

1 tablespoon margarine or butter

¼ cup chopped green bell pepper

¼ cup chopped onion

8 eggs

¼ teaspoon salt

⅛ teaspoon pepper

8 (⅔-oz.) slices American
pasteurized process cheese food

8 slices bacon, cut in half
and crisply cooked

1. Bake biscuits as directed on can. Keep warm.

2. Meanwhile, melt margarine in medium skillet over medium heat. Add bell pepper and onion; cook and stir 2 minutes or until tender.

3. In small bowl, combine eggs, salt and pepper; beat well. Add to mixture in skillet; cook until egg mixture is thoroughly cooked and set but still moist, stirring occasionally.

4. Split warm biscuits. Spoon egg mixture evenly onto bottom half of each biscuit. Top each with 1 slice of cheese, 2 bacon halves and top half of biscuit.

NUTRITION INFORMATION PER SERVING: **Serving Size:** 1 Sandwich; Calories 380; Calories from Fat 220 **% Daily Value:** Total Fat 24g 37%; Saturated Fat 9g 45%; Cholesterol 235mg 78%; Sodium 1,090mg 45%; Total Carbohydrate 25g 8%; Dietary Fiber 1g 4%; Sugars 6g; Protein 16g; Vitamin A 15%; Vitamin C 4%; Calcium 15%; Iron 10% **Dietary Exchanges:** 1½ Starch, 1½ High-Fat Meat, 2½ Fat **OR** 1½ Carbohydrate, 1½ High-Fat Meat, 2½ Fat **Carbohydrate Choices:** 1½

doughboy tip

Store your eggs in their original carton on the refrigerator shelf, not in the refrigerator door. While built-in egg compartments on the door might seem handy, they unfortunately can subject eggs to too many temperature fluctuations in the refrigerator. Keeping them in the carton also prevents the eggs from absorbing odors from other foods.

three-cheese and egg crescent pie

PREP TIME: 15 minutes (Ready in 1 hour 10 minutes)
YIELD: 6 servings

1 (8-oz.) can Pillsbury®
Refrigerated Crescent Dinner Rolls

6 eggs

6 oz. (1½ cups) shredded sharp
Cheddar cheese

½ cup cottage cheese

¼ cup chive and onion
cream cheese spread
(from 8-oz. container)

¼ cup all-purpose flour

½ teaspoon baking powder

1 Italian plum tomato, thinly sliced

1. Heat oven to 350°F. Separate dough into 8 triangles. Place triangles in ungreased 9-inch glass pie pan; press over bottom and up sides to form crust. Turn outside edges under; flute if desired.

2. Beat eggs in large bowl. Add all remaining ingredients except tomato; mix well. Pour egg mixture into crust-lined pan. Bake at 350°F. for 20 minutes.

3. Remove pie from oven. Top with tomato slices. If necessary, cover edge of crust with strips of foil to prevent excessive browning.

4. Return pie to oven; bake an additional 19 to 28 minutes or until knife inserted near center comes out clean. Let stand 5 minutes. Cut into wedges.

NUTRITION INFORMATION PER SERVING: **Serving Size:** ⅙ of Recipe; Calories 390; Calories from Fat 215 **% Daily Value:** Total Fat 24g 37%; Saturated Fat 11g 55%; Cholesterol 255mg 85%; Sodium 840mg 35%; Total Carbohydrate 24g 8%; Dietary Fiber 0g 0%; Sugars 8g; Protein 20g; Vitamin A 16%; Vitamin C 0%; Calcium 22%; Iron 12% **Dietary Exchanges:** 1 Starch, ½ Fruit, 2½ High-Fat Meat, 1 Fat **OR** 1½ Carbohydrate, 2½ High-Fat Meat, 1 Fat **Carbohydrate Choices:** 1½

doughboy tip

For a creative finish, sprinkle sliced ripe olives on top of the pie with the tomato. Try all kinds of different designs. Try arranging the olives and tomatoes in alternating stripes, for example, or concentric circles.

creamy swiss eggs on biscuits

PREP TIME: 25 minutes
YIELD: 4 servings

4 Pillsbury® Home Baked Classics™ Frozen Buttermilk Biscuits (from 25-oz. pkg.)

6 eggs

2 green onions, sliced

2 teaspoons margarine or butter

1 (10¾-oz.) can condensed cream of chicken soup with herbs

⅔ cup milk

4 oz. (1 cup) shredded Swiss cheese

⅛ teaspoon pepper

1. Heat oven to 375°F. Bake frozen biscuits as directed on package.

2. Meanwhile, beat eggs in medium bowl. Stir in green onions. Melt margarine in medium skillet over medium heat. Add egg mixture; cook 4 to 5 minutes or until eggs are thoroughly cooked but still moist, stirring occasionally.

3. In small bowl, combine soup, milk, cheese and pepper; mix well. Add to eggs in skillet; stir in gently. Cook until thoroughly heated.

4. Split warm biscuits; place on individual serving plates. Spoon egg mixture over biscuits.

NUTRITION INFORMATION PER SERVING: Serving Size: ¼ of Recipe; Calories 500; Calories from Fat 270 % Daily Value: Total Fat 30g 46%; Saturated Fat 11g 55%; Cholesterol 350mg 117%; Sodium 1,250mg 52%; Total Carbohydrate 33g 11%; Dietary Fiber 1g 4%; Sugars 9g; Protein 25g; Vitamin A 24%; Vitamin C 0%; Calcium 38%; Iron 14% Dietary Exchanges: 2 Starch, 3½ High-Fat Meat OR 2 Carbohydrate, 3½ High-Fat Meat Carbohydrate Choices: 2

doughboy tip

For a bacon 'n egg breakfast treat, stir ¼ cup real bacon pieces in with the soup mixture. What a nice way to start the day!

denver scrambled egg pizzas

PREP TIME: 25 minutes
YIELD: 4 pizzas

1 (10-oz.) can Pillsbury® Refrigerated Pizza Crust

1 tablespoon margarine or butter

1 cup frozen bell pepper and onion stir-fry

8 eggs

2 tablespoons milk

¼ teaspoon salt

½ cup chopped cooked ham

2 to 3 tablespoons creamy mustard-mayonnaise sauce

1. Heat oven to 400°F. Lightly spray large cookie sheet with nonstick cooking spray. Unroll dough. Cut dough into 4 equal pieces; place on sprayed cookie sheet. Press out each piece of dough to form 6x5-inch rectangle. With fingers, create slight rim on edge of each dough rectangle. Bake at 400°F. for 11 to 15 minutes or until golden brown.

2. Meanwhile, melt margarine in large nonstick skillet over medium heat. Add bell pepper and onion stir-fry; cook 3 to 5 minutes or until tender, stirring occasionally.

3. In medium bowl, combine eggs, milk, salt and ham; beat well. Add mixture to skillet; cook 4 to 5 minutes or until egg mixture is thoroughly cooked and set but still moist, stirring occasionally.

4. Spread each baked crust with mustard-mayonnaise sauce. Spoon egg mixture evenly over sauce. Serve warm.

NUTRITION INFORMATION PER SERVING: Serving Size: 1 Pizza; Calories 410; Calories from Fat 160 % Daily Value: Total Fat 18g 28%; Saturated Fat 6g 30%; Cholesterol 435mg 145%; Sodium 1,230mg 51%; Total Carbohydrate 39g 13%; Dietary Fiber 1g 4%; Sugars 7g; Protein 23g; Vitamin A 20%; Vitamin C 4%; Calcium 8%; Iron 20% Dietary Exchanges: 2 Starch, ½ Fruit, 2½ Medium-Fat Meat, 1 Fat OR 2½ Carbohydrate, 2½ Medium-Fat Meat, 1 Fat Carbohydrate Choices: 2½

doughboy tip

Because you are using a nonstick skillet to cook the eggs in this recipe, very little margarine or butter is needed. To prolong the life of a nonstick pan, use only wooden or plastic utensils and don't store anything in the pan. If you must nest pans for storage, protect the surface with a kitchen towel or double layers of paper towels before stacking the next pan on top.

Doughboy Recommends

chapter 3
Satisfying Sandwiches and Pizzas

MEXICAN BEEF 'N BEAN PIZZA, page 163

mexican beef melts

1 lb. lean ground beef

1 (1.25-oz.) pkg. taco seasoning mix

⅔ cup water

1½ cups chunky-style salsa

1 (16.3-oz.) can Pillsbury® Grands!® Refrigerated Southern Style or Buttermilk Biscuits

4 oz. (1 cup) shredded Monterey Jack cheese or Mexican cheese blend

1 cup sour cream, if desired

1. Heat oven to 375°F. Lightly spray large cookie sheet with nonstick cooking spray. Brown ground beef in large skillet over medium-high heat for 5 to 7 minutes or until thoroughly cooked, stirring frequently. Drain.

2. Add taco seasoning mix, water and ½ cup of the salsa; cook 2 to 4 minutes or until mixture has thickened, stirring occasionally.

3. Separate dough into 8 biscuits. Press or roll each to form 6-inch round. Spoon about ¼ cup beef mixture onto center of each round. Top each with 1 tablespoon of the cheese. Fold dough over filling; press edges firmly with fork to seal. Place on sprayed cookie sheet.

4. Bake at 375°F. for 9 to 14 minutes or until golden brown. To serve, top each sandwich with 1 heaping tablespoon remaining salsa and 1 tablespoon remaining cheese. Serve with sour cream.

NUTRITION INFORMATION PER SERVING: **Serving Size:** 1 Sandwich; Calories 440; Calories from Fat 240 **% Daily Value:** Total Fat 27g 42%; Saturated Fat 12g 60%; Cholesterol 60mg 20%; Sodium 1,470mg 61%; Total Carbohydrate 31g 10%; Dietary Fiber 2g 8%; Sugars 8g; Protein 19g; Vitamin A 15%; Vitamin C 2%; Calcium 20%; Iron 15% **Dietary Exchanges:** 2 Starch, 2 Medium-Fat Meat, 3 Fat **OR** 2 Carbohydrate, 2 Medium-Fat Meat, 3 Fat **Carbohydrate Choices:** 2

doughboy tip

If you're watching fat grams, use reduced-fat sour cream or low-fat or nonfat plain yogurt instead of regular sour cream. To complete the menu, add a crisp green salad of romaine lettuce topped with fresh orange slices drizzled with your favorite low-fat salad dressing.

cheeseburger foldovers

PREP TIME: 20 minutes (Ready in 45 minutes)
YIELD: 8 sandwiches

¾ lb. lean ground beef

½ cup chopped onion

2 tablespoons ketchup

1 tablespoon prepared mustard

1 (16.3-oz.) can Pillsbury®
Grands!® Refrigerated Original
Flaky Layers Biscuits

4 oz. (1 cup) shredded Cheddar
and American cheese blend

16 dill pickle slices

1 egg, beaten

1 teaspoon sesame seed,
if desired

1. Heat oven to 375°F. In large skillet, cook ground beef and onion over medium-high heat for 5 to 7 minutes or until beef is thoroughly cooked, stirring frequently. Drain. Stir in ketchup and mustard.

2. Separate dough into 8 biscuits. On ungreased large cookie sheet, press or roll each biscuit to form 6-inch round. Spoon beef mixture onto one side of each biscuit. Sprinkle each with cheese. Top each with 2 pickles. Fold dough in half over filling; press edges with fork to seal. Make 2 or 3 small slits in top of each for steam to escape. Brush each with beaten egg. Sprinkle with sesame seed.

3. Bake at 375°F. for 18 to 22 minutes or until deep golden brown.

NUTRITION INFORMATION PER SERVING: **Serving Size:** 1 Sandwich; Calories 360; Calories from Fat 180 **% Daily Value:** Total Fat 20g 31%; Saturated Fat 7g 35%; Cholesterol 65mg 22%; Sodium 980mg 41%; Total Carbohydrate 28g 9%; Dietary Fiber 1g 4%; Sugars 5g; Protein 16g; Vitamin A 6%; Vitamin C 0%; Calcium 90%; Iron 15% **Dietary Exchanges:** 2 Starch, 1½ Medium-Fat Meat, 2 Fat **OR** 2 Carbohydrate, 1½ Medium-Fat Meat, 2 Fat **Carbohydrate Choices:** 2

doughboy tip

For quick last-minute prep, stir the ketchup and mustard into the cooked and drained ground beef and onion up to a day in advance. Cover and refrigerate it in a microwave-safe container until needed. Reheat the mixture in the microwave oven before spooning onto the dough.

beef and pepper stromboli

PREP TIME: 15 minutes (Ready in 35 minutes)
YIELD: 6 servings

½ lb. lean ground beef

1 (10-oz.) can Pillsbury®
Refrigerated Pizza Crust

¼ cup pizza sauce

4 oz. (1 cup) shredded
mozzarella cheese

¼ cup chopped green
and/or red bell pepper

¼ teaspoon dried Italian seasoning

1. Heat oven to 400°F. Spray cookie sheet with nonstick cooking spray. Brown ground beef in medium skillet over medium-high heat for 5 to 7 minutes or until thoroughly cooked, stirring frequently. Drain. Set aside.

2. Unroll dough; place on sprayed cookie sheet. Starting at center, press out dough to form 12x8-inch rectangle.

3. Spread pizza sauce over dough to within 2 inches of long sides and ½ inch of short sides. Spoon cooked ground beef lengthwise in 3-inch-wide strip down center of dough to within ½ inch of each short side. Top with cheese, bell pepper and Italian seasoning. Fold long sides of dough over filling; press edges to seal.

4. Bake at 400°F. for 15 to 20 minutes or until crust is golden brown.

NUTRITION INFORMATION PER SERVING: **Serving Size:** ⅙ of Recipe; Calories 250; Calories from Fat 90 **% Daily Value:** Total Fat 10g 15%; Saturated Fat 4g 20%; Cholesterol 35mg 12%; Sodium 500mg 21%; Total Carbohydrate 24g 8%; Dietary Fiber 1g 4%; Sugars 3g; Protein 16g; Vitamin A 4%; Vitamin C 4%; Calcium 15%; Iron 10% **Dietary Exchanges:** 1½ Starch, 1½ Medium-Fat Meat, ½ Fat **OR** 1½ Carbohydrate, 1½ Medium-Fat Meat, ½ Fat **Carbohydrate Choices:** 1½

doughboy tip

Don't be afraid to improvise and add small amounts of other ingredients. Try adding about ½ cup chopped mushrooms or thawed chopped broccoli florets when you spoon the beef onto the dough. For flavor variety, use Italian sausage in place of the ground beef.

crescent beef burritos

PREP TIME: 35 minutes (Ready in 1 hour)
YIELD: 8 servings

½ lb. lean ground beef

2 tablespoons chopped onion

2 tablespoons taco seasoning mix
(from 1.25-oz. pkg.)

½ cup water

½ cup refried beans
(from 16-oz. can)

2 (8-oz.) cans Pillsbury®
Refrigerated Crescent Dinner Rolls

½ cup chunky-style salsa

4 (¾-oz.) slices American cheese,
cut diagonally in half

1 cup sour cream

¼ cup sliced ripe olives

1. Heat oven to 350°F. Spray cookie sheet with nonstick cooking spray. In medium skillet, cook ground beef and onion over medium-high heat until beef is thoroughly cooked, stirring frequently. Drain.

2. Stir in taco seasoning mix and water. Reduce heat to medium; cook until water has evaporated, stirring frequently. Remove from heat. Add beans; mix well.

3. Separate dough into 8 rectangles. Firmly press perforations to seal. Spoon about 2 tablespoons beef mixture and 1 tablespoon of the salsa onto each rectangle; spread to within ½ inch from one short side. Roll up, starting at other short side; pinch edges to seal. Place seam side down on sprayed cookie sheet.

4. Bake at 350°F. for 18 to 23 minutes or until golden brown. Top each burrito with cheese half. Bake an additional 2 to 3 minutes or until cheese is melted. Garnish each with sour cream and olives.

NUTRITION INFORMATION PER SERVING: Serving Size: ⅛ of Recipe; Calories 400; Calories from Fat 205 **% Daily Value:** Total Fat 23g 35%; Saturated Fat 10g 50%; Cholesterol 50mg 17%; Sodium 1,150mg 48%; Total Carbohydrate 34g 11%; Dietary Fiber 2g 8%; Sugars 11g; Protein 14g; Vitamin A 14%; Vitamin C 4%; Calcium 12%; Iron 14% **Dietary Exchanges:** 2 Starch, 1 Vegetable, 1 High-Fat Meat, 3 Fat **OR** 2 Carbohydrate, 1 Vegetable, 1 High-Fat Meat, 3 Fat **Carbohydrate Choices:** 2

doughboy tip

Serve the burritos with extra salsa or guacamole. Then to complete the menu, add a crisp green salad and tall glasses of lemonade or limeade.

sloppy joe loaf

PREP TIME: 20 minutes (Ready in 50 minutes)
YIELD: 6 servings

1 lb. extra-lean ground beef

1 small onion, chopped

1 (8-oz.) can tomato sauce

1 tablespoon all-purpose flour

¼ teaspoon dried basil leaves

¼ teaspoon dried oregano leaves

¼ teaspoon fennel seed

1 (11-oz.) can Pillsbury®
Refrigerated Crusty French Loaf

4 oz. (1 cup) shredded
mozzarella cheese

1. Heat oven to 350°F. Spray cookie sheet and large skillet with nonstick cooking spray. In sprayed skillet, cook ground beef and onion over medium-high heat for 5 to 7 minutes or until beef is thoroughly cooked, stirring frequently. Drain.

2. Add tomato sauce, flour, basil, oregano and fennel seed; mix well. Reduce heat to medium-low; simmer 5 minutes. Remove from heat.

3. Meanwhile, on lightly floured surface, carefully unroll dough. Cut dough in half lengthwise. Press or roll each half to form 16x4-inch rectangle. Place 1 dough rectangle on sprayed cookie sheet, being careful not to change shape.

4. Stir ½ cup of the cheese into ground beef mixture. Spoon and spread mixture over dough rectangle on cookie sheet. Sprinkle with remaining ½ cup cheese. Top with remaining dough rectangle.

5. Bake at 350°F. for 25 to 30 minutes or until golden brown. Cut into slices.

NUTRITION INFORMATION PER SERVING: Serving Size: ⅙ of Recipe; Calories 365; Calories from Fat 125 **% Daily Value:** Total Fat 14g 22%; Saturated Fat 6g 30%; Cholesterol 55mg 18%; Sodium 690mg 29%; Total Carbohydrate 31g 10%; Dietary Fiber 2g 8%; Sugars 3g; Protein 26g; Vitamin A 10%; Vitamin C 4%; Calcium 18%; Iron 20% **Dietary Exchanges:** 2 Starch, 3 Medium-Fat Meat **OR** 2 Carbohydrate, 3 Medium-Fat Meat **Carbohydrate Choices:** 2

doughboy tip

If you wish to substitute fresh herbs for dried, plan on using about three times the amount specified for the dried ingredient. For instance, in this recipe, use ¾ teaspoon chopped fresh basil and ¾ teaspoon chopped fresh oregano.

italian meatball hoagie braids

PREP TIME: 15 minutes (Ready in 35 minutes)
YIELD: 8 sandwiches

2 (8-oz.) cans Pillsbury®
Refrigerated Crescent Dinner Rolls

16 (1½-inch) frozen fully cooked
Italian meatballs (about 1 lb.),
thawed, halved

1 cup tomato-basil pasta sauce

4 oz. (1 cup) shredded
mozzarella cheese

1 egg, slightly beaten

¼ cup grated Parmesan cheese

1. Heat oven to 375°F. Spray 2 cookie sheets with nonstick cooking spray. Separate dough into 8 rectangles. Place rectangles on sprayed cookie sheets. Firmly press perforations to seal.

2. Place 4 meatball halves lengthwise down center of each rectangle. Top each with 2 tablespoons sauce and 2 table-spoons mozzarella cheese. With scissors or sharp knife, make cuts 1 inch apart on each side of filling. Alternately cross strips over filling. Brush dough with beaten egg. Sprinkle with Parmesan cheese.

3. Bake at 375°F. for 15 to 20 minutes or until golden brown.

NUTRITION INFORMATION PER SERVING: Serving Size: 1 Sandwich; Calories 450; Calories from Fat 260 % Daily Value: Total Fat 29g 45%; Saturated Fat 11g 55%; Cholesterol 75mg 25%; Sodium 1,110mg 46%; Total Carbohydrate 28g 9%; Dietary Fiber 3g 12%; Sugars 4g; Protein 19g; Vitamin A 6%; Vitamin C 2%; Calcium 20%; Iron 15% Dietary Exchanges: 2 Starch, 2 High-Fat Meat, 2 Fat OR 2 Carbohydrate, 2 High-Fat Meat, 2 Fat Carbohydrate Choices: 2

doughboy tip

Serve the hoagie braids with a homemade antipasto plate of artfully arranged nibbles. You might include rolled-up salami or ham, chunks or slices of provolone cheese, marinated mushrooms or artichokes, black or ripe olives, pickled vegetables or hot peppers, fresh baby carrots or roasted red bell pepper strips.

italian roast beef focaccia sandwiches

PREP TIME: 25 minutes
YIELD: 4 servings

1 (10-oz.) can Pillsbury®
Refrigerated Pizza Crust

¼ cup purchased Italian
salad dressing

¼ lb. thinly sliced cooked
roast beef

3 thin slices provolone cheese
(about 4½ oz.)

2 Italian plum tomatoes,
thinly sliced

1 cup coarsely shredded lettuce

1. Heat oven to 425°F. Grease cookie sheet or spray with nonstick cooking spray. Unroll dough; place on greased cookie sheet. Starting in center, press out dough to form 13x9-inch rectangle.

2. With fingers or end of wooden spoon handle, make indentations on surface of dough. Drizzle with 4 teaspoons of the salad dressing.

3. Bake at 425°F. for 9 to 12 minutes or until golden brown. Cool 5 minutes.

4. Place bread on cutting board or serving platter. Cut in half lengthwise. On 1 long rectangle, layer beef, cheese, tomato and lettuce. Drizzle with remaining salad dressing. Top with remaining rectangle, top side up; press down gently. Cut into 4 pieces.

NUTRITION INFORMATION PER SERVING: **Serving Size:** ¼ of Recipe; Calories 400; Calories from Fat 170 **% Daily Value:** Total Fat 19g 29%; Saturated Fat 7g 35%; Cholesterol 35mg 12%; Sodium 1,160mg 48%; Total Carbohydrate 37g 12%; Dietary Fiber 1g 4%; Sugars 6g; Protein 20g; Vitamin A 10%; Vitamin C 8%; Calcium 25%; Iron 15% **Dietary Exchanges:** 2½ Starch, 1½ Lean Meat, 2½ Fat OR 2½ Carbohydrate, 1½ Lean Meat, 2½ Fat **Carbohydrate Choices:** 2½

doughboy tip

Do you like assertive flavors? Choose Italian roast beef, with its peppery exterior and garlicky goodness, instead of regular deli roast beef. Top the beef with slices of raw onion and green bell pepper rings for added pizzazz.

grands!® roast beef sandwiches

PREP TIME: 15 minutes (Ready in 40 minutes)
YIELD: 8 sandwiches

1 (16.3-oz.) can Pillsbury® Grands!® Refrigerated Buttermilk Biscuits

2 tablespoons margarine or butter, melted

¼ cup garlic herb dry bread crumbs

⅓ cup mayonnaise or salad dressing

1 (4.5-oz.) can chopped green chiles

8 (1-oz.) slices cooked roast beef

4 oz. (1 cup) finely shredded Monterey Jack cheese

1. Heat oven to 375°F. Separate dough into 8 biscuits. Brush top and sides of each biscuit with margarine; coat with bread crumbs. Place 2 inches apart, crumb side up, on ungreased cookie sheet. Sprinkle any remaining bread crumbs over biscuits.

2. Bake at 375°F. for 14 to 16 minutes or until golden brown. Cool 5 minutes. Set oven to broil.

3. Meanwhile, in small bowl, combine mayonnaise and green chiles; mix well.

4. Split biscuits; place tops and bottoms, cut side up, on same cookie sheet. Spread mayonnaise mixture evenly on top halves of biscuits. Arrange roast beef slices on bottom halves, folding to fit. Top beef with cheese.

5. Broil 4 to 6 inches from heat for 2 to 3 minutes or until cheese is melted and mayonnaise mixture is bubbly. Place top halves of biscuits over bottom halves.

NUTRITION INFORMATION PER SERVING: **Serving Size:** 1 Sandwich; Calories 395; Calories from Fat 215 **% Daily Value:** Total Fat 24g 37%; Saturated Fat 7g 35%; Cholesterol 30mg 10%; Sodium 1,250mg 52%; Total Carbohydrate 32g 11%; Dietary Fiber 1g 4%; Sugars 10g; Protein 13g; Vitamin A 8%; Vitamin C 4%; Calcium 12%; Iron 14% **Dietary Exchanges:** 2 Starch, 1 Lean Meat, 4 Fat **OR** 2 Carbohydrate, 1 Lean Meat, 4 Fat **Carbohydrate Choices:** 2

doughboy tip

To make a tasty sauce for these hearty sandwiches, blend ½ cup mayonnaise with ¼ cup Dijon mustard. Feeling a little adventurous? Add prepared horseradish to taste.

hot corned beef and slaw sandwiches

PREP TIME: 25 minutes
YIELD: 5 sandwiches

1 (10.2-oz.) can (5 biscuits) Pillsbury® Grands!® Refrigerated Buttermilk Biscuits

1 egg white, beaten

½ teaspoon caraway seed

1½ cups purchased coleslaw blend (from 16-oz. pkg.)

¼ cup purchased Thousand Island salad dressing

10 oz. cooked corned beef, thinly sliced

5 (¾-oz.) slices Swiss cheese

1. Heat oven to 375°F. Separate dough into 5 biscuits; place on ungreased cookie sheet. Brush tops with egg white. Sprinkle with caraway seed. Bake at 375°F. for 11 to 13 minutes or until golden brown.

2. Meanwhile, in small bowl, combine coleslaw blend and salad dressing; mix well.

3. Remove biscuits from oven. Split warm biscuits; place bottom halves on same cookie sheet. Set top halves aside. Top each bottom half with coleslaw mixture, beef and cheese.

4. Return to oven; bake an additional 3 to 5 minutes or until cheese is melted and sandwiches are hot. Cover with top halves of biscuits.

NUTRITION INFORMATION PER SERVING: **Serving Size:** 1 Sandwich; Calories 390; Calories from Fat 190 **% Daily Value:** Total Fat 21g 32%; Saturated Fat 8g 40%; Cholesterol 65mg 22%; Sodium 1,140mg 48%; Total Carbohydrate 28g 9%; Dietary Fiber 1g 4%; Sugars 7g; Protein 23g; Vitamin A 15%; Vitamin C 20%; Calcium 25%; Iron 25% **Dietary Exchanges:** 1½ Starch, ½ Fruit, 2½ Lean Meat, 2½ Fat **OR** 2 Carbohydrate, 2½ Lean Meat, 2½ Fat **Carbohydrate Choices:** 2

doughboy tip

For that classic Reuben flavor, use 1½ cups well-drained sauerkraut in place of the coleslaw. Sliced cooked turkey breast in place of the corned beef also makes a tasty sandwich.

pastrami stromboli

PREP TIME: 15 minutes (Ready in 45 minutes)
YIELD: 4 servings

1 (11-oz.) can Pillsbury®
Refrigerated Crusty French Loaf

2 tablespoons mayonnaise

1 teaspoon Dijon mustard

½ lb. thinly sliced pastrami

1 (6-oz.) pkg. sliced provolone
cheese

1 cup french fried onions
(from 2.8-oz. can)

1. Heat oven to 350°F. Spray cookie sheet with nonstick cooking spray. Carefully unroll dough onto sprayed cookie sheet. Press or roll to form 14x12-inch rectangle.

2. In small bowl, combine mayonnaise and mustard; blend well. Spread over dough to within 1 inch of all edges. Layer half each of the pastrami and cheese lengthwise in 5-inch-wide strip down center of dough to within 1 inch of each short side, overlapping pastrami and cheese. Repeat layering with remaining pastrami and cheese. Sprinkle with onions.

3. Fold long sides of dough over filling; pinch edges in center to seal. Fold ends under 1 inch; seal. Cut several slits in top for steam to escape.

4. Bake at 350°F. for 26 to 30 minutes or until deep golden brown. Cool 5 minutes. Cut into crosswise slices.

NUTRITION INFORMATION PER SERVING: Serving Size: ¼ of Recipe; Calories 575; Calories from Fat 280 **% Daily Value:** Total Fat 31g 48%; Saturated Fat 12g 60%; Cholesterol 70mg 23%; Sodium 1,810mg 75%; Total Carbohydrate 46g 15%; Dietary Fiber 2g 8%; Sugars 2g; Protein 30g; Vitamin A 8%; Vitamin C 0%; Calcium 38%; Iron 20% **Dietary Exchanges:** 3 Starch, 3 High-Fat Meat, 1 Fat **OR** 3 Carbohydrate, 3 High-Fat Meat, 1 Fat **Carbohydrate Choices:** 3

doughboy tip

Just before baking, brush the top of the dough with a beaten egg yolk. For a rye-bread flavor similar to a deli pastrami sandwich, sprinkle the dough with caraway seed. Serve the stromboli with coleslaw and dill pickles or pickled green tomatoes.

easy crescent dogs™

PREP TIME: 25 minutes
YIELD: 8 sandwiches

8 hot dogs

4 (¾-oz.) slices American cheese, each cut into 6 strips

1 (8-oz.) can Pillsbury® Refrigerated Crescent Dinner Rolls

1. Heat oven to 375°F. Slit hot dogs to within ½ inch of ends. Insert 3 strips of cheese into each slit.

2. Separate dough into 8 triangles. Wrap dough triangle around each hot dog. Place on ungreased cookie sheet, cheese side up.

3. Bake at 375°F. for 12 to 15 minutes or until golden brown.

NUTRITION INFORMATION PER SERVING: Serving Size: 1 Sandwich; Calories 275; Calories from Fat 180 **% Daily Value:** Total Fat 20g 31%; Saturated Fat 8g 40%; Cholesterol 35mg 12%; Sodium 1,020mg 43%; Total Carbohydrate 15g 5%; Dietary Fiber 0g 0%; Sugars 6g; Protein 9g; Vitamin A 2%; Vitamin C 0%; Calcium 6%; Iron 6% **Dietary Exchanges:** 1 Starch, 1 High-Fat Meat, 2½ Fat OR 1 Carbohydrate, 1 High-Fat Meat, 2½ Fat **Carbohydrate Choices:** 1

doughboy tip

These all-time favorites are great just as they are. But for an added treat, serve the dogs with your favorite condiment—mustard, ketchup, relish, sauerkraut or chopped onions.

pepperoni pizza calzone

PREP TIME: 20 minutes (Ready in 55 minutes)
YIELD: 8 servings

2 (10-oz.) cans Pillsbury®
Refrigerated Pizza Crust

3 oz. small pepperoni slices
(42 slices)

1 (4.5-oz.) jar sliced mushrooms,
well drained

½ cup sliced pimiento-stuffed
green olives

8 oz. thinly sliced
provolone cheese

1 tablespoon grated
Parmesan cheese

1 (14 or 15-oz.) jar pizza
sauce, heated

1. Heat oven to 375°F. Lightly grease 12-inch pizza pan. Unroll 1 can of dough; place in greased pan. Starting at center, press out dough to edge of pan. Layer pepperoni, mushrooms, olives and provolone cheese over dough.

2. Unroll remaining can of dough. Press out dough on work surface to form 12-inch round. Fold dough in half; place over cheese on dough in pan and unfold. Press outside edges to seal. Cut several slits in top crust for steam to escape. Sprinkle with Parmesan cheese.

3. Bake at 375°F. for 30 to 35 minutes or until crust is deep golden brown. Cut pizza into wedges; serve with warm pizza sauce.

NUTRITION INFORMATION PER SERVING: Serving Size: ⅛ of Recipe; Calories 380; Calories from Fat 160 % Daily Value: Total Fat 18g 28%; Saturated Fat 7g 35%; Cholesterol 35mg 12%; Sodium 1,520mg 63%; Total Carbohydrate 39g 13%; Dietary Fiber 2g 8%; Sugars 7g; Protein 17g; Vitamin A 10%; Vitamin C 8%; Calcium 24%; Iron 14% Dietary Exchanges: 2 Starch, ½ Fruit, 1½ High-Fat Meat, 1 Fat OR 2½ Carbohydrate, 1½ High-Fat Meat, 1 Fat Carbohydrate Choices: 2½

doughboy tip

For a time-saver, use a 4-ounce can of sliced ripe olives, drained, for the pimiento-stuffed green olives. If your family loves bacon, you may want to substitute 8 slices of cooked bacon, crumbled, for the pepperoni slices.

ham and biscuit stacks

PREP TIME: 25 minutes
YIELD: 5 servings

1 (12-oz.) can Pillsbury® Golden
Layers™ Refrigerated
Flaky Biscuits

2 tablespoons honey

2 tablespoons prepared mustard

5 (4-inch-square) thin slices
cooked ham

5 (4-inch-square) thin slices
Swiss cheese

10 small lettuce leaves

1. Heat oven to 400°F. Bake biscuits as directed on can.

2. Meanwhile, in small bowl, combine honey and mustard; blend well. Place 1 ham slice on each cheese slice. Cut each stack into 4 squares.

3. Split warm biscuits. Spread each biscuit half with ½ teaspoon honey-mustard mixture. Stack 2 squares of ham and cheese on bottom half of each biscuit. Top with lettuce leaves. Cover with top halves of biscuits.

NUTRITION INFORMATION PER SERVING: Serving Size: ⅕ of Recipe; Calories 340; Calories from Fat 140 % Daily Value: Total Fat 16g 25%; Saturated Fat 6g 30%; Cholesterol 30mg 10%; Sodium 1,140mg 48%; Total Carbohydrate 36g 12%; Dietary Fiber 1g 4%; Sugars 10g; Protein 14g; Vitamin A 4%; Vitamin C 0%; Calcium 20%; Iron 10% Dietary Exchanges: 1½ Starch, 1 Fruit, 1½ Lean Meat, 2 Fat OR 2½ Carbohydrate, 1½ Lean Meat, 2 Fat Carbohydrate Choices: 2½

doughboy tip

Add a spoonful of cranberry-orange relish to each sandwich before topping with the lettuce. Make a mental note to remember the honey-mustard mixture for other uses. It's great to mix up and keep on hand to dress up many kinds of sandwiches.

italian super sub

PREP TIME: 15 minutes (Ready in 1 hour 5 minutes)
YIELD: 4 servings

BREAD

1 (11-oz.) can Pillsbury®
Refrigerated Crusty French Loaf

2 tablespoons shredded fresh
Parmesan cheese

¼ teaspoon garlic salt

¼ teaspoon dried oregano leaves

FILLING

3 tablespoons purchased creamy
Italian salad dressing

2 (1-oz.) slices Swiss cheese

¼ lb. thinly sliced cooked ham

1 small green bell pepper, sliced

2 (1-oz.) slices Cheddar cheese

¼ lb. sliced salami

1 medium tomato, sliced

1 cup shredded lettuce

1. Heat oven to 350°F. Spray cookie sheet with nonstick cooking spray. Remove dough from can; place seam side down on cookie sheet. With sharp or serrated knife, make 4 or 5 (¼-inch-deep) diagonal cuts on top of dough.

2. In small bowl, combine Parmesan cheese, garlic salt and oregano; mix well. Spray dough with nonstick cooking spray. Sprinkle with cheese mixture.

3. Bake at 350°F. for 26 to 30 minutes or until light golden brown. Cool 20 minutes or until completely cooled.

4. Cut bread in half lengthwise. Brush cut sides of bread with salad dressing. Layer bottom half with Swiss cheese, ham, bell pepper, Cheddar cheese, salami, tomato and lettuce. Cover with top half of bread. Secure sandwich with toothpicks. Cut into 4 pieces.

NUTRITION INFORMATION PER SERVING: **Serving Size:** ¼ of Recipe; Calories 530; Calories from Fat 250 **% Daily Value:** Total Fat 28g 43%; Saturated Fat 12g 60%; Cholesterol 65mg 22%; Sodium 1,770mg 74%; Total Carbohydrate 40g 13%; Dietary Fiber 2g 8%; Sugars 6g; Protein 28g; Vitamin A 10%; Vitamin C 20%; Calcium 30%; Iron 15% **Dietary Exchanges:** 2½ Starch, 3 High-Fat Meat, ½ Fat OR 2½ Carbohydrate, 3 High-Fat Meat, ½ Fat **Carbohydrate Choices:** 2½

doughboy tip

This is a great "grab and go" sandwich. Wrap sections of the finished sub in plastic wrap, and store in the refrigerator. When family members need a quick snack to take on the road, it's ready and waiting.

ham 'n cheese breadstick wraps

PREP TIME: 25 minutes
YIELD: 6 sandwiches

1 (7-oz.) can (6 breadsticks) Pillsbury® Refrigerated Breadsticks

6 leaf lettuce leaves

6 thin slices baby Swiss cheese

6 thin slices cooked ham

1 tablespoon prepared mustard

1. Heat oven to 375°F. Prepare and bake breadsticks as directed on can. Cool 10 minutes or until completely cooled.

2. Meanwhile, place lettuce leaves on work surface. Top each with cheese slice and ham slice. Spread mustard over ham.

3. Place cooled breadstick over ham in center of each. Wrap lettuce, cheese and ham around breadsticks. Secure each with toothpick.

NUTRITION INFORMATION PER SERVING: Serving Size: 1 Sandwich; Calories 230; Calories from Fat 90 **% Daily Value:** Total Fat 10g 15%; Saturated Fat 6g 30%; Cholesterol 40mg 13%; Sodium 590mg 25%; Total Carbohydrate 18g 6%; Dietary Fiber 1g 4%; Sugars 3g; Protein 15g; Vitamin A 8%; Vitamin C 2%; Calcium 30%; Iron 6% **Dietary Exchanges:** 1 Starch, 1½ High-Fat Meat **OR** 1 Carbohydrate, 1½ High-Fat Meat **Carbohydrate Choices:** 1

doughboy tip

Let the toothpick fastener do double duty on these "inside out" sandwiches. Secure an edible garnish, such as a pitted olive, cherry tomato, seedless green grape or pickle slice, on one end of each toothpick.

cheesy sausage 'n broccoli loaf

1 (12-oz.) pkg. bulk sage-flavored pork sausage

1 (11-oz.) can Pillsbury® Refrigerated Crusty French Loaf

2 cups frozen cut broccoli, cooked, drained

4 oz. (1 cup) shredded mozzarella cheese

4 oz. (1 cup) shredded Cheddar cheese

PREP TIME: 15 minutes (Ready in 45 minutes)
YIELD: 4 servings

1. Heat oven to 350°F. Cook sausage in medium skillet over medium-high heat until no longer pink, stirring frequently. Drain.

2. Carefully unroll dough onto ungreased cookie sheet. Press to form 14x12-inch rectangle. Spoon sausage down center of dough. Top with cooked broccoli and cheeses. Fold long sides of dough over filling, meeting in center; press edges and ends to seal.

3. Bake at 350°F. for 20 to 30 minutes or until golden brown. Cut into crosswise slices.

NUTRITION INFORMATION PER SERVING: **Serving Size:** ¼ of Recipe; Calories 540; Calories from Fat 260 **% Daily Value:** Total Fat 29g 45%; Saturated Fat 14g 70%; Cholesterol 80mg 27%; Sodium 1,320mg 55%; Total Carbohydrate 38g 13%; Dietary Fiber 2g 8%; Sugars 5g; Protein 30g; Vitamin A 15%; Vitamin C 25%; Calcium 45%; Iron 15% **Dietary Exchanges:** 2 Starch, 1 Vegetable, 3 High-Fat Meat, 1 Fat **OR** 2 Carbohydrate, 1 Vegetable, 3 High-Fat Meat, 1 Fat **Carbohydrate Choices:** 2½

doughboy tip

This tasty loaf is easy to "dress up for company." Serve each slice on a pool of warm chunky tomato pasta sauce in a pasta bowl. Sprinkle with fresh basil or parsley and shredded fresh Parmesan cheese. If you like, Italian sausage can be used instead of the sage-flavored pork sausage.

italian sausage crescent sandwiches

PREP TIME: 25 minutes (Ready in 45 minutes)
YIELD: 8 sandwiches

1 lb. bulk Italian sausage, crumbled

½ cup chopped green bell pepper

⅓ cup chopped onion

1 (16-oz.) can pizza sauce

2 (8-oz.) cans Pillsbury®
Refrigerated Crescent Dinner Rolls

1 (6-oz.) pkg. mozzarella cheese
slices, halved, folded

1. Heat oven to 375°F. In large skillet, cook sausage, bell pepper and onion over medium-high heat until sausage is no longer pink and vegetables are tender, stirring frequently. Drain. Add 3 tablespoons of the pizza sauce; mix well.

2. Separate dough into 8 rectangles. Firmly press perforations to seal. Place about ¼ cup sausage mixture and ½ slice of cheese, folded, on one end of each rectangle. Fold dough in half over filling; press edges with fork to seal. Place on ungreased cookie sheet.

3. Bake at 375°F. for 15 to 18 minutes or until golden brown. Meanwhile, in small saucepan, heat remaining pizza sauce over low heat until hot. Serve sandwiches with warm pizza sauce.

NUTRITION INFORMATION PER SERVING: **Serving Size:** 1 Sandwich; Calories 430; Calories from Fat 240 **% Daily Value:** Total Fat 27g 42%; Saturated Fat 9g 45%; Cholesterol 45mg 15%; Sodium 1,280mg 53%; Total Carbohydrate 29g 10%; Dietary Fiber 1g 4%; Sugars 9g; Protein 18g; Vitamin A 8%; Vitamin C 10%; Calcium 20%; Iron 10% **Dietary Exchanges:** 2 Starch, 1½ High-Fat Meat, 3 Fat **OR** 2 Carbohydrate, 1½ High-Fat Meat, 3 Fat **Carbohydrate Choices:** 2

doughboy tip

Bulk pork sausage can be used instead of the Italian sausage. After the pork sausage mixture has been thoroughly cooked, taste it. You might want to add a shake of fennel seed, dried oregano or dried Italian seasoning.

savory crescent
chicken squares

PREP TIME: 20 minutes (Ready in 50 minutes)
YIELD: 4 sandwiches

1 (3-oz.) pkg. cream cheese,
softened

1 tablespoon margarine
or butter, softened

2 cups cubed cooked chicken

1 tablespoon chopped fresh chives

¼ teaspoon salt

⅛ teaspoon pepper

2 tablespoons milk

1 tablespoon chopped pimientos,
if desired

1 (8 oz.) can Pillsbury®
Refrigerated Crescent Dinner Rolls

1 tablespoon margarine
or butter, melted

¾ cup seasoned croutons,
crushed

1. Heat oven to 350°F. In medium bowl, combine cream cheese and 1 tablespoon softened margarine; beat until smooth. Add chicken, chives, salt, pepper, milk and pimientos; mix well.

2. Separate dough into 4 rectangles. Firmly press perforations to seal. Spoon ½ cup chicken mixture onto center of each rectangle. Pull 4 corners of dough to center of chicken mixture; twist firmly. Pinch edges to seal. Place on ungreased cookie sheet.

3. Brush tops of sandwiches with 1 tablespoon melted margarine. Sprinkle with crushed croutons.

4. Bake at 350°F. for 25 to 30 minutes or until golden brown.

NUTRITION INFORMATION PER SERVING: **Serving Size:** 1 Sandwich; Calories 500; Calories from Fat 280 **% Daily Value:** Total Fat 31g 48%; Saturated Fat 10g 50%; Cholesterol 85mg 28%; Sodium 850mg 35%; Total Carbohydrate 28g 9%; Dietary Fiber 1g 4%; Sugars 5g; Protein 27g; Vitamin A 15%; Vitamin C 4%; Calcium 6%; Iron 15% **Dietary Exchanges:** 2 Starch, 3 Lean Meat, 4 Fat **OR** 2 Carbohydrate, 3 Lean Meat, 4 Fat **Carbohydrate Choices:** 2

doughboy tip

If you don't have chives, you can substitute 1 tablespoon finely chopped onions. Green onions are ideal, as they add a mild flavor and the same attractive color contrast as the chives.

muffuletta

PREP TIME: 15 minutes (Ready in 1 hour)
YIELD: 6 servings

BREAD

2 (11-oz.) cans Pillsbury®
Refrigerated Breadsticks

Nonstick cooking spray

¼ cup grated Parmesan cheese

FILLING

⅓ cup pitted ripe olives, sliced

⅓ cup pimiento-stuffed green
olives, chopped or sliced

¼ cup finely chopped red onion

3 tablespoons sweet pickle relish,
well drained

1 tablespoon grated
Parmesan cheese

¼ cup purchased creamy
Italian salad dressing

½ lb. thinly sliced cooked deli
meat of your choice (such as ham,
turkey and/or hard salami)

4 oz. thinly sliced provolone or
Swiss cheese

1. Heat oven to 375°F. Spray pizza pan or cookie sheet with nonstick cooking spray. Remove dough from both cans; do not unroll. Separate coils of dough. Place 1 coil of dough in center of sprayed pan. Carefully unroll each strip and wrap around center coil, pinching ends together securely as strips are added. Continue with all strips to make 1 large round.

2. Lightly spray top of dough with nonstick cooking spray. Sprinkle with ¼ cup Parmesan cheese.

3. Bake at 375°F. for 20 to 24 minutes or until golden brown. Remove from pan; place on wire rack. Cool 15 minutes.

4. Meanwhile, in medium bowl, combine ripe olives, pimiento-stuffed olives, onion, relish, 1 tablespoon Parmesan cheese and salad dressing; mix well.

5. Cut baked bread loaf horizontally to make 2 rounds. Spread bottom half of bread with olive mixture. Top with deli meat and sliced cheese. Cover with top half of bread. Serve warm, cut into wedges, or wrap tightly and refrigerate until serving time.

NUTRITION INFORMATION PER SERVING: **Serving Size:** ⅙ of Recipe; Calories 545; Calories from Fat 215 **% Daily Value:** Total Fat 24g 37%; Saturated Fat 8g 40%; Cholesterol 45mg 15%; Sodium 1,900mg 79%; Total Carbohydrate 58g 19%; Dietary Fiber 3g 12%; Sugars 6g; Protein 25g; Vitamin A 6%; Vitamin C 0%; Calcium 32%; Iron 24% **Dietary Exchanges:** 4 Starch, 2 Lean Meat, 2½ Fat **OR** 4 Carbohydrate, 2 Lean Meat, 2½ Fat **Carbohydrate Choices:** 4

doughboy tip

For the best flavor, plan to use freshly sliced deli meats within a day or two of purchase. If the store packaging is deli paper, rewrap the cold cuts tightly in plastic wrap, and slip the package into a resealable food storage plastic bag.

barbecue chicken crescent pinwheels

PREP TIME: 15 minutes (Ready in 35 minutes)
YIELD: 6 sandwiches

1 (15.5-oz.) can Pillsbury®
Grands!® Refrigerated
Crescent Dinner Rolls

½ lb. thinly sliced roasted
chicken breast

1 to 2 tablespoons barbecue
sauce

6 (¾-oz.) thin slices
mozzarella cheese

1 egg white, beaten

1 tablespoon sesame seed

Barbecue sauce

1. Heat oven to 375°F. Spray large cookie sheet with nonstick cooking spray. Separate dough into 3 rectangles. Firmly press perforations to seal. Cut rectangles in half crosswise to make 6 pieces, each about 5½x4 inches. Place dough pieces on sprayed cookie sheet. Press each to form 5½-inch square.

2. Arrange chicken evenly on dough squares, folding under edges of chicken as necessary to fit dough. Spread chicken with 1 to 2 tablespoons barbecue sauce. Top each with cheese slice to fit.

3. With kitchen scissors, cut into each sandwich from each corner to within 1 inch of center. Fold alternating points to center of each, overlapping and pressing center to seal. (See diagram.) Brush each with egg white. Sprinkle dough with sesame seed.

4. Bake at 375°F. for 13 to 18 minutes or until golden brown. Serve sandwiches with additional barbecue sauce.

NUTRITION INFORMATION PER SERVING: **Serving Size:** 1 Sandwich; Calories 400; Calories from Fat 180 **% Daily Value:** Total Fat 20g 31%; Saturated Fat 6g 30%; Cholesterol 30mg 10%; Sodium 1,230mg 51%; Total Carbohydrate 34g 11%; Dietary Fiber 1g 4%; Sugars 6g; Protein 20g; Vitamin A 10%; Vitamin C 2%; Calcium 20%; Iron 10% **Dietary Exchanges:** 2½ Starch, 2 Very Lean Meat, 3 Fat **OR** 2½ Carbohydrate, 2 Very Lean Meat, 3 Fat **Carbohydrate Choices:** 2

doughboy tip

A sprinkling of sesame seed gives the pinwheels a polka-dot surface. Other finishing touches you might like to try include poppy seed, chili powder or a salt-free herb blend mixture.

thai chicken
sandwiches

PREP TIME: 15 minutes (Ready in 35 minutes)
YIELD: 4 sandwiches

2 tablespoons plain yogurt
or sour cream

1 tablespoon peanut butter

2 teaspoons curry powder

1 teaspoon ginger

½ teaspoon garlic powder

1½ teaspoons soy sauce

1½ cups shredded carrots
(from 10-oz. pkg.)

1 cup frozen diced cooked chicken
breast (from 9-oz. pkg.), thawed

4 oz. (1 cup) shredded hot pepper
Monterey Jack cheese

1 (8-oz.) can Pillsbury®
Refrigerated Crescent Dinner Rolls

½ cup mango chutney, heated

1. Heat oven to 375°F. Spray cookie sheet with nonstick cooking spray. In large bowl, combine yogurt, peanut butter, curry powder, ginger, garlic powder and soy sauce; mix well. Add carrots, chicken and cheese; mix well.

2. Separate dough into 4 rectangles. Place on sprayed cookie sheet. Firmly press perforations to seal. Press each rectangle to form 5-inch square. Spoon chicken mixture onto squares. Bring 4 corners of each dough square up over filling; press edges to seal.

3. Bake at 375°F. for 15 to 20 minutes or until golden brown. Serve sandwiches with warm chutney.

NUTRITION INFORMATION PER SERVING: **Serving Size:** 1 Sandwich; Calories 540; Calories from Fat 220 **% Daily Value:** Total Fat 24g 37%; Saturated Fat 10g 50%; Cholesterol 60mg 20%; Sodium 1,160mg 48%; Total Carbohydrate 58g 19%; Dietary Fiber 3g 12%; Sugars 26g; Protein 23g; Vitamin A 260%; Vitamin C 6%; Calcium 25%; Iron 10% **Dietary Exchanges:** 1½ Starch, 2 Fruit, 1 Vegetable, 2½ Lean Meat, 3 Fat **OR** 3½ Carbohydrate, 1 Vegetable, 2½ Lean Meat, 3 Fat **Carbohydrate Choices:** 4

doughboy tip

Feel free to make the pockets with chopped cooked chicken or turkey that you have on hand or buy from a deli instead of using the thawed frozen chicken. Try purchased peanut sauce for dipping rather than the warm chutney.

chicken breast club sandwiches

PREP TIME: 25 minutes
YIELD: 5 sandwiches

1 (10.2-oz.) can (5 biscuits)
Pillsbury® Grands!® Refrigerated
Original Flaky Layers Biscuits

10 slices bacon

⅓ cup mayonnaise

1½ cups shredded lettuce

10 thin slices tomato

2 (6-oz.) pkg. sliced chicken breast

1. Heat oven to 375°F. Separate dough into 5 biscuits. Split each into 2 rounds. Press or roll each round to form 4-inch round; place on ungreased cookie sheets. Bake at 375°F. for 7 to 9 minutes or until golden brown.

2. Meanwhile, cook bacon until crisp. Drain on paper towels.

3. To serve, spread bottom of each baked biscuit round evenly with mayonnaise. Top 5 biscuit rounds, mayonnaise side up, with lettuce, tomato, chicken and cooked bacon. Top each with biscuit round, mayonnaise side down. Cut each sandwich into quarters. If desired, insert toothpick into each quarter.

NUTRITION INFORMATION PER SERVING: Serving Size: 1 Sandwich; Calories 460; Calories from Fat 250 % Daily Value: Total Fat 28g 43%; Saturated Fat 7g 35%; Cholesterol 55mg 18%; Sodium 1,400mg 58%; Total Carbohydrate 28g 9%; Dietary Fiber 2g 8%; Sugars 5g; Protein 23g; Vitamin A 8%; Vitamin C 10%; Calcium 2%; Iron 10% Dietary Exchanges: 2 Starch, 2½ High-Fat Meat, 1 Fat OR 2 Carbohydrate, 2½ High-Fat Meat, 1 Fat Carbohydrate Choices: 2

doughboy tip
Iceberg lettuce is the green most traditionally used in a club sandwich, but it's fun to try the sandwich with other salad leaves, too. Some possibilities are crisp romaine, tender green-leaf or Bibb, crunchy endive or the pleasantly bitter radicchio. Cook the bacon in the microwave or purchase cooked bacon to save a few minutes in the kitchen.

grands!® tuna melts

PREP TIME: 15 minutes (Ready in 35 minutes)
YIELD: 8 sandwiches

2 (6-oz.) cans water-packed tuna, well drained

⅓ cup chopped onion

⅓ cup mayonnaise

⅛ teaspoon salt

⅛ teaspoon pepper

1 (16.3-oz.) can Pillsbury® Grands!® Refrigerated Original Flaky Layers Biscuits

4 oz. (1 cup) shredded Cheddar cheese

Sour cream, if desired

Chopped tomato, if desired

Shredded lettuce, if desired

1. Heat oven to 350°F. Grease cookie sheet. In medium bowl, combine tuna, onion, mayonnaise, salt and pepper; mix well.

2. Separate dough into 8 biscuits. Place 4 biscuits on greased cookie sheet. Press or roll each to form 5-inch round. Spoon tuna mixture evenly onto center of each biscuit. Top each with cheese. Press or roll remaining 4 biscuits to form 5-inch rounds. Place over filling. Press edges to seal.

3. Bake at 350°F. for 15 to 20 minutes or until golden brown. Cut each sandwich in half. Top each with sour cream, tomato and lettuce.

NUTRITION INFORMATION PER SERVING: Serving Size: 1 Sandwich; Calories 380; Calories from Fat 210 **% Daily Value:** Total Fat 23g 35%; Saturated Fat 7g 35%; Cholesterol 35mg 12%; Sodium 870mg 36%; Total Carbohydrate 27g 9%; Dietary Fiber 1g 4%; Sugars 5g; Protein 17g; Vitamin A 8%; Vitamin C 4%; Calcium 15%; Iron 10% **Dietary Exchanges:** 2 Starch, 1½ Lean Meat, 3½ Fat **OR** 2 Carbohydrate, 1½ Lean Meat, 3½ Fat **Carbohydrate Choices:** 2

doughboy tip

Serve the tuna melts, a nice rendition of a lunch-counter classic, with crunchy dill pickles. Add a bowl of tomato soup topped with a sprinkle of fresh or dried dill weed or seasoned croutons.

salmon salad crescent sandwiches

PREP TIME: 20 minutes
YIELD: 6 sandwiches

1 (15.5-oz.) can Pillsbury®
Grands!® Refrigerated
Crescent Dinner Rolls

1 (14.75 to 16-oz.) can salmon,
drained, flaked

2 hard-cooked eggs,
peeled, chopped

¼ cup chopped celery

2 tablespoons drained dill
pickle relish

½ teaspoon onion salt

⅓ cup mayonnaise or
salad dressing

6 small leaves leaf or
iceberg lettuce

1. Bake crescent rolls as directed on can.

2. Meanwhile, in medium bowl, combine salmon, eggs, celery, relish, onion salt and mayonnaise; mix well.

3. Carefully cut each warm crescent roll in half to make 2 layers. Line bottom halves of rolls with lettuce. Top each with salmon mixture. Cover with top halves of rolls.

NUTRITION INFORMATION PER SERVING: Serving Size: 1 Sandwich; Calories 480; Calories from Fat 280 **% Daily Value:** Total Fat 31g 48%; Saturated Fat 6g 30%; Cholesterol 105mg 35%; Sodium 1,120mg 47%; Total Carbohydrate 31g 10%; Dietary Fiber 1g 4%; Sugars 8g; Protein 20g; Vitamin A 10%; Vitamin C 2%; Calcium 20%; Iron 15% **Dietary Exchanges:** 1½ Starch, ½ Fruit, 2 Lean Meat, 5 Fat **OR** 2 Carbohydrate, 2 Lean Meat, 5 Fat **Carbohydrate Choices:** 2

doughboy tip

Salmon generally has a more vibrant color than tuna, but either fish tastes delicious in these crescent sandwiches. Use a 12-ounce can of tuna if you are substituting it for the salmon. Not in the mood for fish but hungry for a sandwich? Use 1½ cups chopped cooked ham instead of the salmon.

grands!® crescent shrimp salad sandwiches

PREP TIME: 15 minutes (Ready in 35 minutes)
YIELD: 6 sandwiches

1 (15.5-oz.) can Pillsbury® Grands!® Refrigerated Crescent Dinner Rolls

2 (5-oz.) pkg. frozen cooked salad shrimp, thawed (about 1¾ cups)

¼ cup chopped celery

2 tablespoons sliced green onions

⅓ cup tartar sauce

8 to 10 drops hot pepper sauce

6 leaves leaf lettuce

1. Bake crescent dinner rolls as directed on can. Cool 15 minutes.

2. Meanwhile, in medium bowl, combine all remaining ingredients except lettuce leaves.

3. Split crescent rolls. Spoon about ¼ cup filling evenly onto bottom half of each roll. Top with lettuce leaves and top halves of rolls.

NUTRITION INFORMATION PER SERVING: **Serving Size:** 1 Sandwich; Calories 390; Calories from Fat 210 **% Daily Value:** Total Fat 23g 35%; Saturated Fat 5g 25%; Cholesterol 100mg 33%; Sodium 720mg 30%; Total Carbohydrate 30g 10%; Dietary Fiber 1g 4%; Sugars 6g; Protein 15g; Vitamin A 6%; Vitamin C 6%; Calcium 4%; Iron 20% **Dietary Exchanges:** 2 Starch, 1½ Very Lean Meat, 4 Fat **OR** 2 Carbohydrate, 1½ Very Lean Meat, 4 Fat **Carbohydrate Choices:** 2

doughboy tip

Forget to buy tartar sauce? No problem. Improvise by blending 1½ tablespoons pickle relish into ¼ cup mayonnaise. If you prefer a more pickle-flavored tartar sauce, increase the amount of relish.

grands!® grilled cheese sandwiches

PREP TIME: 20 minutes
YIELD: 4 sandwiches

1 (16.3-oz.) can Pillsbury®
Grands!® Refrigerated
Buttermilk Biscuits

2 teaspoons oil

8 (⅔-oz.) slices American cheese

1. Separate dough into 8 biscuits. Press or roll each to form 5½-inch round.

2. Heat oil in large skillet over medium heat until hot. Add biscuit rounds, a few at a time; cook 3 minutes. Turn; cook an additional 3 minutes or until light golden brown. Remove from skillet.

3. Place 2 slices of cheese on each of 4 biscuit rounds. Top with remaining biscuit rounds.

4. Return sandwiches to skillet; cook 2 to 3 minutes. Turn; cook an additional 2 minutes or until cheese is melted.

NUTRITION INFORMATION PER SERVING: Serving Size: 1 Sandwich; Calories 550; Calories from Fat 290 **% Daily Value:** Total Fat 32g 49%; Saturated Fat 13g 65%; Cholesterol 40mg 13%; Sodium 1,730mg 72%; Total Carbohydrate 49g 16%; Dietary Fiber 1g 4%; Sugars 9g; Protein 16g; Vitamin A 10%; Vitamin C 0%; Calcium 30%; Iron 15% **Dietary Exchanges:** 3 Starch, ½ Fruit, 1 High Fat Meat, 4½ Fat **OR** 3½ Carbohydrate, 1 High-Fat Meat, 4½ Fat **Carbohydrate Choices:** 3

doughboy tip

Sandwich thin tomato slices and a sprinkling of real bacon pieces or crumbled cooked bacon between the cheese slices before topping with the remaining biscuit rounds.

vegetable calzones

PREP TIME: 45 minutes
YIELD: 4 calzones

1 (10-oz.) can Pillsbury®
Refrigerated Pizza Crust

⅓ cup ricotta cheese

2 tablespoons prepared ranch
salad dressing

4 oz. (1 cup) shredded
Monterey Jack cheese

1 cup chopped fresh broccoli

½ cup chopped tomato

¼ cup chopped green bell pepper

1 egg white, beaten

1. Heat oven to 425°F. Spray cookie sheet with nonstick cooking spray. Unroll dough; cut into fourths. Place dough on sprayed cookie sheet; press each section to form 6-inch square.

2. In small bowl, combine ricotta cheese and salad dressing; mix well. Spoon about 1 heaping tablespoonful cheese mixture onto half of each dough square to within ½ inch of edge. Top each with ¼ cup Monterey Jack cheese.

3. In medium bowl, combine broccoli, tomato and bell pepper; mix well. Spoon scant ½ cup vegetable mixture on top of cheese on each square. Bring remaining half of each dough square over filling; press edges with fork to seal. Brush calzones with beaten egg white. Cut 2 or 3 slits in top of each for steam to escape.

4. Bake at 425°F. for 12 to 14 minutes or until golden brown.

NUTRITION INFORMATION PER SERVING: Serving Size: 1 Calzone; Calories 365; Calories from Fat 145 **% Daily Value:** Total Fat 16g 25%; Saturated Fat 7g 35%; Cholesterol 35mg 12%; Sodium 810mg 34%; Total Carbohydrate 38g 13%; Dietary Fiber 2g 8%; Sugars 7g; Protein 17g; Vitamin A 18%; Vitamin C 26%; Calcium 28%; Iron 12% **Dietary Exchanges:** 2 Starch, 1 Vegetable, 1½ High-Fat Meat **OR** 2 Carbohydrate, 1 Vegetable, 1½ High-Fat Meat **Carbohydrate Choices:** 2½

doughboy tip

These meatless calzones are delicious as they are, but you may want to try adding about ¼ cup chopped fresh basil, parsley or green onion to the ricotta cheese mixture for an extra touch of added flavor and color.

cheese and roasted pepper calzones

PREP TIME: 25 minutes
YIELD: 5 calzones

1 (10.2-oz.) can (5 biscuits) Pillsbury® Grands!® Refrigerated Buttermilk Biscuits

2 oz. (½ cup) shredded Swiss cheese

2 oz. (½ cup) shredded Cheddar cheese

¼ cup grated Parmesan cheese

⅓ cup roasted red bell pepper (from a jar), cut into strips

1. Heat oven to 375°F. Separate dough into 5 biscuits. Press or roll each to form 5½-inch round.

2. Sprinkle all cheeses evenly onto biscuits. Top each with pepper strips. Fold half of biscuit over filling; seal edges. Press edges firmly with fork to seal. Cut 3 slits in top of each for steam to escape. Place on ungreased cookie sheet.

3. Bake at 375°F. for 12 to 15 minutes or until deep golden brown.

NUTRITION INFORMATION PER SERVING: **Serving Size:** 1 Calzone; Calories 315; Calories from Fat 155 **% Daily Value:** Total Fat 17g 26%; Saturated Fat 8g 40%; Cholesterol 25mg 8%; Sodium 890mg 37%; Total Carbohydrate 29g 10%; Dietary Fiber 1g 4%; Sugars 9g; Protein 12g; Vitamin A 14%; Vitamin C 12%; Calcium 24%; Iron 8% **Dietary Exchanges:** 1½ Starch, ½ Fruit, 1 High-Fat Meat, 1½ Fat OR 2 Carbohydrate, 1 High-Fat Meat, 1½ Fat **Carbohydrate Choices:** 2

doughboy tip

To roast your own bell peppers, broil or grill them. As the skin on the side near the heat blackens, turn the peppers to expose a new side. When the peppers are completely blackened, remove them from the heat. When they're cool enough to handle, peel off the blackened skin to reveal sweet roasted pepper that you can cut into strips and use for tasty additions to salads and sandwiches—as well as calzones.

beef 'n pepperoni pizza pie

PREP TIME: 35 minutes (Ready in 55 minutes)
YIELD: 6 servings

¾ lb. lean ground beef

½ cup pizza sauce

2 tablespoons ketchup

2½ oz. (½ cup) sliced pepperoni, quartered

¼ cup grated Parmesan cheese

1 (10-oz.) can Pillsbury® Refrigerated Pizza Crust

1 (4.5-oz.) jar sliced mushrooms, drained

⅓ cup chopped green bell pepper

¼ cup sliced ripe olives

6 oz. (1½ cups) shredded mozzarella cheese

1. Heat oven to 400°F. Spray 9-inch pie pan with nonstick cooking spray. Brown ground beef in medium skillet over medium-high heat for 5 to 7 minutes or until thoroughly cooked, stirring frequently. Drain.

2. Stir pizza sauce, ketchup, pepperoni and Parmesan cheese into beef. Cook 3 to 5 minutes or until thoroughly heated, stirring occasionally.

3. Unroll dough into sprayed pan, stretching dough while pressing firmly in bottom and up sides of pan. Spoon hot beef mixture into crust. Top with mushrooms, bell pepper, olives and cheese.

4. Bake at 400°F. for 15 to 20 minutes or until crust is golden brown. Let stand 10 minutes before serving.

NUTRITION INFORMATION PER SERVING: **Serving Size:** ⅙ of Recipe; Calories 410; Calories from Fat 190 **% Daily Value:** Total Fat 21g 32%; Saturated Fat 9g 45%; Cholesterol 65mg 22%; Sodium 1,100mg 46%; Total Carbohydrate 28g 9%; Dietary Fiber 2g 8%; Sugars 5g; Protein 27g; Vitamin A 8%; Vitamin C 8%; Calcium 30%; Iron 15% **Dietary Exchanges:** 2 Starch, 3 Medium-Fat Meat, 1 Fat **OR** 2 Carbohydrate, 3 Medium-Fat Meat, 1 Fat **Carbohydrate Choices:** 2

doughboy tip

This truly is a "pie" pizza as it's baked in a pie pan. For a more colorful presentation, instead of green bell pepper, use a combination of red, green and yellow bell peppers. If you like, ground turkey breast can be used in place of the ground beef.

mexican beef 'n bean pizza **pictured on page 129**

PREP TIME: 35 minutes
YIELD: 6 servings

1 (10-oz.) can Pillsbury®
Refrigerated Pizza Crust

½ lb. lean ground beef

¼ teaspoon salt

⅛ teaspoon pepper

1 (16-oz.) can refried beans

1 cup taco sauce or
chunky-style salsa

1 (11-oz.) can vacuum-packed
whole kernel corn with red and
green peppers, well drained

4 oz. (1 cup) shredded
Cheddar cheese

1 cup shredded lettuce

1 medium tomato, chopped

½ cup sliced green onions,
if desired

1. Heat oven to 400°F. Grease 12-inch pizza pan. Unroll dough; place in greased pan. Starting at center, press out dough to edge of pan. Bake at 400°F. for 9 to 11 minutes or until crust begins to brown.

2. Meanwhile, in medium skillet, brown ground beef with salt and pepper over medium-high heat for 5 to 7 minutes or until thoroughly cooked, stirring frequently. Drain.

3. Remove partially baked crust from oven. Spread refried beans evenly over crust. Spread ½ cup of the taco sauce over beans. Top with ground beef mixture, corn and cheese.

4. Return to oven; bake an additional 12 to 15 minutes or until crust is golden brown and cheese is melted. Top with lettuce, tomatoes and green onions. Serve with remaining ½ cup taco sauce.

NUTRITION INFORMATION PER SERVING: Serving Size: ⅙ of Recipe; Calories 410; Calories from Fat 130 **% Daily Value:** Total Fat 14g 22%; Saturated Fat 6g 30%; Cholesterol 45mg 15%; Sodium 1,460mg 61%; Total Carbohydrate 49g 16%; Dietary Fiber 7g 28%; Sugars 10g; Protein 21g; Vitamin A 8%; Vitamin C 15%; Calcium 20%; Iron 20% **Dietary Exchanges:** 3 Starch, 1 Vegetable, 1½ Medium-Fat Meat, 1 Fat **OR** 3 Carbohydrate, 1 Vegetable, 1½ Medium-Fat Meat, 1 Fat **Carbohydrate Choices:** 3

doughboy tip

Choose a sturdy, crisp-leaf lettuce, such as iceberg or romaine, to shred as topping for the baked pizza. Softer varieties will wilt more quickly when they come in contact with the hot pizza.

beef and spinach deep-dish pizza

PREP TIME: 25 minutes (Ready in 1 hour 15 minutes)
YIELD: 8 servings

1 (9-oz.) pkg. frozen spinach In a pouch

1 lb. lean ground beef

1 small onion, chopped

1 (8-oz.) can pizza sauce

1 (11-oz.) can Pillsbury® Refrigerated Crusty French Loaf

4 oz. sliced pepperoni

8 oz. (2 cups) shredded Italian cheese blend

1 egg

1 teaspoon olive oil

1. Heat oven to 350°F. Spray 9½-inch deep-dish glass pie pan with nonstick cooking spray. Cook spinach as directed on package. Drain well; set aside to cool.

2. Meanwhile, in medium skillet, cook ground beef and onion over medium-high heat for 5 to 7 minutes or until beef is thoroughly cooked, stirring frequently. Drain. Stir in pizza sauce until well mixed.

3. Carefully unroll dough. Place in sprayed pie pan so edges extend over sides of pan. Pat dough in bottom and up sides of pan, leaving dough extended over sides. Spoon ground beef mixture into crust. Top with pepperoni slices and half of the cheese.

4. Squeeze spinach to remove moisture. Slightly beat egg in small bowl. Add spinach; mix well. Spoon spinach mixture over cheese. Top with remaining half of cheese.

5. Fold extended edges of dough up and over filling; seal all edges. Cut several slits in top for steam to escape. Brush crust with oil.

6. Bake at 350°F. for 38 to 48 minutes or until deep golden brown. Let stand 10 minutes before serving.

NUTRITION INFORMATION PER SERVING: Serving Size: ⅛ of Recipe; Calories 425; Calories from Fat 235 **% Daily Value:** Total Fat 26g 40%; Saturated Fat 11g 55%; Cholesterol 95mg 32%; Sodium 960mg 40%; Total Carbohydrate 24g 8%; Dietary Fiber 2g 8%; Sugars 2g; Protein 26g; Vitamin A 46%; Vitamin C 6%; Calcium 28%; Iron 16% **Dietary Exchanges:** 1½ Starch, 3 High-Fat Meat **OR** 1½ Carbohydrate, 3 High-Fat Meat **Carbohydrate Choices:** 1½

doughboy tip

Stock up on ground beef when it's on sale. Divide it into quarter-pound patties, and wrap each individually in plastic wrap; store the wrapped patties in a resealable freezer bag. With quarter-pound patties, it's easy and quick to thaw exactly the amount you need.

pepperoni pizzas

PREP TIME: 45 minutes
YIELD: 8 pizzas

1 (16.3-oz.) can Pillsbury®
Grands!® Refrigerated
Buttermilk Biscuits

1 (15-oz.) can Italian-style
tomato sauce

4 oz. (1 cup) shredded
Cheddar cheese

4 oz. (1 cup) shredded
mozzarella cheese

32 slices pepperoni (about 2 oz.)

1. Heat oven to 375°F. Lightly grease 2 large cookie sheets.

2. Separate dough into 8 biscuits. Place 4 inches apart on greased cookie sheets. Press out each to form 6-inch round. Spread 2 to 3 tablespoons sauce on each round. Sprinkle each with Cheddar cheese and mozzarella cheese. Top each with 4 pepperoni slices.

3. Bake at 375°F. for 10 to 12 minutes or until crust edges are golden brown and cheese is melted.

NUTRITION INFORMATION PER SERVING: Serving Size: 1 Pizza; Calories 340; Calories from Fat 170 % Daily Value: Total Fat 19g 29%; Saturated Fat 8g 40%; Cholesterol 30mg 10%; Sodium 910mg 38%; Total Carbohydrate 28g 9%; Dietary Fiber 1g 4%; Sugars 7g; Protein 13g; Vitamin A 15%; Vitamin C 15%; Calcium 25%; Iron 10% Dietary Exchanges: 2 Starch, 1 High-Fat Meat, 2 Fat OR 2 Carbohydrate, 1 High-Fat Meat, 2 Fat Carbohydrate Choices: 2

doughboy tip

To give these pizzas Mexican flair, substitute salsa for the Italian tomato sauce. Then top each pizza with a dollop of sour cream, a little guacamole and a sprinkle of chopped green onions.

ham and swiss grands!® pizzas

PREP TIME: 30 minutes
YIELD: 5 pizzas

1 (10.2-oz.) can (5 biscuits)
Pillsbury® Grands!® Refrigerated
Buttermilk Biscuits

5 teaspoons creamy
mustard-mayonnaise sauce

6 oz. (1½ cups) shredded
Swiss cheese

¾ cup coarsely chopped
cooked ham

2 tablespoons sliced green onions

3 Italian plum tomatoes

1. Heat oven to 375°F. Spray large cookie sheet with nonstick cooking spray or lightly grease. Separate dough into 5 biscuits; place on sprayed cookie sheet. Press out each biscuit to form 6-inch round.

2. Spread each with mustard-mayonnaise sauce. Top each with cheese, ham and green onions. Cut each tomato into 5 slices. Place 3 tomato slices on each pizza.

3. Bake at 375°F. for 10 to 15 minutes or until bottoms of crusts are deep golden brown and cheese is melted.

NUTRITION INFORMATION PER SERVING: Serving Size: 1 Pizza; Calories 360; Calories from Fat 180 % Daily Value: Total Fat 20g 31%; Saturated Fat 9g 45%; Cholesterol 40mg 13%; Sodium 1,040mg 43%; Total Carbohydrate 28g 9%; Dietary Fiber 1g 4%; Sugars 5g; Protein 18g; Vitamin A 10%; Vitamin C 6%; Calcium 35%; Iron 10% Dietary Exchanges: 2 Starch, 1½ Lean Meat, 3 Fat OR 2 Carbohydrate, 1½ Lean Meat, 3 Fat Carbohydrate Choices: 2

doughboy tip

If you don't have the purchased creamy mustard-mayonnaise sauce on hand, you can substitute by blending 1 teaspoon prepared mustard with 4 teaspoons mayonnaise.

lumpy pan pizza

PREP TIME: 10 minutes (Ready in 40 minutes)
YIELD: 6 servings

1 (16.3-oz.) can Pillsbury®
Grands!® Refrigerated Original
Flaky Layers Biscuits

1 (8-oz.) can pizza sauce

8 oz. (2 cups) finely shredded
mozzarella cheese

16 (1½-inch) slices pepperoni

1. Heat oven to 375°F. Separate dough into 8 biscuits. Cut each biscuit into 8 pieces; place in medium bowl. Add pizza sauce and 1 cup of the cheese; toss to coat.

2. Spoon and spread mixture in ungreased 9-inch square (2-quart) glass baking dish. Top with pepperoni and remaining 1 cup cheese.

3. Bake at 375°F. for 22 to 28 minutes or until golden brown and bubbly.

NUTRITION INFORMATION PER SERVING: **Serving Size:** ⅙ of Recipe; Calories 460; Calories from Fat 230 **% Daily Value:** Total Fat 26g 40%; Saturated Fat 9g 45%; Cholesterol 30mg 10%; Sodium 1,500mg 63%; Total Carbohydrate 37g 12%; Dietary Fiber 1g 4%; Sugars 7g; Protein 19g; Vitamin A 8%; Vitamin C 0%; Calcium 30%; Iron 15% **Dietary Exchanges:** 2 Starch, ½ Fruit, 2 Medium-Fat Meat, 3 Fat **OR** 2½ Carbohydrate, 2 Medium-Fat Meat, 3 Fat **Carbohydrate Choices:** 2½

doughboy tip

If you like additional toppings, try sprinkling with cooked Italian sausage, sliced mushrooms or sliced green onions with or in place of the pepperoni.

barbecue beef pizza

PREP TIME: 30 minutes
YIELD: 4 servings

1 (10-oz.) can Pillsbury®
Refrigerated Pizza Crust

2 cups refrigerated barbecue
sauce with sliced fully cooked beef
(from 32-oz. container)

6 oz. (1½ cups) shredded
Monterey Jack cheese

½ medium red onion, thinly sliced

1 green bell pepper,
cut into thin strips

1. Heat oven to 425°F. Spray cookie sheet with nonstick cooking spray. Unroll dough; place on sprayed cookie sheet. Starting at center, press out dough to form 13x9-inch rectangle. Bake at 425°F. for 7 to 9 minutes or until light golden brown.

2. Remove partially baked crust from oven. Top with beef in sauce, cheese, onion and bell pepper.

3. Return to oven; bake an additional 10 to 12 minutes or until crust is golden brown and cheese is melted.

NUTRITION INFORMATION PER SERVING: **Serving Size:** ¼ of Recipe; Calories 520; Calories from Fat 170 **% Daily Value:** Total Fat 19g 29%; Saturated Fat 11g 55%; Cholesterol 70mg 23%; Sodium 1,410mg 59%; Total Carbohydrate 54g 18%; Dietary Fiber 4g 16%; Sugars 17g; Protein 34g; Vitamin A 20%; Vitamin C 25%; Calcium 40%; Iron 30% **Dietary Exchanges:** 2½ Starch, 1 Fruit, 4 Lean Meat, 1 Fat **OR** 3½ Carbohydrate, 4 Lean Meat, 1 Fat **Carbohydrate Choices:** 3½

doughboy tip
For a quick salad accompaniment, purchase a bag of prewashed romaine, mesclun (baby lettuce mix) or coleslaw blend (shredded cabbage and carrots). Add any other chopped fresh vegetables you may have on hand, then toss with your favorite purchased dressing.

pineapple-canadian bacon pizza ring **pictured on page 172**

PREP TIME: 25 minutes (Ready in 45 minutes)
YIELD: 5 servings

1 (12-oz.) can Pillsbury® Golden Layers™ Refrigerated Flaky Biscuits

3 tablespoons purchased sweet-and-sour sauce

1 (8-oz.) can pineapple tidbits in unsweetened juice, well drained

1 (5-oz.) pkg. thinly sliced Canadian bacon, chopped

4 oz. (1 cup) shredded Monterey Jack cheese

¼ cup chopped bell pepper (any color)

2 tablespoons sliced green onions

1. Heat oven to 400°F. Separate dough into 10 biscuits. Press or roll each to form 4½-inch round. On ungreased cookie sheet, arrange biscuits, slightly overlapping, to form 12-inch-diameter ring.

2. Spread sweet-and-sour sauce evenly over biscuits. Top each biscuit with pineapple and Canadian bacon. Sprinkle with cheese. Top with bell pepper and green onions.

3. Bake at 400°F. for 15 to 20 minutes or until crust is golden brown. Cool 5 minutes. To serve, pull apart into individual pizzas.

NUTRITION INFORMATION PER SERVING: **Serving Size:** ⅕ of Recipe; Calories 415; Calories from Fat 180 **% Daily Value:** Total Fat 20g 31%; Saturated Fat 8g 40%; Cholesterol 40mg 13%; Sodium 1,430mg 60%; Total Carbohydrate 43g 14%; Dietary Fiber 1g 4%; Sugars 19g; Protein 17g; Vitamin A 6%; Vitamin C 8%; Calcium 18%; Iron 12% **Dietary Exchanges:** 2 Starch, 1 Fruit, 1½ Medium-Fat Meat, 1½ Fat **OR** 3 Carbohydrate, 1½ Medium-Fat Meat, 1½ Fat **Carbohydrate Choices:** 3

doughboy tip

Don't throw away the juice drained from the canned pineapple. Use it to keep apples and bananas bright in a fruit salad, drizzle over a scoop of cottage cheese or stir into your favorite fruit juice.

chili-dog pizza

PREP TIME: 30 minutes
YIELD: 6 servings

1 (10-oz.) can Pillsbury®
Refrigerated Pizza Crust

1 (7.5-oz.) can chili with beans

½ lb. hot dogs, cut into
½-inch slices

¼ cup drained sweet pickle relish

1 cup (2 to 4 medium) chopped
Italian plum tomatoes

4 oz. (1 cup) finely shredded
mozzarella cheese

1. Heat oven to 425°F. Grease 12-inch pizza pan. Unroll dough; place in greased pan. Starting at center, press out dough to edge of pan, forming ½-inch rim. Bake at 425°F. for 7 to 9 minutes or until light golden brown.

2. Remove partially baked crust from oven. Spoon and spread chili over crust. Sprinkle with hot dogs, relish, tomatoes and cheese.

3. Return to oven; bake an additional 15 to 18 minutes or until crust is deep golden brown.

NUTRITION INFORMATION PER SERVING: **Serving Size:** ⅙ of Recipe; Calories 350; Calories from Fat 160 **% Daily Value:** Total Fat 18g 28%; Saturated Fat 7g 35%; Cholesterol 35mg 12%; Sodium 1,090mg 45%; Total Carbohydrate 32g 11%; Dietary Fiber 2g 8%; Sugars 8g; Protein 15g; Vitamin A 8%; Vitamin C 4%; Calcium 15%; Iron 15% **Dietary Exchanges:** 2 Starch, 1½ High-Fat Meat, 1 Fat **OR** 2 Carbohydrate, 1½ High-Fat Meat, 1 Fat **Carbohydrate Choices:** 2

doughboy tip

Set out a dish of chopped onions or green onions for those who want even more "chili dog" experience. Try using shredded Cheddar or Monterey Jack cheese in place of the mozzarella cheese for a nice flavor change.

TOP: CHICKEN AND ARTICHOKE PIZZA
BOTTOM: PINEAPPLE-CANADIAN BACON PIZZA RING, PAGE 170

chicken and artichoke pizza

PREP TIME: 15 minutes (Ready in 35 minutes)
YIELD: 8 servings

1 (10-oz.) can Pillsbury® Refrigerated Pizza Crust

¼ cup purchased creamy Caesar salad dressing

3 tablespoons grated Parmesan cheese

2 cups chopped cooked chicken or turkey

1 (6 1/2-oz.) jar marinated artichoke hearts, drained, coarsely chopped

6 oz. (1½ cups) shredded fontina cheese

2 Italian plum tomatoes, seeded, chopped

1. Heat oven to 400°F. Lightly grease 12-inch pizza pan. Unroll dough; place in greased pan. Starting at center, press out dough to edge of pan.

2. Bake at 400°F. for 6 to 8 minutes or until crust begins to dry. Meanwhile, in small bowl, combine salad dressing and Parmesan cheese.

3. Remove partially baked crust from oven. Spread dressing mixture over crust. Top with chicken and artichokes. Sprinkle with fontina cheese. Top with tomatoes.

4. Return to oven; bake an additional 15 to 20 minutes or until crust is golden brown and cheese is melted.

NUTRITION INFORMATION PER SERVING: **Serving Size:** ⅛ of Recipe; Calories 290; Calories from Fat 125 **% Daily Value:** Total Fat 14g 22%; Saturated Fat 6g 30%; Cholesterol 55mg 18%; Sodium 610mg 25%; Total Carbohydrate 21g 7%; Dietary Fiber 1g 4%; Sugars 3g; Protein 20g; Vitamin A 8%; Vitamin C 4%; Calcium 20%; Iron 10% **Dietary Exchanges:** 1½ Starch, 2 Lean Meat, 1½ Fat **OR** 1½ Carbohydrate, 2 Lean Meat, 1½ Fat **Carbohydrate Choices:** 1½

doughboy tip

If you don't have an "official" pizza pan, press the dough out to form a 13x9-inch rectangle on a lightly greased cookie sheet. You'll need to reduce the baking time slightly: In Step 2, bake the crust at 400°F. for 5 to 7 minutes. After the toppings go onto the partially baked crust, continue baking for an additional 10 to 12 minutes.

italian chicken pizza

PREP TIME: 25 minutes (Ready in 40 minutes)
YIELD: 6 servings

1 (10-oz.) can Pillsbury®
Refrigerated Pizza Crust

1 (9-oz.) pkg. frozen spinach
in a pouch

1 tablespoon oil

½ cup coarsely chopped onion

1 (6-oz.) pkg. refrigerated
cooked Italian-style chicken
breast strips, chopped

8 oz. (2 cups) shredded
mozzarella cheese

1 (2.8 to 3-oz.) pkg. precooked
bacon slices, cut into
½-inch pieces

1. Heat oven to 400°F. Grease 15x10x1-inch baking pan. Unroll dough; place in greased pan. Starting at center, press out dough to edge of pan. Bake at 400°F. for 9 to 13 minutes or until edges are light golden brown.

2. Meanwhile, cook spinach as directed on package. Drain well; squeeze to remove liquid. Heat oil in small skillet over medium-high heat until hot. Add onion; cook 3 to 4 minutes or until tender, stirring frequently.

3. Remove partially baked crust from oven. Top crust with spinach, onion, chicken, cheese and bacon.

4. Return to oven; bake an additional 9 to 12 minutes or until cheese is melted.

NUTRITION INFORMATION PER SERVING: Serving Size: ⅙ of Recipe; Calories 385; Calories from Fat 170 % Daily Value: Total Fat 19g 29%; Saturated Fat 7g 35%; Cholesterol 55mg 18%; Sodium 890mg 37%; Total Carbohydrate 26g 9%; Dietary Fiber 2g 8%; Sugars 4g; Protein 28g; Vitamin A 54%; Vitamin C 2%; Calcium 32%; Iron 12% Dietary Exchanges: 2 Starch, 3 Medium-Fat Meat OR 2 Carbohydrate, 3 Medium-Fat Meat Carbohydrate Choices: 2

doughboy tip

We like this easy pizza as a main dish, but it would also be great as an appetizer. Just prepare as directed, then cut into small squares and arrange on a pretty platter.

deluxe turkey club pizza

PREP TIME: 35 minutes
YIELD: 6 servings

CRUST

1 (10-oz.) can Pillsbury®
Refrigerated Pizza Crust

2 teaspoons sesame seed

TOPPING

6 slices bacon, cut into
1-inch pieces

¼ cup light or regular mayonnaise

½ to 1 teaspoon grated
lemon peel

4 oz. (1 cup) shredded
Monterey Jack cheese

1 tablespoon thinly sliced fresh
basil or 1 teaspoon dried
basil leaves

¼ lb. cooked turkey breast slices,
cut into 1-inch strips

2 small Italian plum tomatoes
or 1 small tomato, thinly sliced

2 oz. (½ cup) shredded Swiss
cheese

Fresh basil leaves, if desired

1. Heat oven to 425°F. Lightly spray 12-inch pizza pan or 13x9-inch pan with nonstick cooking spray. Unroll dough; place in sprayed pan. Starting at center, press out dough to edge of pan. Sprinkle sesame seed evenly over dough. Bake at 425°F. for 10 to 12 minutes or until crust is light golden brown.

2. Meanwhile, cook bacon in large skillet over medium heat until crisp. Drain on paper towels. Discard drippings. In small bowl, combine mayonnaise and lemon peel; blend well.

3. Remove partially baked crust from oven. Spread mayonnaise mixture over crust. Top with Monterey Jack cheese, sliced basil, turkey strips, cooked bacon and tomatoes. Sprinkle with Swiss cheese.

4. Return to oven; bake an additional 7 to 9 minutes or until crust is golden brown and cheese is melted. Garnish with fresh basil leaves.

NUTRITION INFORMATION PER SERVING: **Serving Size:** ⅙ of Recipe; Calories 320; Calories from Fat 150 **% Daily Value:** Total Fat 17g 26%; Saturated Fat 8g 40%; Cholesterol 40mg 13%; Sodium 920mg 38%; Total Carbohydrate 24g 8%; Dietary Fiber 1g 4%; Sugars 3g; Protein 18g; Vitamin A 8%; Vitamin C 4%; Calcium 25%; Iron 10% **Dietary Exchanges:** 1½ Starch, 2 Lean Meat, 2 Fat OR 1½ Carbohydrate, 2 Lean Meat, 2 Fat **Carbohydrate Choices:** 1½

doughboy tip

Ripe fresh tomatoes are the secret to success. To maintain the best flavor and texture, store tomatoes unwrapped and unrefrigerated. A woven basket is ideal, as it allows air to circulate, preventing the accumulation of surface moisture that can lead to spoilage. Underripe tomatoes will continue to ripen if you set them in a sunny window.

chicken cordon bleu pizza

PREP TIME: 15 minutes (Ready in 40 minutes)
YIELD: 4 servings

1 (10-oz.) can Pillsbury® Refrigerated Pizza Crust

⅓ cup purchased garlic ranch salad dressing

4 oz. (1 cup) shredded smoked provolone cheese

4 oz. refrigerated roasted chicken breast strips

2 oz. sliced cooked Canadian bacon, halved

2 tablespoons cooked real bacon pieces or imitation bacon bits

4 green onions, sliced

¼ cup chopped tomato

4 oz. (1 cup) shredded mozzarella cheese

1. Heat oven to 425°F. Grease 12-inch pizza pan. Unroll dough; place in greased pan. Starting at center, press out dough to edge of pan.

2. Spread salad dressing over crust. Sprinkle with provolone cheese. Top with chicken, Canadian bacon, bacon, green onions, tomato and mozzarella cheese.

3. Bake at 425°F. for 18 to 22 minutes or until crust is deep golden brown.

NUTRITION INFORMATION PER SERVING: Serving Size: ¼ of Recipe; Calories 550; Calories from Fat 250 % Daily Value: Total Fat 28g 43%; Saturated Fat 10g 50%; Cholesterol 80mg 27%; Sodium 1,500mg 63%; Total Carbohydrate 39g 13%; Dietary Fiber 2g 8%; Sugars 8g; Protein 35g; Vitamin A 12%; Vitamin C 4%; Calcium 46%; Iron 16% Dietary Exchanges: 2½ Starch, 4 Medium-Fat Meat, 1 Fat OR 2½ Carbohydrate, 4 Medium-Fat Meat, 1 Fat Carbohydrate Choices: 2½

doughboy tip

Thinly sliced ham can be substituted for the Canadian bacon, and regular provolone or Swiss cheese can used instead of the smoked provolone. If you have an extra cooked chicken breast in the refrigerator, cut it into strips and use it instead of the purchased chicken breast strips.

tomato, blue cheese and pine nut pizza

PREP TIME: 25 minutes
YIELD: 4 servings

1 (10-oz.) can Pillsbury® Refrigerated Pizza Crust

4 large Italian plum tomatoes, sliced (about 2 cups)

2 (¼-inch) slices red onion, separated into rings

2 oz. blue or Gorgonzola cheese, crumbled (½ cup)

3 oz. (¾ cup) shredded mozzarella cheese

¼ cup pine nuts

1. Heat oven to 425°F. Grease cookie sheet. Unroll dough; place on greased cookie sheet. Starting at center, press out dough to form 12x10-inch rectangle. Bake at 425°F. for 7 minutes.

2. Remove partially baked crust from oven. Top with tomato slices, onion, blue cheese, mozzarella cheese and pine nuts.

3. Return to oven; bake an additional 10 to 12 minutes or until crust is light golden brown and cheese is melted.

NUTRITION INFORMATION PER SERVING: **Serving Size:** ¼ of Recipe; Calories 350; Calories from Fat 130 **% Daily Value:** Total Fat 14g 22%; Saturated Fat 6g 30%; Cholesterol 20mg 7%; Sodium 790mg 33%; Total Carbohydrate 38g 13%; Dietary Fiber 2g 8%; Sugars 6g; Protein 17g; Vitamin A 10%; Vitamin C 10%; Calcium 25%; Iron 15% **Dietary Exchanges:** 2 Starch, 1 Vegetable, 1½ High-Fat Meat **OR** 2 Carbohydrate, 1 Vegetable, 1½ High-Fat Meat **Carbohydrate Choices:** 2½

doughboy tip

Red onions are often very large. If you don't use all of a fresh onion, wrap the unused portion tightly in plastic wrap and store it in the refrigerator for a day or two. Slivered almonds can be used instead of the pine nuts.

tomato-basil-cheese pizza

PREP TIME: 20 minutes
YIELD: 4 servings

1 (10-oz.) can Pillsbury®
Refrigerated Pizza Crust

8 oz. (2 cups) shredded
mozzarella cheese

2 Italian plum tomatoes, sliced

¼ teaspoon salt

⅛ teaspoon pepper

¼ cup chopped fresh basil

1 tablespoon olive or vegetable oil

1. Heat oven to 425°F. Lightly grease cookie sheet. Unroll dough; place on greased cookie sheet. Starting at center, press out dough to form 12-inch round with ½-inch rim.

2. Sprinkle 1 cup of the cheese over dough to within ½ inch of edge. Arrange tomato slices over cheese. Sprinkle with salt, pepper and 2 tablespoons of the basil. Sprinkle with remaining 1 cup cheese. Drizzle with oil.

3. Bake at 425°F. for 18 to 20 minutes or until crust is golden brown and cheese is melted. Sprinkle with remaining 2 tablespoons basil before serving.

NUTRITION INFORMATION PER SERVING: Serving Size: ¼ of Recipe; Calories 380; Calories from Fat 145 **% Daily Value:** Total Fat 16g 25%; Saturated Fat 7g 35%; Cholesterol 30mg 10%; Sodium 960mg 40%; Total Carbohydrate 37g 12%; Dietary Fiber 1g 4%; Sugars 6g; Protein 22g; Vitamin A 16%; Vitamin C 4%; Calcium 42%; Iron 12% **Dietary Exchanges:** 2½ Starch, 4 Medium-Fat Meat **OR** 2½ Carbohydrate, 4 Medium-Fat Meat **Carbohydrate Choices:** 2½

doughboy tip

This Italian classic is made with fresh tomatoes, basil and mozzarella cheese. Substitute fresh mozzarella, usually available at the deli counter, for the regular. Instead of shredding, which is difficult to do because of the soft texture of the fresh cheese, cut it into thin slices with a sharp serrated knife.

spinach and mushroom pizza pie

PREP TIME: 10 minutes (Ready in 50 minutes)
YIELD: 6 servings

2 (10-oz.) cans Pillsbury®
Refrigerated Pizza Crust

1 (8-oz.) can (1 cup) pizza sauce

1 (4.5-oz.) jar sliced mushrooms,
drained

¼ cup sliced ripe olives

6 oz. (1½ cups) shredded
mozzarella cheese

2 (9-oz.) pkg. frozen spinach in a
pouch, thawed, squeezed to drain

1 teaspoon olive or vegetable oil

1 tablespoon grated
Parmesan cheese

1. Heat oven to 400°F. Lightly grease 9-inch pie pan. Unroll 1 can of dough into greased pan. Press in bottom and up sides of pan to form crust.

2. In small bowl, combine pizza sauce and mushrooms; mix well. Spoon onto dough. Layer olives, ¾ cup of the mozzarella cheese, spinach and remaining ¾ cup mozzarella cheese over mushroom mixture.

3. Unroll remaining can of dough. Press dough to form 9-inch round; place over filling. Pinch edges of dough to seal; roll up edge of dough or flute to form rim. Cut several slits in top crust for steam to escape. Brush with oil. Sprinkle with Parmesan cheese.

4. Bake at 400°F. for 35 to 40 minutes or until crust is deep golden brown.

NUTRITION INFORMATION PER SERVING: **Serving Size:** ⅙ of Recipe; Calories 460; Calories from Fat 135 **% Daily Value:** Total Fat 15g 23%; Saturated Fat 5g 25%; Cholesterol 15mg 5%; Sodium 1,000mg 42%; Total Carbohydrate 63g 21%; Dietary Fiber 5g 20%; Sugars 0g; Protein 19g; Vitamin A 0%; Vitamin C 0%; Calcium 0%; Iron 0% **Dietary Exchanges:** 3½ Starch, 2 Vegetable, 1 High-Fat Meat **OR** 3½ Carbohydrate, 2 Vegetable, 1 High-Fat Meat **Carbohydrate Choices:** 4

doughboy tip

For a heartier pie, add about ½ pound cooked bulk Italian turkey sausage or ground beef along with the olives in Step 2, then continue with the recipe as directed.

easy cheesy pizzas

PREP TIME: 15 minutes (Ready in 35 minutes)
YIELD: 8 pizzas

1 (16.3-oz.) can Pillsbury®
Grands!® Refrigerated
Buttermilk Biscuits

1 (14 or 15-oz.) jar pizza sauce

6 oz. (1½ cups) shredded
mozzarella cheese

1. Heat oven to 375°F. Spray 2 cookie sheets with nonstick cooking spray. Separate dough into 8 biscuits; place 2 inches apart on sprayed cookie sheets. Press or roll each to form 6-inch round.

2. Spread 3 tablespoons pizza sauce evenly over each round. Sprinkle each with cheese. If desired, add favorite pizza toppings.

3. Bake at 375°F. for 12 to 17 minutes or until biscuits are golden brown and cheese is bubbly.

NUTRITION INFORMATION PER SERVING: Serving Size: 1 Pizza; Calories 280; Calories from Fat 130
% Daily Value: Total Fat 14g 22%; Saturated Fat 5g 25%; Cholesterol 15mg 5%; Sodium 1,040mg 43%;
Total Carbohydrate 28g 9%; Dietary Fiber 1g 4%; Sugars 7g; Protein 10g; Vitamin A 6%; Vitamin C 2%;
Calcium 20%; Iron 10% Dietary Exchanges: 1 Starch, 1 Fruit, 1 Medium-Fat Meat, 1½ Fat OR
2 Carbohydrate, 1 Medium-Fat Meat, 1½ Fat Carbohydrate Choices: 2

doughboy tip

What's your favorite pizza topping? Dress up these homemade pizzas with sliced olives, chopped marinated artichoke hearts, sliced mushrooms, sliced pepperoni, cooked ground beef or Italian sausage, diced bell pepper, shredded Cheddar cheese or even crushed pineapple. For a party, fill bowls with a variety of ingredients and let everyone create a "personal pizza."

beef stroganoff pot pie

PREP TIME: 30 minutes (Ready in 1 hour 25 minutes)
YIELD: 6 servings

1 (15-oz.) pkg. Pillsbury®
Refrigerated Pie Crusts, softened
as directed on package

1 lb. extra-lean ground beef

1 cup chopped onions

1 garlic clove, minced

1 cup soft bread crumbs

1 cup chopped fresh parsley

½ teaspoon pepper

2 eggs

1 (10¾-oz.) can condensed cream
of mushroom soup

1 (8-oz.) pkg. cream cheese,
softened

1 (4.5-oz.) jar sliced mushrooms,
drained

1 egg white, slightly beaten

1. Prepare pie crust as directed on package for *two-crust pie* using 9-inch glass pie pan.

2. Heat oven to 375°F. In large skillet, cook ground beef, onions and garlic over medium-high heat until beef is browned and thoroughly cooked, stirring frequently. Drain. Stir in all remaining ingredients except egg white; mix well. Pour into crust-lined pan.

3. Unfold second crust. Using leaf-shaped canapé or cookie cutter, cut out leaf shapes in several places. Place crust over filling; flute edge. Brush with beaten egg white. Arrange leaf cutouts on top crust; brush with egg white.

4. Bake at 375°F. for 45 to 55 minutes or until crust is deep golden brown. If necessary, cover edge of pie crust with strips of foil after 15 to 20 minutes of baking to prevent excessive browning. Let stand 10 minutes before serving.

NUTRITION INFORMATION PER SERVING: **Serving Size:** ⅙ of Recipe; Calories 710; Calories from Fat 420 **% Daily Value:** Total Fat 47g 72%; Saturated Fat 21g 105%; Cholesterol 175mg 58%; Sodium 920mg 38%; Total Carbohydrate 48g 16%; Dietary Fiber 2g 8%; Sugars 6g; Protein 24g; Vitamin A 25%; Vitamin C 20%; Calcium 10%; Iron 20% **Dietary Exchanges:** 3 Starch, 2 Lean Meat, 8 Fat **OR** 3 Carbohydrate, 2 Lean Meat, 8 Fat **Carbohydrate Choices:** 3

doughboy tip

Fresh parsley can sometimes have a bit of sand stuck on the leaves. Pinch the leaves from the stems, and soak the leaves in enough cold water to cover. Lift the leaves out, fill the bowl with fresh water and repeat until no trace of grit remains when you lift out the parsley. Roll the parsley in a paper towel to absorb excess moisture before chopping.

beef 'n beans with cheesy biscuits

PREP TIME: 15 minutes (Ready in 40 minutes)
YIELD: 5 servings

1 lb. lean ground beef

½ cup chopped onion

1 (16-oz.) can barbecue beans or pork and beans with molasses

1 (10¾-oz.) can condensed tomato soup

1 teaspoon chili powder

¼ teaspoon garlic powder

1 (12-oz.) can Pillsbury® Golden Layers™ Refrigerated Flaky Biscuits

4 oz. (1 cup) shredded Cheddar or American cheese

1. Heat oven to 375°F. In large skillet, cook ground beef and onion over medium-high heat until beef is thoroughly cooked, stirring frequently. Drain.

2. Stir in beans, soup, chili powder and garlic powder; mix well. Bring to a boil. Reduce heat; simmer 5 minutes.

3. Separate dough into 10 biscuits. Spoon hot beef mixture into ungreased 8-inch square (2-quart) glass baking dish or 2-quart casserole. Arrange biscuits over hot mixture. Sprinkle with cheese.

4. Bake at 375°F. for 20 to 25 minutes or until mixture is bubbly, and biscuits are golden brown and no longer doughy.

NUTRITION INFORMATION PER SERVING: Serving Size: ⅕ of Recipe; Calories 640; Calories from Fat 270 **% Daily Value:** Total Fat 30g 46%; Saturated Fat 12g 60%; Cholesterol 80mg 27%; Sodium 1,570mg 65%; Total Carbohydrate 61g 20%; Dietary Fiber 6g 24%; Sugars 16g; Protein 32g; Vitamin A 15%; Vitamin C 40%; Calcium 25%; Iron 35% **Dietary Exchanges:** 4 Starch, 3 Medium-Fat Meat, 2½ Fat **OR** 4 Carbohydrate, 3 Medium-Fat Meat, 2½ Fat **Carbohydrate Choices:** 4

doughboy tip

Chili powder is a mixture of dried ground chiles and various spices. The blend differs from brand to brand, so flavors and "heat" can vary quite a bit. Once the beef and bean mixture has had a chance to warm through, taste it and adjust the seasonings, if necessary, to suit your family's taste.

biscuit-topped lasagna

PREP TIME: 30 minutes (Ready in 1 hour)
YIELD: 6 servings

1 lb. lean ground beef

1 (14-oz.) jar tomato pasta sauce

1 (4-oz.) can mushroom pieces
and stems, drained

1 cup ricotta cheese

1 cup chopped fresh spinach

8 oz. (2 cups) shredded
mozzarella cheese

1 (12-oz.) can Pillsbury® Golden
Layers™ Refrigerated
Flaky Biscuits

1 tablespoon chopped
fresh parsley

1. Heat oven to 375°F. Spray 12x8-inch (2-quart) glass baking dish with nonstick cooking spray. Brown ground beef in large skillet over medium-high heat until thoroughly cooked, stirring frequently. Drain. Stir in pasta sauce and mushrooms. Cook until thoroughly heated, stirring frequently.

2. In small bowl, combine ricotta cheese and spinach; mix well. In sprayed baking dish, layer half each of beef mixture, ricotta cheese mixture and mozzarella cheese. Repeat layers.

3. Separate dough into 10 biscuits; separate each into 3 layers. Arrange biscuits over cheese layer, overlapping slightly. Sprinkle with parsley.

4. Bake at 375°F. for 25 to 30 minutes or until golden brown. Let stand 5 minutes before serving.

NUTRITION INFORMATION PER SERVING: Serving Size: 1/6 of Recipe; Calories 530; Calories from Fat 260 **% Daily Value:** Total Fat 29g 45%; Saturated Fat 12g 60%; Cholesterol 80mg 27%; Sodium 1,230mg 51%; Total Carbohydrate 33g 11%; Dietary Fiber 3g 12%; Sugars 4g; Protein 34g; Vitamin A 25%; Vitamin C 10%; Calcium 45%; Iron 20% **Dietary Exchanges:** 2 Starch, 1 Vegetable, 4 Medium-Fat Meat, 1½ Fat **OR** 2 Carbohydrate, 1 Vegetable, 4 Medium-Fat Meat, 1½ Fat **Carbohydrate Choices:** 2

doughboy tip

Fresh spinach can sometimes require extra cleaning. Trim the spinach stems, then soak the leaves in successive changes of cold water until no dirt remains in the bottom of the pan when you lift out the leaves. Or to save time, use prewashed packaged fresh spinach that is available in the produce area of the grocery store.

cheeseburger skillet hash

PREP TIME: 15 minutes (Ready in 40 minutes)
YIELD: 5 servings

4 slices bacon

1 lb. lean ground beef

3 tablespoons chopped onion

3 tablespoons oil

2½ cups frozen hash-brown potatoes, thawed

1 (11-oz.) can vacuum-packed whole kernel corn with red and green peppers, drained

1 (4.5-oz.) can chopped green chiles, drained

½ cup barbecue sauce

8 oz. (2 cups) shredded Cheddar cheese

¼ teaspoon salt, if desired

¼ teaspoon pepper, if desired

1 (16.3-oz.) can Pillsbury® Grands!® Refrigerated Buttermilk Biscuits

1. Heat oven to 400°F. Cook bacon until crisp. Drain on paper towel; crumble. Set aside.

2. In 12-inch cast-iron or ovenproof skillet, brown ground beef and onion over medium heat until beef is thoroughly cooked, stirring frequently. Drain. Place beef mixture in medium bowl; cover to keep warm.

3. Add oil to same skillet. Heat over medium-high heat until hot. Add potatoes; cook 3 to 5 minutes or until browned, stirring constantly. Add cooked ground beef, corn, chiles, barbecue sauce, cheese, salt and pepper; mix well. Cook until thoroughly heated, stirring occasionally. Sprinkle with bacon.

4. Separate dough into 8 biscuits. Arrange biscuits over hot mixture.

5. Bake at 400°F. for 16 to 24 minutes or until biscuits are deep golden brown and bottoms are no longer doughy.

NUTRITION INFORMATION PER SERVING: **Serving Size:** ⅕ of Recipe; Calories 880; Calories from Fat 480 **% Daily Value:** Total Fat 53g 82%; Saturated Fat 20g 100%; Cholesterol 110mg 37%; Sodium 1,950mg 81%; Total Carbohydrate 62g 21%; Dietary Fiber 4g 16%; Sugars 12g; Protein 38g; Vitamin A 20%; Vitamin C 15%; Calcium 45%; Iron 30% **Dietary Exchanges:** 3 Starch, 1 Fruit, 4 Medium-Fat Meat, 6 Fat **OR** 4 Carbohydrate, 4 Medium-Fat Meat, 6 Fat **Carbohydrate Choices:** 4

doughboy tip

For very hearty appetites or a super brunch dish, convert this dish to "Hash Ranchero" by serving it with fried or poached eggs. Offer sour cream, salsa and guacamole to top off each serving.

poppin' fresh® barbecups

PREP TIME: 20 minutes (Ready in 35 minutes)
YIELD: 10 servings

1 lb. lean ground beef

½ cup barbecue sauce

¼ cup chopped onion

1 to 2 tablespoons brown sugar

1 (12-oz.) can Pillsbury® Golden Layers™ Refrigerated Flaky Biscuits

2 oz. (½ cup) shredded Cheddar or American cheese

1. Heat oven to 400°F. Grease 10 muffin cups. Brown ground beef in large skillet over medium heat until thoroughly cooked, stirring frequently. Drain. Stir in barbecue sauce, onion and brown sugar. Cook 1 minute to blend flavors, stirring constantly.

2. Separate dough into 10 biscuits. Place 1 biscuit in each greased muffin cup. Firmly press in bottom and up sides, forming ¼-inch rim over edge of cup. Spoon about ¼ cup beef mixture into each biscuit-lined cup. Sprinkle each with cheese.

3. Bake at 400°F. for 10 to 12 minutes or until edges of biscuits are golden brown. Cool 1 minute; remove from muffin cups.

NUTRITION INFORMATION PER SERVING: **Serving Size:** ⅒ of Recipe; Calories 240; Calories from Fat 120 **% Daily Value:** Total Fat 13g 20%; Saturated Fat 5g 25%; Cholesterol 35mg 12%; Sodium 520mg 22%; Total Carbohydrate 19g 6%; Dietary Fiber 1g 4%; Sugars 5g; Protein 11g; Vitamin A 4%; Vitamin C 0%; Calcium 6%; Iron 10% **Dietary Exchanges:** 1 Starch, ½ Fruit, 1 Medium-Fat Meat, 1½ Fat **OR** 1½ Carbohydrate, 1 Medium-Fat Meat, 1½ Fat **Carbohydrate Choices:** 1

doughboy tip

If your family loves spicy food, set out assorted zesty condiments for the Barbecups. You could include salsa, hot red-pepper flakes, chopped fresh chiles or bottled hot-pepper sauce.

mexican beef pie

PREP TIME: 15 minutes (Ready in 40 minutes)
YIELD: 6 servings

1 lb. lean ground beef

1 (1.25-oz.) pkg. taco
seasoning mix

½ cup water

⅓ cup sliced olives

1 (8-oz.) can Pillsbury®
Refrigerated Crescent Dinner Rolls

1 cup crushed corn chips

1 (8-oz.) container sour cream

4 oz. (1 cup) shredded
Cheddar cheese

1 cup corn chips

Shredded lettuce, if desired

Salsa, if desired

1. Heat oven to 375°F. Brown ground beef in large skillet over medium-high heat for 5 to 7 minutes or until thoroughly cooked, stirring frequently. Drain. Stir in taco seasoning mix, water and olives. Reduce heat to low; simmer 5 minutes.

2. Meanwhile, separate dough into 8 triangles. Place triangles in ungreased 9-inch pie pan; press in bottom and up sides to form crust. Sprinkle 1 cup crushed corn chips evenly in bottom of crust.

3. Spoon hot beef mixture over corn chips. Spread sour cream over beef mixture. Sprinkle with cheese and remaining 1 cup corn chips.

4. Bake at 375°F. for 20 to 25 minutes or until crust is golden brown. Cut into wedges. Top with lettuce and salsa.

NUTRITION INFORMATION PER SERVING: Serving Size: ⅙ of Recipe; Calories 640; Calories from Fat 390 **% Daily Value:** Total Fat 43g 66%; Saturated Fat 16g 80%; Cholesterol 85mg 28%; Sodium 1,050mg 44%; Total Carbohydrate 38g 13%; Dietary Fiber 3g 12%; Sugars 6g; Protein 24g; Vitamin A 15%; Vitamin C 2%; Calcium 25%; Iron 15% **Dietary Exchanges:** 2½ Starch, 2½ Medium-Fat Meat, 5½ Fat **OR** 2½ Carbohydrate, 2½ Medium-Fat Meat, 5½ Fat **Carbohydrate Choices:** 2½

doughboy tip

To make the pie in advance, prepare it through the end of Step 3, but don't sprinkle with the corn chips. Cover the prepared pie with foil and refrigerate it for up to 2 hours before topping with the corn chips and baking as directed. To reheat, cover the baked pie with foil and bake at 375°F. for 25 to 30 minutes or until thoroughly heated.

sloppy joe casserole

PREP TIME: 15 minutes (Ready in 35 minutes)
YIELD: 4 servings

1 lb. lean ground beef

½ cup sliced green onions

1 (15.5-oz.) can sloppy Joe
sandwich sauce

1 (11-oz.) can vacuum-packed
whole kernel corn with red and
green peppers, undrained

1 (6-oz.) can (5 biscuits) Pillsbury®
Golden Layers™ Refrigerated
Buttermilk Biscuits

1. Heat oven to 375°F. In large skillet, cook ground beef and
   green onions until beef is browned and thoroughly cooked,
   stirring frequently. Drain.

2. Stir in sandwich sauce and corn. Cook 2 to 3 minutes or
   until thoroughly heated, stirring occasionally. Spoon mixture
   into ungreased 1- to 1½-quart casserole.

3. Separate dough into 5 biscuits; cut each in half. Arrange cut
   side down over hot mixture around outer edge of casserole
   with sides of biscuits touching.

4. Bake at 375°F. for 15 to 20 minutes or until biscuits are
   deep golden brown.

NUTRITION INFORMATION PER SERVING: Serving Size: ¼ of Recipe; Calories 480; Calories from Fat 190
% Daily Value: Total Fat 21g 32%; Saturated Fat 8g 40%; Cholesterol 70mg 23%; Sodium 1,620mg 68%;
Total Carbohydrate 45g 15%; Dietary Fiber 4g 16%; Sugars 19g; Protein 27g; Vitamin A 45%;
Vitamin C 6%; Calcium 4%; Iron 25% **Dietary Exchanges:** 2 Starch, 1 Fruit, 3 Medium-Fat Meat, 1 Fat
OR 3 Carbohydrate, 3 Medium-Fat Meat, 1 Fat **Carbohydrate Choices:** 3

doughboy tip

If you like, ground turkey can be
used in place of the ground beef.
And if you don't have green
onions, use ½ cup chopped
onion or 1 tablespoon instant
chopped or minced onion or
¾ teaspoon onion powder.

spicy jamaican meat pies with island salsa

PREP TIME: 15 minutes (Ready in 35 minutes)
YIELD: 4 servings

MEAT PIES

1 lb. lean ground beef

½ cup chopped onion

1 jalapeño chile, minced

2 garlic cloves, minced

4 teaspoons curry powder

½ teaspoon dried thyme leaves

½ teaspoon turmeric

¼ teaspoon freshly ground black pepper

⅛ teaspoon ground red pepper (cayenne)

Salt to taste

¼ cup unseasoned dry bread crumbs

¼ cup water

2 (8-oz.) cans Pillsbury® Refrigerated Crescent Dinner Rolls

SALSA

1 cup chunky-style salsa

1 (15.25-oz.) can tropical mixed fruit, coarsely chopped, drained and reserving 1 tablespoon liquid

¼ teaspoon nutmeg

doughboy tip

Salsa can be made up to a day ahead. Stir all ingredients together, cover and store in the refrigerator. Serve leftover salsa with grilled or broiled chicken, pork chops or fish.

1. Heat oven to 375°F. In large skillet, combine ground beef, onion, chile and garlic; cook over medium-high heat until beef is thoroughly cooked, stirring frequently. Drain. Add curry powder, thyme, turmeric, pepper, ground red pepper and salt; mix well. Add bread crumbs and water; stir until thickened.

2. Separate dough into 8 rectangles. Firmly press perforations to seal. Place 2 heaping tablespoons meat mixture on long half of each rectangle. Fold dough over filling; press edges to seal. Place on ungreased cookie sheet.

3. Bake at 375°F. for 15 to 20 minutes or until golden brown. Meanwhile, in medium bowl, combine all salsa ingredients; mix well. Serve salsa with meat pies.

NUTRITION INFORMATION PER SERVING: Serving Size: ¼ of Recipe; Calories 760; Calories from Fat 340 **% Daily Value:** Total Fat 38g 58%; Saturated Fat 11g 55%; Cholesterol 70mg 23%; Sodium 1,580mg 66%; Total Carbohydrate 75g 25%; Dietary Fiber 5g 20%; Sugars 27g; Protein 30g; Vitamin A 25%; Vitamin C 45%; Calcium 8%; Iron 30% **Dietary Exchanges:** 3 Starch, 2 Fruit, 3 Medium-Fat Meat, 4 Fat **OR** 5 Carbohydrate, 3 Medium-Fat Meat, 4 Fat **Carbohydrate Choices:** 5

most requested recipe

biscuit bowls with chili

PREP TIME: 45 minutes
YIELD: 8 servings

1 (16.3-oz.) can Pillsbury®
Grands!® Refrigerated
Buttermilk Biscuits

2 (15-oz.) cans chili with beans or
chili without beans

Sliced green onions, if desired

Sour cream, if desired

Shredded Cheddar cheese,
if desired

1. Heat oven to 350°F. Cut 8 (25x12-inch) pieces of aluminum foil. Shape each into 3½-inch ball by slightly crushing foil; flatten balls slightly. Place foil balls on large cookie sheets.

2. Separate dough into 8 biscuits. Press or roll each to form 5½-inch round. Place 1 biscuit round over each foil ball, shaping biscuit gently to fit. (Dough should not touch cookie sheets.)

3. Bake at 350°F. for 15 to 18 minutes or until golden brown. Meanwhile, in large saucepan, heat chili until thoroughly heated.

4. Carefully remove biscuit bowls from foil balls; place in individual shallow soup bowls or on plates. Spoon ½ cup chili into each bowl. Top each with onions, sour cream and cheese.

NUTRITION INFORMATION PER SERVING: Serving Size: ⅛ of Recipe; Calories 275; Calories from Fat 80 % Daily Value: Total Fat 9g 14%; Saturated Fat 2g 10%; Cholesterol 0mg 0%; Sodium 1,040mg 43%; Total Carbohydrate 40g 13%; Dietary Fiber 4g 16%; Sugars 11g; Protein 8g; Vitamin A 10%; Vitamin C 12%; Calcium 4%; Iron 16% Dietary Exchanges: 2½ Starch, 2 Fat OR 2½ Carbohydrate, 2 Fat Carbohydrate Choices: 2½

doughboy tip

You can use 10-ounce custard cups in place of the foil balls. Invert 8 custard cups in ungreased 15x10-inch baking pans or on cookie sheets. Place 1 biscuit over each cup, shaping the dough gently to fit, being sure the dough doesn't touch the pan, then bake as directed in the recipe.

biscuit-topped green bean and beef casserole

PREP TIME: 25 minutes (Ready in 55 minutes)
YIELD: 5 servings

1 lb. lean ground beef

2 cups frozen cut green beans

1 (10¾-oz.) can condensed cream of mushroom soup

1 (8-oz.) can sliced water chestnuts, drained

½ cup milk

1 (2.8-oz.) can french fried onions

1 (12-oz.) can Pillsbury® Golden Layers™ Refrigerated Flaky Biscuits

1. Heat oven to 350°F. Spray 8-inch square (2-quart) glass baking dish with nonstick cooking spray. Brown ground beef in large skillet over medium-high heat until thoroughly cooked, stirring frequently. Drain.

2. Add beans, soup, water chestnuts and milk; mix well. Reduce heat to medium; cover and cook 8 to 10 minutes or until bubbly, stirring occasionally. Stir in half of onions. Spoon mixture into sprayed baking dish.

3. Separate dough into 10 biscuits; cut each into quarters. Place biscuit pieces, points up, over beef mixture.

4. Bake at 350°F. for 15 minutes. Slightly crush remaining half of onions; sprinkle over biscuits. Bake an additional 10 to 15 minutes or until biscuits are deep golden brown.

NUTRITION INFORMATION PER SERVING: **Serving Size:** ⅕ of Recipe; Calories 600; Calories from Fat 310 **% Daily Value:** Total Fat 34g 52%; Saturated Fat 10g 50%; Cholesterol 60mg 20%; Sodium 1,310mg 55%; Total Carbohydrate 50g 17%; Dietary Fiber 3g 12%; Sugars 8g; Protein 24g; Vitamin A 4%; Vitamin C 6%; Calcium 8%; Iron 20% **Dietary Exchanges:** 3 Starch, 1 Vegetable, 2 Medium-Fat Meat, 4½ Fat **OR** 3 Carbohydrate, 1 Vegetable, 2 Medium-Fat Meat, 4½ Fat **Carbohydrate Choices:** 3

doughboy tip

This soon-to-be family favorite is based on the very popular green bean, mushroom soup and french-fried onion side dish. Serve the hearty main dish with buttered steamed baby carrots on the side. If you wish, sprinkle the carrots with fresh or dried dill weed or tarragon.

meatball stew
with dill biscuits

PREP TIME: 30 minutes (Ready in 50 minutes)
YIELD: 5 servings

MEATBALLS

1 egg, beaten

¼ cup milk

¼ cup Italian-style dry
bread crumbs

½ teaspoon salt

¼ teaspoon pepper

1 lb. lean ground beef

STEW

1 (10¾-oz.) can condensed
tomato soup

1¼ cups water

2 tablespoons Worcestershire
sauce

1 (1-lb.) pkg. frozen mixed
vegetables

BISCUITS

1 (12-oz.) can Pillsbury®
Golden Layers™ Refrigerated
Flaky Biscuits

1 tablespoon margarine
or butter, melted

1 tablespoon cornmeal

¾ teaspoon dried dill weed

doughboy tip

To save time, use frozen cooked
meatballs. About half of a 16-ounce
package will give you 36 frozen
meatballs. Heat the meatballs as
directed on the package.

1. Heat oven to 425°F. Spray 13x9-inch pan with nonstick cooking spray. In large bowl, combine all meatball ingredients; mix well. Shape mixture into 36 (1¼-inch) meatballs; place in sprayed pan.

2. Bake at 425°F. for 12 to 15 minutes or until meatballs are thoroughly cooked. Reduce oven temperature to 400°F.

3. Meanwhile, in large ovenproof skillet, combine all stew ingredients; mix well. Cook over medium heat for 10 to 12 minutes or until mixture comes to a boil, stirring occasionally.

4. Drain meatballs; add to stew. Separate dough into 10 biscuits. Dip 1 side of each biscuit in melted margarine; place margarine side up over stew. In small bowl, combine cornmeal and dill; mix well. Sprinkle over biscuits.

5. Bake at 400°F. for 13 to 16 minutes or until biscuits are golden brown and bottoms are no longer doughy.

NUTRITION INFORMATION PER SERVING: **Serving Size:** ⅕ of Recipe; Calories 560; Calories from Fat 230 **% Daily Value:** Total Fat 26g 40%; Saturated Fat 8g 40%; Cholesterol 100mg 33%; Sodium 1,550mg 65%; Total Carbohydrate 54g 18%; Dietary Fiber 4g 16%; Sugars 9g; Protein 27g; Vitamin A 45%; Vitamin C 45%; Calcium 8%; Iron 30% **Dietary Exchanges:** 3 Starch, ½ Fruit, 2½ Medium-Fat Meat, 2½ Fat **OR** 3½ Carbohydrate, 2½ Medium-Fat Meat, 2½ Fat **Carbohydrate Choices:** 3½

zesty italian crescent casserole

PREP TIME: 25 minutes (Ready in 50 minutes)
YIELD: 6 servings

1 lb. lean ground beef

¼ cup chopped onion

1 cup tomato pasta sauce

6 oz. (1½ cups) shredded mozzarella or Monterey Jack cheese

½ cup sour cream

1 (8-oz.) can Pillsbury® Refrigerated Crescent Dinner Rolls

⅓ cup grated Parmesan cheese

2 tablespoons margarine or butter, melted

1. Heat oven to 375°F. In large skillet, cook ground beef and onion over medium heat for 8 to 10 minutes or until beef is thoroughly cooked, stirring frequently. Drain. Stir in pasta sauce; cook until thoroughly heated.

2. In medium bowl, combine mozzarella cheese and sour cream; mix well.

3. Pour hot beef mixture into ungreased 12x8-inch (2-quart) glass baking dish, or 9½- or 10-inch deep-dish pie pan. Spoon cheese mixture over beef mixture.

4. Unroll dough over cheese mixture. (If using pie pan, separate dough into 8 triangles; arrange points toward center over cheese mixture, crimping outside edges if necessary.) In small bowl, combine Parmesan cheese and margarine; mix well. Spread evenly over dough.

5. Bake at 375°F. for 18 to 25 minutes or until deep golden brown.

NUTRITION INFORMATION PER SERVING: **Serving Size:** ⅙ of Recipe; Calories 490, Calories from Fat 300 **% Daily Value:** Total Fat 33g 51%; Saturated Fat 13g 65%; Cholesterol 75mg 25%; Sodium 780mg 33%; Total Carbohydrate 21g 7%; Dietary Fiber 1g 4%; Sugars 4g, Protein 27g; Vitamin A 15%; Vitamin C 4%; Calcium 30%; Iron 15% **Dietary Exchanges:** 1½ Starch, 3 Medium-Fat Meat, 3½ Fat **OR** 1½ Carbohydrate, 3 Medium-Fat Meat, 3½ Fat **Carbohydrate Choices:** 1½

doughboy tip

Herb lovers can decorate each serving with shredded fresh basil leaves or a blend of minced fresh basil, parsley and chives. Chop the basil just before serving to prevent the leaves from discoloring.

beef pepper steak casserole

PREP TIME: 25 minutes (Ready in 45 minutes)
YIELD: 6 servings

2 tablespoons oil

1 medium green bell pepper,
cut into bite-sized strips

1 medium red bell pepper,
cut into bite-sized strips

1 medium onion,
cut into thin wedges

1 lb. beef strips for stir-frying

1 (12-oz.) jar beef gravy

1 (10-oz.) can diced tomatoes
and green chiles, undrained

1 egg

1 tablespoon water

1 (7-oz.) can (6 breadsticks)
Pillsbury® Refrigerated Breadsticks

1. Heat oven to 375°F. Heat oil in 12-inch skillet over medium-high heat until hot. Add bell peppers and onion; cook and stir 3 minutes. Add beef strips; cook and stir 3 to 5 minutes or until beef is lightly browned and vegetables are softened.

2. Add gravy and tomatoes; mix well. Cook until mixture is hot and bubbly, stirring occasionally. Remove from heat. Pour mixture into ungreased 8-inch square (2-quart) glass baking dish.

3. In small bowl, beat egg and water until well blended. Separate dough into 6 breadsticks. Tie each into loose knot. Arrange knots on top of hot beef mixture. Brush knots with egg mixture. Discard any remaining egg mixture.

4. Bake at 375°F. for 15 to 20 minutes or until breadsticks are deep golden brown.

NUTRITION INFORMATION PER SERVING: Serving Size: 1/6 of Recipe; Calories 290; Calories from Fat 110 **% Daily Value:** Total Fat 12g 18%; Saturated Fat 3g 15%; Cholesterol 75mg 25%; Sodium 700mg 29%; Total Carbohydrate 25g 8%; Dietary Fiber 2g 8%; Sugars 5g; Protein 20g; Vitamin A 20%; Vitamin C 50%; Calcium 4%; Iron 20% **Dietary Exchanges:** 1½ Starch, 2 Lean Meat, 1 Fat **OR** 1½ Carbohydrate, 2 Lean Meat, 1 Fat **Carbohydrate Choices:** 1½

doughboy tip

Beef strips for stir-frying are thin strips of steak that are often available in the meat section of your supermarket. If they aren't available, purchase a pound of sirloin or flank steak and cut your own strips. Freeze the meat for about half an hour to firm it up for easier slicing, then cut across the grain into thin strips.

swedish meatball and biscuit casserole

PREP TIME: 15 minutes (Ready in 45 minutes)
YIELD: 4 servings

1 (12-oz.) pkg. frozen Swedish-style meatballs, thawed

1 (12-oz.) jar beef gravy

1 (4.5-oz.) jar sliced mushrooms, drained

½ cup frozen pearl onions, thawed

½ cup sour cream

2 teaspoons Worcestershire sauce

4 Pillsbury® Home Baked Classics™ Frozen Buttermilk Biscuits (from 25-oz. pkg.)

1 tablespoon chopped fresh parsley, if desired

1. Heat oven to 375°F. Spray 8-inch square (2-quart) glass baking dish with nonstick cooking spray.

2. In medium saucepan, combine all ingredients except biscuits and parsley; mix well. Cook over medium-high heat for 5 to 8 minutes or until mixture is bubbly and thoroughly heated, stirring frequently. Pour mixture into sprayed baking dish. Arrange frozen biscuits over top.

3. Bake at 375°F. for 25 to 30 minutes or until biscuits are deep golden brown and filling is bubbly. Serve meatball mixture over biscuits. Sprinkle each serving with parsley.

NUTRITION INFORMATION PER SERVING: **Serving Size:** ¼ of Recipe; Calories 535; Calories from Fat 280 **% Daily Value:** Total Fat 31g 48%; Saturated Fat 13g 65%; Cholesterol 115mg 38%; Sodium 1,720mg 72%; Total Carbohydrate 40g 13%; Dietary Fiber 2g 8%; Sugars 7g; Protein 26g; Vitamin A 8%; Vitamin C 2%; Calcium 14%; Iron 24% **Dietary Exchanges:** 2 Starch, ½ Fruit, 3 High-Fat Meat, 1 Fat **OR** 2½ Carbohydrate, 3 High-Fat Meat, 1 Fat **Carbohydrate Choices:** 2½

doughboy tip

Don't have a package of frozen Swedish-style meatballs? Use your favorite meatball recipe and add ½ teaspoon ground allspice or nutmeg with the salt and pepper. Cook the meatballs, then add them to the gravy mixture.

beef stew pot pie

PREP TIME: 40 minutes (Ready in 1 hour 20 minutes)
YIELD: 6 servings

1 (15-oz.) pkg. Pillsbury®
Refrigerated Pie Crusts, softened
as directed on package

¾ lb. boneless beef sirloin steak,
cut into ½-inch cubes

2 small onions,
cut into thin wedges

1½ cups cubed (¾-inch)
peeled baking potatoes

¾ cup cut (1x½x½-inch) carrot

½ cup frozen sweet peas

1 (4.5-oz.) jar whole mushrooms,
drained

1 (12-oz.) jar brown gravy

2 tablespoons cornstarch

½ teaspoon dried thyme leaves

½ teaspoon salt

¼ teaspoon pepper

1 egg yolk

2 teaspoons water

1 teaspoon sesame seed

1. Heat oven to 425°F. Prepare pie crusts as directed on package for *two-crust pie* using 9-inch glass pie pan.

2. In large nonstick skillet, cook beef and onions over medium-high heat for 4 to 6 minutes or until beef is browned, stirring frequently. Stir in potatoes, carrot, peas and mushrooms.

3. In small bowl, combine gravy, cornstarch, thyme, salt and pepper; mix well. Stir into beef mixture; cook until thoroughly heated. Pour mixture into crust-lined pan. Top with second crust; seal edges and flute. Cut small slits in several places in top crust.

4. In another small bowl, beat egg yolk and water until well blended. Brush top crust with egg mixture. Sprinkle with sesame seed.

5. Bake at 425°F. for 30 to 40 minutes or until crust is golden brown and filling is bubbly. Cover edge of crust with strips of foil after first 15 to 20 minutes of baking to prevent excessive browning. Let stand 10 minutes before serving.

NUTRITION INFORMATION PER SERVING: Serving Size: ⅙ of Recipe; Calories 490; Calories from Fat 210 **% Daily Value:** Total Fat 23g 35%; Saturated Fat 9g 45%; Cholesterol 85mg 28%; Sodium 880mg 37%; Total Carbohydrate 53g 18%; Dietary Fiber 3g 12%; Sugars 5g; Protein 17g; Vitamin A 90%; Vitamin C 10%; Calcium 4%; Iron 15% **Dietary Exchanges:** 3½ Starch, 1 Lean Meat, 3½ Fat **OR** 3½ Carbohydrate, 1 Lean Meat, 3½ Fat **Carbohydrate Choices:** 3½

doughboy tip

This hearty supper pie is chock-full of vegetables and beef. If you like, you don't have to peel the potatoes, but just give them a good scrub and cut into pieces. The skins add color and nutrients.

easy beef pot pie

PREP TIME: 15 minutes (Ready in 1 hour)
YIELD: 8 servings

1 (15-oz.) pkg. Pillsbury®
Refrigerated Pie Crusts, softened
as directed on package

1 (12-oz.) jar beef gravy

1 tablespoon cornstarch

2 cups frozen mixed vegetables

1 (4.5-oz.) jar sliced mushrooms,
drained

1 tablespoon Worcestershire sauce

1 lb. thickly sliced cooked
roast beef, cubed

1. Heat oven to 425°F. Prepare pie crust as directed on package for *two-crust pie* using 9-inch glass pie pan.

2. In large saucepan, combine gravy and cornstarch; blend well. Add frozen mixed vegetables, mushrooms and Worcestershire sauce; mix well. Cook over medium-high heat until bubbly. Stir in roast beef. Pour into crust-lined pan. Top with second crust; seal edges and flute. Cut decorative slits in several places in top crust.

3. Bake at 425°F. for 30 to 45 minutes or until crust is golden brown and filling is bubbly. Cover edge of crust with strips of foil after first 15 minutes of baking to prevent excessive browning.

NUTRITION INFORMATION PER SERVING: **Serving Size:** ⅛ of Recipe; Calories 350; Calories from Fat 140 **% Daily Value:** Total Fat 16g 25%; Saturated Fat 7g 35%; Cholesterol 40mg 13%; Sodium 1,100mg 46%; Total Carbohydrate 35g 12%; Dietary Fiber 2g 8%; Sugars 2g; Protein 16g; Vitamin A 10%; Vitamin C 2%; Calcium 0%; Iron 10% **Dietary Exchanges:** 2½ Starch, 1 Lean Meat, 2 Fat **OR** 2½ Carbohydrate, 1 Lean Meat, 2 Fat **Carbohydrate Choices:** 2

doughboy tip

To make this hearty pot pie, go ahead and use that leftover cooked beef roast that's tucked in your refrigerator! Or you can pick it up at the deli. Either way, you'll need about 2 cups cubed beef. If mixed vegetables aren't your family's favorite, try other frozen vegetables such as 2 cups of whole kernel corn, green beans or peas.

bbq beef biscuit bake

PREP TIME: 10 minutes (Ready in 1 hour 15 minutes)
YIELD: 5 servings

1 (32-oz.) container refrigerated barbecue sauce with sliced fully cooked beef

1 (8.3-oz.) can (¾ cup) baked beans, undrained

1 (10.2-oz.) can (5 biscuits) Pillsbury® Grands!® Refrigerated Buttermilk Biscuits

1. Heat oven to 375°F. In ungreased 11x7-inch (2-quart) glass baking dish, combine beef and beans; mix well. Cover with foil. Bake at 375°F. for 40 minutes or until bubbly.

2. Meanwhile, separate dough into 5 biscuits; cut each into 8 pieces.

3. Remove baking dish from oven. Uncover; place biscuit pieces evenly over hot mixture in baking dish.

4. Return to oven; bake, uncovered, an additional 12 to 15 minutes or until biscuits are deep golden brown.

NUTRITION INFORMATION PER SERVING: **Serving Size:** ⅕ of Recipe; Calories 430; Calories from Fat 115 **% Daily Value:** Total Fat 13g 20%; Saturated Fat 3g 15%; Cholesterol 30mg 10%; Sodium 1,990mg 83%; Total Carbohydrate 61g 20%; Dietary Fiber 3g 12%; Sugars 32g; Protein 20g; Vitamin A 8%; Vitamin C 0%; Calcium 4%, Iron 16% **Dietary Exchanges:** 4 Starch, 1 High-Fat Meat **OR** 4 Carbohydrate, 1 High-Fat Meat **Carbohydrate Choices:** 4

doughboy tip
This is a tasty home-style dish just as it is, but for a bit of added flavor, stir 4 slices of cooked bacon, crumbled, and ½ cup finely chopped green bell pepper into the beef and bean mixture. For a picnic-style supper, serve the casserole with deli potato salad and a variety of crisp relishes.

baked pork chops
with biscuit stuffin'

PREP TIME: 20 minutes (Ready in 1 hour 15 minutes)
YIELD: 6 servings

1 tablespoon oil

6 (1/2-inch-thick) pork loin chops

1 (10¾-oz.) can condensed cream of chicken soup

1 cup chopped celery

1 cup chopped onions

1 egg

¼ teaspoon pepper

⅛ teaspoon poultry seasoning

1 (7.5-oz.) can Pillsbury® Refrigerated Buttermilk Biscuits

1. Heat oven to 350°F. Heat oil in large skillet over medium heat until hot. Add pork chops; cook until browned on both sides. Place pork chops in ungreased 13x9-inch pan.

2. In medium bowl, combine soup, celery, onions, egg, pepper and poultry seasoning; mix well.

3. Separate dough into 10 biscuits; cut each into 8 pieces. Stir biscuit pieces into soup mixture. Spoon over pork chops.

4. Bake at 350°F. for 45 to 55 minutes or until biscuit pieces are golden brown and no longer doughy in center.

NUTRITION INFORMATION PER SERVING: Serving Size: 1/6 of Recipe; Calories 340; Calories from Fat 155 **% Daily Value:** Total Fat 17g 26%; Saturated Fat 5g 25%; Cholesterol 110mg 37%; Sodium 860mg 36%; Total Carbohydrate 23g 8%; Dietary Fiber 1g 4%; Sugars 7g; Protein 24g; Vitamin A 6%; Vitamin C 4%; Calcium 4%; Iron 10% **Dietary Exchanges:** 1½ Starch, 3 Medium-Fat Meat **OR** 1½ Carbohydrate, 3 Medium-Fat Meat **Carbohydrate Choices:** 1½

doughboy tip

This is a nice home-style dish to serve on a cool evening. If you need to substitute for the poultry seasoning, use ⅛ teaspoon ground sage and a dash of ground thyme. No thyme? Use all ground sage, and it will still be tasty.

pork and sweet potato supper

PREP TIME: 20 minutes (Ready in 40 minutes)
YIELD: 5 servings

2 tablespoons oil

1 lb. pork tenderloins, cut into 1-inch pieces

2 cups cubed peeled dark-orange sweet potatoes (about 2 medium)

½ cup chopped onion

⅔ cup maple-flavored syrup

2 tablespoons all-purpose flour

½ to 1 teaspoon ginger

¼ teaspoon salt

⅛ teaspoon pepper

1 cup frozen sweet peas

1 pear, peeled, chopped, if desired

1 (12-oz.) can Pillsbury® Golden Layers™ Refrigerated Flaky Biscuits

1. Heat oven to 375°F. Heat oil in large ovenproof skillet over medium-high heat until hot. Add pork, sweet potatoes and onion; cook 8 to 10 minutes or until pork is browned and sweet potatoes are crisp-tender, stirring occasionally.

2. In small bowl, combine syrup, flour, ginger, salt and pepper; blend well. Stir syrup mixture, peas and pear into pork mixture. Cook 1 to 2 minutes or until hot, stirring frequently.

3. Separate dough into 10 biscuits; cut each into quarters. Arrange biscuit pieces over pork mixture in skillet.

4. Bake at 375°F. for 15 to 20 minutes or until biscuits are golden brown.

NUTRITION INFORMATION PER SERVING: Serving Size: ⅕ of Recipe; Calories 640; Calories from Fat 170. **% Daily Value: Total Fat** 19g 29%, Saturated Fat 5g 25%; Cholesterol 55mg 18%; Sodium 1,060mg 44%; Total Carbohydrate 94g 31%; Dietary Fiber 5g 20%; Sugars 41g; Protein 28g; Vitamin A 100%; Vitamin C 18%; Calcium 4%; Iron 22% **Dietary Exchanges:** 3½ Starch, 2½ Fruit, 2½ Lean Meat, 2 Fat **OR** 6 Carbohydrate, 2½ Lean Meat, 2 Fat **Carbohydrate Choices:** 6

doughboy tip

You'll enjoy the combination of sweet and savory in this flavorful one-dish meal. Be sure to peel and cut the sweet potatoes just before using so they don't discolor. Any type of pear, such as Bosc or Bartlett, would be delicious in this recipe. And if you like, apple can be substituted for the pear.

ham, broccoli and rice pie

PREP TIME: 25 minutes (Ready in 1 hour 5 minutes)
YIELD: 6 servings

1 Pillsbury® Refrigerated Pie Crust (from 15-oz. pkg.), softened as directed on package

3 eggs

¼ cup milk

1½ cups finely chopped cooked ham

2 (10-oz.) pkg. frozen long-gain white rice and broccoli with cheese flavored sauce, thawed

8 oz. (2 cups) shredded Swiss cheese

⅛ teaspoon pepper

1. Heat oven to 425°F. Prepare pie crust as directed on package for *one-crust baked shell* using 9-inch glass pie pan. DO NOT PRICK CRUST. Bake at 425°F. for 7 to 8 minutes or until crust begins to brown.

2. Meanwhile, beat eggs in large bowl. Add milk, ham, rice and broccoli mixture, 1 cup of the Swiss cheese and pepper; mix well.

3. Remove partially baked crust from oven. Reduce oven temperature to 400°F. Pour ham mixture into crust. Top with remaining 1 cup cheese.

4. Return to oven; bake at 400°F. for an additional 35 to 40 minutes or until knife inserted in center comes out clean. If necessary, cover edge of crust with strips of foil after 15 to 20 minutes of baking to prevent excessive browning. Let stand 10 minutes before serving.

NUTRITION INFORMATION PER SERVING: Serving Size: ⅙ of Recipe; Calories 500; Calories from Fat 245 **% Daily Value:** Total Fat 27g 42%; Saturated Fat 13g 65%; Cholesterol 170mg 57%; Sodium 1,110mg 46%; Total Carbohydrate 38g 13%; Dietary Fiber 0g 0%; Sugars 5g; Protein 26g; Vitamin A 36%; Vitamin C 6%; Calcium 42%; Iron 10% **Dietary Exchanges:** 2½ Starch, 2½ Medium-Fat Meat, 2½ Fat **OR** 2½ Carbohydrate, 2½ Medium-Fat Meat, 2½ Fat **Carbohydrate Choices:** 2½

doughboy tip

Because it is a custard pie, overbaking can cause the egg filling to break down, giving the pie a curdled appearance. It will still taste great but just won't look as good. Start testing for doneness at the minimum bake time and remove the pie from the oven as soon as the knife inserted in the center comes out clean.

chili-cheese dog fondue

PREP TIME: 20 minutes
YIELD: 8 servings

1 (11-oz.) can Pillsbury®
Refrigerated Breadsticks

24 cocktail-sized smoked link
sausages (from 16-oz. pkg.)

1 (1-lb.) pkg. pasteurized prepared
cheese product, cubed

2 (15-oz.) cans chili without beans

1. Heat oven to 375°F. Unroll dough; separate into strips. Cut dough strips in half crosswise. Wrap 1 breadstick half around center of each sausage; pinch ends of dough strip to seal. Place seam side down and about 1 inch apart on ungreased cookie sheet. Bake immediately, or cover and refrigerate up to 4 hours.

2. Bake at 375°F. for 13 to 15 minutes or until golden brown.

3. Meanwhile, in fondue pot or medium saucepan, combine cheese and chili. Cook over medium heat until cheese is melted, stirring frequently.

4. Serve hot fondue with warm wrapped sausages to be speared with fondue forks for dipping.

NUTRITION INFORMATION PER SERVING: **Serving Size:** $\frac{1}{8}$ of Recipe; Calories 450; Calories from Fat 230 **% Daily Value:** Total Fat 25g 38%; Saturated Fat 12g 60%; Cholesterol 65mg 22%; Sodium 1,760mg 73%; Total Carbohydrate 32g 11%; Dietary Fiber 2g 8%; Sugars 9g; Protein 23g; Vitamin A 30%; Vitamin C 0%; Calcium 35%; Iron 15% **Dietary Exchanges:** 2 Starch, 2½ Medium-Fat Meat, 2½ Fat **OR** 2 Carbohydrate, 2½ Medium-Fat Meat, 2½ Fat **Carbohydrate Choices:** 2

doughboy tip

Brush the breadstick dough with a little of your favorite mustard before wrapping it around the cocktail sausages. Or brush the outside of the dough with melted butter and sprinkle with ground cumin or chili powder before baking. Chances are you won't have any leftover fondue, but if you do, heat it and serve over corn or tortilla chips for a quick nacho snack.

cheesy hot-dog pie

PREP TIME: 25 minutes (Ready in 1 hour 10 minutes)
YIELD: 8 servings

1 (15-oz.) pkg. Pillsbury® Refrigerated Pie Crusts, softened as directed on package

1½ cups frozen whole kernel corn, thawed

1 (16-oz.) pkg. miniature hot dogs

1 (15.5-oz.) can sloppy Joe sandwich sauce

1 tablespoon all-purpose flour

4 oz. (1 cup) finely shredded American and Cheddar cheese blend

2 teaspoons milk

1 tablespoon cornmeal

1. Heat oven to 400°F. Prepare pie crust as directed on package for *two-crust pie* using 9-inch glass pie pan.

2. In large bowl, combine corn, hot dogs, sloppy Joe sauce and flour; mix well. Spoon mixture into crust-lined pan. Sprinkle with cheese.

3. Top pie with second crust; seal edges and flute. Brush crust with milk. Sprinkle with cornmeal. Cut slits in several places in top crust.

4. Bake at 400°F. for 40 to 45 minutes or until deep golden brown. If necessary, cover edge of crust with strips of foil after 15 minutes of baking to prevent excessive browning. Let stand 10 minutes before serving.

NUTRITION INFORMATION PER SERVING: Serving Size: ⅛ of Recipe; Calories 530; Calories from Fat 320 **% Daily Value:** Total Fat 35g 54%; Saturated Fat 15g 75%; Cholesterol 55mg 18%; Sodium 1,330mg 55%; Total Carbohydrate 40g 13%; Dietary Fiber 2g 8%; Sugars 10g; Protein 13g; Vitamin A 25%; Vitamin C 2%; Calcium 90%; Iron 10% **Dietary Exchanges:** 2 Starch, ½ Fruit, 1 High-Fat Meat, 5 Fat **OR** 2½ Carbohydrate, 1 High-Fat Meat, 5 Fat **Carbohydrate Choices:** 2½

doughboy tip

Everyone loves sloppy Joes, so who wouldn't enjoy this yummy sloppy Joe-style pie? Serve the family-pleasing dish with your favorite hot-dog toppings, such as ketchup, pickle relish, chopped onions and assorted types of mustard.

chicken cacciatore with biscuits

PREP TIME: 25 minutes (Ready in 1 hour 30 minutes)
YIELD: 5 servings

2½ to 3 lb. cut-up frying chicken

½ medium green bell pepper, cut into strips

2 cups whole fresh mushrooms

1 (28 to 30-oz.) jar tomato pasta sauce

¼ cup chopped onion

1 teaspoon dried oregano leaves, crushed

1 (12-oz.) can Pillsbury® Golden Layers™ Refrigerated Buttermilk Biscuits

1 tablespoon margarine or butter, melted

2 tablespoons grated Parmesan cheese

1. Heat oven to 375°F. Spray large nonstick skillet with non-stick cooking spray. Heat over medium-high heat until hot. Add chicken pieces; cook until browned on all sides. Place browned chicken in ungreased 13x9-inch (3-quart) glass baking dish. Top with bell pepper and mushrooms.

2. In small bowl, combine pasta sauce, onion and oregano; mix well. Pour over chicken; spread evenly around edges of baking dish. Cover with foil. Bake at 375°F. for 45 minutes.

3. Remove chicken from oven; uncover. Separate dough into 10 biscuits. Arrange over hot mixture around outer edges of dish. Brush biscuits with margarine. Sprinkle with Parmesan cheese.

4. Return to oven; bake an additional 14 to 20 minutes or until biscuits are deep golden brown, and chicken is fork-tender and juices run clear.

NUTRITION INFORMATION PER SERVING: Serving Size: ⅕ of Recipe; Calories 590; Calories from Fat 260 **% Daily Value:** Total Fat 29g 45%; Saturated Fat 7g 35%; Cholesterol 95mg 32%; Sodium 1,570mg 65%; Total Carbohydrate 45g 15%; Dietary Fiber 4g 16%; Sugars 4g; Protein 37g; Vitamin A 20%; Vitamin C 25%; Calcium 10%; Iron 25% **Dietary Exchanges:** 3 Starch, 4 Lean Meat, 3 Fat **OR** 3 Carbohydrate, 4 Lean Meat, 3 Fat **Carbohydrate Choices:** 3

doughboy tip

Cacciatore is simply the Italian word for "hunter" and refers to dishes prepared "hunter style" with mushrooms, tomatoes, onions and herbs. Serve this tasty version of the classic chicken dish with cut green beans and spaghetti topped with a generous sprinkle of shredded Parmesan cheese.

most requested recipe
baked chicken and biscuits

PREP TIME: 10 minutes (Ready in 1 hour 25 minutes)
YIELD: 5 servings

2½ to 3 lb. cut-up frying chicken, skin removed

1 (10¾-oz.) can condensed cream of mushroom soup

1 (8-oz.) container sour cream

½ cup dry sherry or water

1 (4.5-oz.) jar whole mushrooms, drained

1 (12-oz.) can Pillsbury® Golden Layers™ Refrigerated Flaky Biscuits

Paprika

Chopped fresh parsley, if desired

1. Heat oven to 350°F. Place chicken in 13x9-inch (3-quart) glass baking dish.

2. In medium bowl, combine soup, sour cream and sherry; blend well. Stir in mushrooms. Pour over chicken.

3. Bake at 350°F. for 45 to 55 minutes or until chicken is fork-tender and juices run clear.

4. Remove chicken from oven. Separate dough into 10 biscuits. Arrange over hot mixture around outer edges of dish. Sprinkle with paprika.

5. Return to oven; bake an additional 11 to 18 minutes or until biscuits are golden brown and bottoms are no longer doughy. Garnish with fresh parsley.

NUTRITION INFORMATION PER SERVING: Serving Size: ⅕ of Recipe; Calories 520; Calories from Fat 245 **% Daily Value:** Total Fat 27g 42%; Saturated Fat 10g 50%; Cholesterol 110mg 37%; Sodium 1,310mg 55%; Total Carbohydrate 37g 12%; Dietary Fiber 2g 8%; Sugars 12g; Protein 32g; Vitamin A 8%; Vitamin C 0%; Calcium 10%; Iron 16% **Dietary Exchanges:** 2½ Starch, 3½ Medium-Fat Meat, 1 Fat **OR** 2½ Carbohydrate, 3½ Medium-Fat Meat, 1 Fat **Carbohydrate Choices:** 2½

doughboy tip
Curly parsley and flat-leaf (or Italian) parsley can be used interchangeably in most recipes. You'll find that flat-leaf parsley, however, is stronger flavored but not as readily available as the more decorative curly variety. Either type adds a fresh, vibrant touch to almost any entrée.

one-pan crispy chicken and biscuits

PREP TIME: 5 minutes (Ready in 40 minutes)
YIELD: 4 servings

⅔ cup corn flake crumbs

1 teaspoon seasoned salt

¼ cup milk

4 boneless skinless chicken breast halves

1 (16.3-oz.) can Pillsbury® Grands!® Refrigerated Buttermilk Biscuits

1. Heat oven to 375°F. Line 15x10x1-inch baking pan with foil.

2. In shallow dish, combine corn flake crumbs and seasoned salt; mix well. Place milk in another shallow dish. Dip chicken in milk; coat with crumb mixture. Arrange chicken in center of foil-lined pan.

3. Bake at 375°F. for 15 minutes. Remove chicken from oven. Separate dough into 8 biscuits. Place biscuits in pan around chicken.

4. Return to oven; bake an additional 15 to 17 minutes or until biscuits are golden brown and chicken is fork-tender and juices run clear.

NUTRITION INFORMATION PER SERVING: **Serving Size:** ¼ of Recipe; Calories 605; Calories from Fat 190 **% Daily Value:** Total Fat 21g 32%; Saturated Fat 6g 30%; Cholesterol 75mg 25%; Sodium 1,960mg 82%; Total Carbohydrate 68g 23%; Dietary Fiber 2g 8%; Sugars 18g; Protein 36g; Vitamin A 8%; Vitamin C 6%; Calcium 6%; Iron 46% **Dietary Exchanges:** 4½ Starch, 3 Medium-Fat Meat, 1 Fat **OR** 4½ Carbohydrate, 3 Medium-Fat Meat, 1 Fat **Carbohydrate Choices:** 4½

doughboy tip

It's easy to make your own corn flake crumbs. You'll need about 1⅓ cups corn flake cereal to get ⅔ cup crumbs. Place the cereal in a resealable food storage plastic bag and crush with a rolling pin, the bottom of a small saucepan or your hands. This is a job the kids will love to help you with.

chicken taco *grande*

PREP TIME: 25 minutes (Ready in 50 minutes)
YIELD: 8 servings

TACO RING

1 tablespoon oil

1¼ lb. boneless skinless chicken breast halves, cut into ¼ to ½-inch pieces

2 cups frozen whole kernel corn

½ cup chopped green bell pepper

⅓ cup water

1 (1.25-oz.) pkg. taco seasoning mix

4 oz. (1 cup) shredded Cheddar cheese

2 (8-oz.) cans Pillsbury® Refrigerated Crescent Dinner Rolls

TOPPING

1 cup shredded lettuce

½ cup chopped tomato

¼ cup sliced ripe olives

GARNISH

½ cup sour cream

½ cup chunky-style salsa

doughboy tip

If you like, serve guacamole as well as the sour cream and salsa, and sprinkle chopped green onion or avocado over the top. Add a side of Mexican rice or refried beans, and you will have a *grande* Mexican meal!

1. Heat oven to 375°F. Spray large cookie sheet with nonstick cooking spray. Heat oil in medium skillet over medium heat until hot. Add chicken; cook 5 minutes or until no longer pink in center, stirring frequently.

2. Add corn, bell pepper, water and taco seasoning mix; mix well. Heat until bubbly. Reduce heat to medium; cook 10 to 15 minutes or until liquid evaporates, stirring occasionally. Remove from heat. Stir in cheese. Set aside.

3. Separate both cans of dough into 16 triangles. Arrange triangles on sprayed cookie sheet with short sides of triangles toward center, overlapping into wreath shape and leaving 5-inch round opening in center. Lightly press short sides of dough to flatten slightly.

4. Spoon chicken filling onto widest part of dough. Pull end points of triangles over filling and tuck under dough to form ring. (Filling will be visible.)

5. Bake at 375°F. for 20 to 25 minutes or until golden brown. Meanwhile, in small bowl, combine lettuce, tomato and olives; toss gently to mix.

6. Loosen baked ring with spatula; slide onto serving platter. Spoon lettuce mixture into center of ring. Serve with sour cream and salsa.

NUTRITION INFORMATION PER SERVING: **Serving Size:** ⅛ of Recipe; Calories 450; Calories from Fat 220 **% Daily Value:** Total Fat 24g 37%; Saturated Fat 8g 40%; Cholesterol 65mg 22%; Sodium 1,130mg 47%; Total Carbohydrate 34g 11%; Dietary Fiber 2g 8%; Sugars 7g; Protein 24g; Vitamin A 15%; Vitamin C 15%; Calcium 15%; Iron 15% **Dietary Exchanges:** 2½ Starch, 2½ Very Lean Meat, 4 Fat **OR** 2½ Carbohydrate, 2½ Very Lean Meat, 4 Fat **Carbohydrate Choices:** 2

slow-cooker chicken and dumplings

PREP TIME: 20 minutes (Ready in 9 hours 50 minutes)
YIELD: 5 servings

1 teaspoon oil

1 lb. boneless skinless chicken thighs, cut into 1-inch pieces

1½ cups sliced celery

1½ cups fresh baby carrots

1 cup sliced fresh mushrooms

1 (1.8-oz.) pkg. dry leek soup mix

4 cups water

1 (10.2-oz.) can (5 biscuits) Pillsbury® Grands!® Refrigerated Original Flaky Layers Biscuits

1 tablespoon cornmeal

1½ cups frozen sweet peas

¼ teaspoon pepper

1. Heat oil in medium skillet over medium-high heat until hot. Add chicken; cook and stir until browned.

2. In 4- to 6-quart slow cooker, combine chicken, celery, carrots, mushrooms, soup mix and water; mix well.

3. Cover; cook on low setting for 7 to 9 hours.

4. About 35 minutes before serving, separate dough into 5 biscuits; cut each into 8 wedges. Sprinkle wedges with cornmeal. Stir coated biscuits pieces into hot chicken mixture.

5. Increase heat setting to high; cover and cook an additional 25 to 30 minutes or until biscuits are no longer doughy in center.

6. About 10 minutes before serving, microwave peas in covered microwave-safe dish on HIGH for 3 to 4 minutes or until hot. Just before serving, stir peas and pepper into chicken mixture.

NUTRITION INFORMATION PER SERVING: **Serving Size:** ⅕ of Recipe; Calories 440; Calories from Fat 170 **% Daily Value:** Total Fat 19g 29%; Saturated Fat 5g 25%; Cholesterol 60mg 20%; Sodium 1,220mg 51%; Total Carbohydrate 43g 14%; Dietary Fiber 4g 16%; Sugars 8g; Protein 24g; Vitamin A 200%; Vitamin C 15%; Calcium 6%; Iron 20% **Dietary Exchanges:** 2½ Starch, 1 Vegetable, 2 Lean Meat, 2 Fat **OR** 2½ Carbohydrate, 1 Vegetable, 2 Lean Meat, 2 Fat **Carbohydrate Choices:** 3

doughboy tip

Don't peek! Lifting the slow-cooker lid ahead of time lets heat escape and prolongs the cooking time. Wait until the minimum amount of cooking time has passed before uncovering the pot. If you're purchasing a new slow cooker, choose one with a removable lining for the easiest cleanup. Many of the inserts now double as attractive serving dishes, too.

grands!® chicken and biscuits

PREP TIME: 20 minutes (Ready in 45 minutes)
YIELD: 6 servings

2 (10¾-oz.) cans condensed creamy chicken mushroom soup

½ cup milk

¼ teaspoon dried thyme leaves, crushed

¼ teaspoon pepper

4 cups frozen broccoli, carrots and cauliflower, drained, rinsed

2 cups cubed cooked chicken or turkey

1 (16.3-oz.) can Pillsbury® Grands!® Refrigerated Buttermilk Biscuits

1. Heat oven to 375°F. In medium saucepan, combine both cans of soup, milk, thyme and pepper; mix well. Stir in vegetables and chicken. Cook over medium-high heat until mixture just begins to bubble, stirring occasionally. Reduce heat; cook an additional 3 to 4 minutes. Pour into an ungreased 13x9-inch (3-quart) glass baking dish.

2. Separate dough into 8 biscuits; cut each into quarters. Arrange biscuit pieces over hot chicken mixture around outer edges of dish.

3. Bake at 375°F. for 18 to 22 minutes or until biscuits are golden brown and bottoms are no longer doughy.

NUTRITION INFORMATION PER SERVING: **Serving Size:** ⅙ of Recipe; Calories 500; Calories from Fat 200 **% Daily Value:** Total Fat 22g 34%; Saturated Fat 6g 30%; Cholesterol 50mg 17%; Sodium 1,740mg 73%; Total Carbohydrate 53g 18%; Dietary Fiber 4g 16%; Sugars 14g; Protein 23g; Vitamin A 100%; Vitamin C 22%; Calcium 8%; Iron 20% **Dietary Exchanges:** 3 Starch, 2 Vegetable, 1½ Medium-Fat Meat, 2 Fat **OR** 3 Carbohydrate, 2 Vegetable, 1½ Medium-Fat Meat, 2 Fat **Carbohydrate Choices:** 3½

doughboy tip
It is important that the chicken mixture be hot when placing the biscuit pieces on top. If the mixture isn't hot, the biscuits may be golden brown on top but they may not be cooked through and will be doughy on the bottom.

chicken à la grands!®

1 (10.2-oz.) can (5 biscuits) Pillsbury® Grands!® Refrigerated Buttermilk Biscuits

1 (9-oz.) pkg. frozen diced cooked chicken breast

¼ cup margarine or butter

⅓ cup all-purpose flour

1 (10½-oz.) can condensed chicken broth

1¼ cups milk

1 cup frozen sweet peas

1 (4-oz.) can mushroom pieces and stems, drained

1 (2-oz.) jar diced pimientos, drained

¼ teaspoon salt

¼ teaspoon pepper

1. Bake biscuits as directed on can.

2. Meanwhile, place chicken on microwave-safe plate. Microwave on HIGH for 1½ to 2½ minutes or until thawed. Melt margarine in large saucepan over medium-low heat. Add flour; stir until well blended. Gradually stir in broth and milk, cooking and stirring until bubbly and thickened.

3. Add chicken and all remaining ingredients; mix well. Simmer 5 minutes or until thoroughly heated.

4. Split warm biscuits; place bottom halves on individual serving plates. Spoon hot chicken mixture over each biscuit half. Place top halves of biscuits over chicken mixture.

NUTRITION INFORMATION PER SERVING: Serving Size: ⅕ of Recipe; Calories 490; Calories from Fat 220 % Daily Value: Total Fat 24g 37%; Saturated Fat 6g 30%; Cholesterol 55mg 18%; Sodium 1,480mg 62%; Total Carbohydrate 40g 13%; Dietary Fiber 3g 12%; Sugars 10g; Protein 28g; Vitamin A 20%; Vitamin C 20%; Calcium 15%; Iron 20% Dietary Exchanges: 2½ Starch, 3 Lean Meat, 3 Fat OR 2½ Carbohydrate, 3 Lean Meat, 3 Fat Carbohydrate Choices: 2½

doughboy tip

If you don't have frozen peas on hand, use a cup of frozen cut green beans, chopped broccoli or whole kernel corn. And you can substitute 1⅓ cups cubed cooked chicken or turkey in place of the package of frozen cooked chicken breast.

most requested recipe
classic chicken pot pie

PREP TIME: 25 minutes (Ready in 1 hour 5 minutes)
YIELD: 6 servings

CRUST

1 (15-oz.) pkg. Pillsbury®
Refrigerated Pie Crusts, softened
as directed on package

FILLING

⅓ cup margarine or butter

⅓ cup chopped onion

⅓ cup all-purpose flour

½ teaspoon salt

¼ teaspoon pepper

1 (14-oz.) can chicken broth

½ cup milk

2½ cups shredded cooked
chicken or turkey

2 cups frozen mixed vegetables,
thawed

1. Heat oven to 425°F. Prepare pie crust as directed on package for *two-crust pie* using 9-inch glass pie pan.

2. Melt margarine in medium saucepan over medium heat. Add onion; cook and stir 2 minutes or until tender. Add flour, salt and pepper; stir until well blended. Gradually stir in broth and milk, cooking and stirring until bubbly and thickened.

3. Add chicken and mixed vegetables; mix well. Remove from heat. Spoon chicken mixture into crust-lined pan. Top with second crust; seal edges and flute. Cut slits in several places in top crust.

4. Bake at 425°F. for 30 to 40 minutes or until crust is golden brown. If necesary, cover edge of crust with strips of foil during last 15 to 20 minutes of baking to prevent excessive browning. Let stand 5 minutes before serving.

NUTRITION INFORMATION PER SERVING: Serving Size: ⅙ of Recipe; Calories 590; Calories from Fat 310 **% Daily Value:** Total Fat 34g 52%; Saturated Fat 11g 55%; Cholesterol 70mg 23%; Sodium 860mg 36%; Total Carbohydrate 47g 16%; Dietary Fiber 2g 8%; Sugars 4g; Protein 23g; Vitamin A 25%; Vitamin C 4%; Calcium 6%; Iron 10% **Dietary Exchanges:** 3 Starch, 2 Lean Meat, 5½ Fat **OR** 3 Carbohydrate, 2 Lean Meat, 5½ Fat **Carbohydrate Choices:** 3

doughboy tip

Instead of cutting slits into the top crust for steam vents, cut out tiny shapes using small cookie cutters or the tip of a knife. Be creative and cut out a tiny chicken, or use a small chicken-shaped cookie cutter to make cutouts and dress up the pie.

grands!® chicken and dumplings

PREP TIME: 45 minutes
YIELD: 8 servings

¼ cup margarine or butter

½ cup chopped onion

⅔ cup all-purpose flour

½ teaspoon salt

1 (10½-oz.) can condensed chicken broth

1 cup water

3 drops hot pepper sauce

2½ cups cubed cooked chicken or turkey

1½ cups frozen mixed vegetables, thawed

1 cup sour cream

1 (16.3-oz.) can Pillsbury® Grands!® Refrigerated Buttermilk or Southern Style Biscuits

Chopped fresh parsley, if desired

Paprika, if desired

1. Melt margarine in large heavy skillet over medium heat. Add onion; cook and stir until tender. Add flour and salt; stir until smooth. Add broth, water and hot pepper sauce; cook until bubbly and thickened, stirring constantly. Stir in chicken, mixed vegetables and sour cream. Reduce heat to low; simmer until thoroughly heated.

2. Separate dough into 8 biscuits; cut each in half. Arrange biscuit halves on top of hot chicken mixture. Simmer, uncovered, 10 minutes.

3. Cover; simmer an additional 15 to 20 minutes or until biscuits are no longer doughy. Sprinkle with parsley and paprika.

NUTRITION INFORMATION PER SERVING: Serving Size: ⅛ of Recipe; Calories 450; Calories from Fat 220 **% Daily Value:** Total Fat 24g 37%; Saturated Fat 8g 40%; Cholesterol 55mg 18%; Sodium 1,090mg 45%; Total Carbohydrate 37g 12%; Dietary Fiber 2g 8%; Sugars 7g; Protein 21g; Vitamin A 20%; Vitamin C 4%; Calcium 10%; Iron 15% **Dietary Exchanges:** 2 Starch, ½ Fruit, 2 Lean Meat, 3½ Fat **OR** 2½ Carbohydrate, 2 Lean Meat, 3½ Fat **Carbohydrate Choices:** 2½

doughboy tip

Start testing the dumplings for doneness at the minimum cooking time: Go ahead and cut into one. It should look dry inside and have the texture of moist bread. If the center still looks wet and dough-like, cook the dumplings a little longer.

crunchy biscuit chicken casserole

PREP TIME: 15 minutes (Ready in 45 minutes)
YIELD: 6 servings

2 (5-oz.) cans chunk chicken or 2 cups cubed cooked chicken

1 (10¾-oz.) can condensed cream of chicken soup

1 (8.25-oz.) can half-inch diagonal-cut green beans, drained

1 (2.5-oz.) jar sliced mushrooms, undrained

4 oz. (1 cup) shredded Cheddar or American cheese

½ cup mayonnaise or salad dressing

1 teaspoon lemon juice

1 (16.3-oz.) can Pillsbury® Grands!® Refrigerated Buttermilk Biscuits

1 to 2 tablespoons margarine or butter, melted

¼ to ½ cup crushed Cheddar cheese flavor or seasoned croutons

1. Heat oven to 375°F. In medium saucepan, combine chicken, soup, green beans, mushrooms, cheese, mayonnaise and lemon juice. Bring to a boil, stirring occasionally. Pour hot chicken mixture into ungreased 13x9-inch (3-quart) glass baking dish.

2. Separate dough into 8 biscuits. Arrange over hot chicken mixture in dish. Brush each biscuit with margarine. Sprinkle with crushed croutons.

3. Bake at 375°F. for 23 to 27 minutes or until biscuits are deep golden brown and bottoms are no longer doughy.

NUTRITION INFORMATION PER SERVING: Serving Size: ⅙ of Recipe; Calories 630; Calories from Fat 380 % Daily Value: Total Fat 42g 65%; Saturated Fat 12g 60%; Cholesterol 65mg 22%; Sodium 1,920mg 80%; Total Carbohydrate 41g 14%; Dietary Fiber 2g 8%; Sugars 8g; Protein 23g; Vitamin A 15%; Vitamin C 2%; Calcium 20%; Iron 20% Dietary Exchanges: 2½ Starch, 2 Medium-Fat Meat, 6 Fat OR 2½ Carbohydrate, 2 Medium-Fat Meat, 6 Fat Carbohydrate Choices: 3

doughboy tip

Out of cream of chicken soup? You can still make this family favorite using any canned cream soup you might have on hand— and you might discover a great new flavor combination! Why not try cream of broccoli, cream of mushroom, cream of asparagus or cream of celery?

chicken taco stew
in bread bowls

PREP TIME: 10 minutes (Ready in 35 minutes)
YIELD: 3 servings

1 (11-oz.) can Pillsbury® Refrigerated Crusty French Loaf

1 (6-oz.) pkg. refrigerated Southwestern-flavor chicken strips, coarsely chopped

1 (15 or 15.5-oz.) can kidney beans, drained, rinsed

1 (10-oz.) can diced tomatoes and green chiles, undrained

1 cup frozen whole kernel corn

1 cup chicken broth

1 tablespoon cornstarch

2 oz. (½ cup) shredded Cheddar cheese

1. Heat oven to 350°F. Spray cookie sheet with nonstick cooking spray. Cut dough into 3 equal pieces. Shape each into ball, placing seam at bottom so dough is smooth on top. Place dough balls seam side down on sprayed cookie sheet.

2. Bake at 350°F. for 18 to 22 minutes or until golden brown. Cool 5 minutes.

3. Meanwhile, in medium saucepan, combine all remaining ingredients except cheese; mix well. Cook over medium heat until mixture boils and thickens, stirring occasionally.

4. Cut top off each bread loaf. Lightly press center of bread down to form bowls. Place each bread bowl in individual shallow soup plate. Spoon about 1 cup stew into each bread bowl. Sprinkle with cheese. Place top of each bread bowl next to filled bowl.

NUTRITION INFORMATION PER SERVING: Serving Size: ⅓ of Recipe; Calories 655; Calories from Fat 125 **% Daily Value:** Total Fat 14g 22%; Saturated Fat 6g 30%; Cholesterol 70mg 23%; Sodium 1,920mg 80%; Total Carbohydrate 98g 33%; Dietary Fiber 13g 52%; Sugars 12g; Protein 47g; Vitamin A 10%; Vitamin C 12%; Calcium 18%; Iron 46% **Dietary Exchanges:** 5 Starch, 1 Fruit, 1 Vegetable, 4 Very Lean Meat, 1½ Fat **OR** 6 Carbohydrate, 1 Vegetable, 4 Very Lean Meat, 1½ Fat **Carbohydrate Choices:** 6

doughboy tip

If you like black beans, go ahead and substitute them for the kidney beans in this recipe. Chickpeas (garbanzos) can also be used, but the kidney and black beans offer the advantage of adding one more deep color to the finished dish.

warm chicken salad pie

PREP TIME: 15 minutes (Ready in 55 minutes)
YIELD: 8 servings

CRUST

1 Pillsbury® Refrigerated Pie Crust (from 15-oz. pkg.), softened as directed on package

FILLING

2 cups cubed cooked chicken or turkey

2 cups chopped celery

2 cups frozen broccoli florets

½ cup chopped pecans

1 tablespoon instant minced onion

½ teaspoon dried tarragon leaves

1½ cups mayonnaise

3 tablespoons dry white wine or water

1½ teaspoons lemon juice

1 oz. (¼ cup) grated fresh Parmesan cheese

1. Heat oven to 425°F. Place pie crust in 9-inch glass pie pan as directed on package for *one-crust filled pie*. DO NOT PRICK CRUST. Bake at 425°F. for 8 minutes.

2. Meanwhile, in large bowl, combine all filling ingredients except cheese; mix well.

3. Remove partially baked crust from oven. Reduce oven temperature to 400°F. Spoon filling into crust. Sprinkle with cheese.

4. Return to oven; bake at 400°F. for 25 to 35 minutes or until golden brown.

NUTRITION INFORMATION PER SERVING: Serving Size: ⅛ of Recipe; Calories 635; Calories from Fat 440 **% Daily Value:** Total Fat 49g 75%; Saturated Fat 10g 50%; Cholesterol 60mg 20%; Sodium 470mg 20%; Total Carbohydrate 18g 6%; Dietary Fiber 2g 8%; Sugars 3g; Protein 14g; Vitamin A 8%; Vitamin C 16%; Calcium 8%; Iron 6% **Dietary Exchanges:** 1 Starch, 1 Vegetable, 1 High-Fat Meat, 9 Fat **OR** 1 Carbohydrate, 1 Vegetable, 1 High-Fat Meat, 9 Fat **Carbohydrate Choices:** 1

doughboy tip

Garnish each serving of this tasty pie with a sprinkle of coarsely chopped pecans and a little extra Parmesan cheese. Add a cluster of red or green grapes alongside for a bit of color. If you wish, try walnuts or hazelnuts instead of the pecans in the recipe and for the garnish.

most requested recipe

individual chicken pot pies pictured on page 185

PREP TIME: 25 minutes (Ready in 45 minutes)
YIELD: 8 servings

¼ cup margarine or butter

⅓ cup all-purpose flour

Dash pepper

1 (10½-oz.) can condensed chicken broth

¾ cup milk

2 cups cubed cooked chicken or turkey

⅓ cup chopped onion

1 (4-oz.) can mushroom pieces and stems, drained

1 cup frozen sweet peas

1 cup frozen sliced carrots

1 (16.3-oz.) can Pillsbury® Grands!® Refrigerated Original Flaky Layers Biscuits

Milk, if desired

1. Heat oven to 350°F. Grease 8 (10-oz.) ramekins, custard cups or large muffin cups.

2. Melt margarine in large skillet; stir in flour and pepper. Cook 1 minute or until smooth and bubbly, stirring constantly. Gradually stir in broth and milk; cook until mixture boils and thickens, stirring constantly. Add chicken, onion, mushrooms, peas and carrots; cook until hot and bubbly. Spoon mixture evenly into greased custard cups.

3. Separate dough into 8 biscuits. Press or roll each biscuit to form 4½-inch round. Place biscuit rounds on top of filled custard cups. Cut slits in biscuit tops. Brush biscuit tops with milk. Sprinkle with sesame seed.

4. Bake at 350°F. for 17 to 20 minutes or until biscuits are golden brown.

NUTRITION INFORMATION PER SERVING: Serving Size: ⅛ of Recipe; Calories 395; Calories from Fat 160 % Daily Value: Total Fat 18g 28%; Saturated Fat 4g 20%; Cholesterol 32mg 11%; Sodium 1,170mg 49%; Total Carbohydrate 41g 14%; Dietary Fiber 3g 12%; Sugars 13g; Protein 18g; Vitamin A 100%; Vitamin C 4%; Calcium 6%; Iron 16% Dietary Exchanges: 2½ Starch, 1½ Medium-Fat Meat, 2 Fat OR 2½ Carbohydrate, 1½ Medium-Fat Meat, 2 Fat Carbohydrate Choices: 3

doughboy tip

For a nice flavor twist, add 1 tablespoon chopped fresh thyme or 1 tablespoon chopped fresh rosemary leaves to the chicken mixture. Then garnish each little pie with a sprig of fresh thyme or rosemary.

easy chicken pot pies

PREP TIME: 15 minutes (Ready in 35 minutes)
YIELD: 8 servings

1 (16.3-oz.) can Pillsbury®
Grands!® Refrigerated Original
Flaky Layers Biscuits

1 (19-oz.) can ready-to-serve
roasted white meat chicken, pasta
and Italian garden vegetables or
chicken noodle soup

1 to 2 tablespoons margarine
or butter, melted

1 teaspoon dried Italian seasoning

½ teaspoon garlic powder

1 oz. (¼ cup) shredded
mozzarella cheese

1. Heat oven to 375°F. Lightly spray 8 (2¼x1¼-inch) muffin cups with nonstick cooking spray. Separate dough into 8 biscuits; separate each biscuit into 2 layers. Place 8 biscuit halves in sprayed muffin cups, pressing in bottom and up sides to cover.

2. Drain soup; discard liquid or freeze for a later use. Spoon drained soup evenly into biscuit-lined cups. Place remaining biscuit halves over soup; gently seal each biscuit.

3. Brush biscuit tops with margarine. Sprinkle with Italian seasoning and garlic powder. Top each with ½ tablespoon cheese.

4. Bake at 375°F. for 15 to 18 minutes or until edges are golden brown.

NUTRITION INFORMATION PER SERVING: Serving Size: ⅛ of Recipe; Calories 260; Calories from Fat 120 % Daily Value: Total Fat 13g 20%; Saturated Fat 4g 20%; Cholesterol 15mg 5%; Sodium 890mg 37%; Total Carbohydrate 28g 9%; Dietary Fiber 1g 4%; Sugars 4g; Protein 8g; Vitamin A 8%; Vitamin C 0%; Calcium 4%; Iron 10% Dietary Exchanges: 2 Starch, ½ Medium-Fat Meat, 1½ Fat OR 2 Carbohydrate, ½ Medium-Fat Meat, 1½ Fat Carbohydrate Choices: 2

doughboy tip
The liquid, or broth, drained from the canned soup can be frozen in ice-cube trays. Remove the frozen cubes from the trays and place in a resealable food storage plastic bag or freezer container so they are ready when you need a bit of added flavor or broth. Add a few cubes to the water when cooking vegetables, pasta or rice. Or use several cubes to enhance the flavor of soup or stew.

turkey stew
with biscuits

PREP TIME: 30 minutes (Ready in 50 minutes)
YIELD: 6 servings

4 slices bacon, cut into ½-inch pieces

1 (¾ to 1-lb.) fresh turkey breast tenderloin, cut into ½-inch pieces

2 (10¾-oz.) cans condensed cream of chicken soup

1 (1-lb.) pkg. frozen broccoli, carrots and cauliflower

¼ to ½ teaspoon poultry seasoning

¾ cup sour cream

1 (6-oz.) can (5 biscuits) Pillsbury® Golden Layers™ Refrigerated Buttermilk Biscuits

1. Heat oven to 375°F. Cook bacon in large skillet over medium heat until crisp. Reserve bacon and 1 tablespoon drippings in skillet. Add turkey to skillet; cook and stir until browned and no longer pink.

2. Stir in soup, vegetables and poultry seasoning. Cook until bubbly, stirring frequently. Reduce heat; cover and simmer 5 to 7 minutes or until vegetables are crisp-tender.

3. Stir in sour cream. Spoon mixture into ungreased 2½-quart oval casserole or 12x8-inch (2-quart) glass baking dish.

4. Separate dough into 5 biscuits; cut each in half. Arrange cut side down over hot mixture around outer edges of casserole.

5. Bake at 375°F. for 14 to 18 minutes or until biscuits are deep golden brown and bottoms are no longer doughy.

NUTRITION INFORMATION PER SERVING: **Serving Size:** ⅙ of Recipe; Calories 360; Calories from Fat 170 **% Daily Value:** Total Fat 19g 29%; Saturated Fat 7g 35%; Cholesterol 70mg 23%; Sodium 1,190mg 50%; Total Carbohydrate 27g 9%; Dietary Fiber 3g 12%; Sugars 6g; Protein 21g; Vitamin A 54%; Vitamin C 20%; Calcium 6%; Iron 12% **Dietary Exchanges:** 1½ Starch, 1 Vegetable, 2 Lean Meat, 2½ Fat **OR** 1½ Carbohydrate, 1 Vegetable, 2 Lean Meat, 2½ Fat **Carbohydrate Choices:** 2

doughboy tip

You can make this tasty stew using ¾ to 1 pound boneless chicken breasts or thighs in place of the turkey tenderloin. To substitute for the ½ teaspoon of poultry seasoning, use ¼ teaspoon ground thyme plus ¼ teaspoon ground sage, or simply use ½ teaspoon of ground sage.

ham and swiss crescent braid

PREP TIME: 25 minutes (Ready in 1 hour)
YIELD: 8 servings

¾ lb. cooked ham, chopped (2¼ cups)

1 cup frozen broccoli florets, thawed

4 oz. (1 cup) shredded Swiss cheese

1 (4.5-oz.) jar sliced mushrooms, drained

½ cup mayonnaise or salad dressing

1 tablespoon honey mustard

2 (8-oz.) cans Pillsbury® Refrigerated Crescent Dinner Rolls

1 egg white, beaten

2 tablespoons slivered almonds

1. Heat oven to 375°F. Spray cookie sheet with nonstick cooking spray. In large bowl, combine ham, broccoli, cheese, mushrooms, mayonnaise and mustard; mix well.

2. Unroll both cans of dough into 2 large rectangles. Place dough with long sides together on sprayed cookie sheet, forming 15x12-inch rectangle. Press edges and perforations to seal.

3. Spoon and spread ham mixture lengthwise in 6-inch-wide strip down center of dough. With scissors or sharp knife, make cuts 1½ inches apart on long sides of dough to within ½ inch of filling. Twisting each strip once, alternately cross strips over filling. Tuck short ends under; press to seal. Brush dough with egg white. Sprinkle with almonds.

4. Bake at 375°F. for 28 to 33 minutes or until deep golden brown. Cool 5 minutes. Cut crosswise into slices.

NUTRITION INFORMATION PER SERVING: Serving Size: ⅛ of Recipe; Calories 440, Calories from Fat 260 % Daily Value: Total Fat 29g 45%; Saturated Fat 7g 35%; Cholesterol 40mg 13%; Sodium 1,230mg 51%; Total Carbohydrate 26g 9%; Dietary Fiber 1g 4%; Sugars 5g; Protein 18g; Vitamin A 4%; Vitamin C 4%; Calcium 15%; Iron 10% Dietary Exchanges: 1½ Starch, 2 Lean Meat, 4½ Fat OR 1½ Carbohydrate, 2 Lean Meat, 4½ Fat Carbohydrate Choices: 2

doughboy tip

This recipe is a great way to use up your leftover ham. If you're planning ahead and purchasing precooked meat, order a chunk rather than slices of ham at the deli counter. Choose boiled ham if you prefer its mildness, or for a deeper flavor, buy baked or smoked ham.

salmon à la king casserole

PREP TIME: 15 minutes (Ready in 35 minutes)
YIELD: 6 servings

1 (1-lb.) jar Alfredo sauce

1 (9-oz.) pkg. frozen baby early peas in pouch, thawed

1 (4.5-oz.) jar sliced mushrooms, drained

2 (14¾-oz.) cans pink salmon, drained, skin and bones removed

1 (2-oz.) jar chopped pimientos, drained

1 (8-oz.) can Pillsbury® Refrigerated Crescent Dinner Rolls

1. Heat oven to 375°F. Spray 12x8-inch (2 quart) glass baking dish with nonstick cooking spray. In medium saucepan, combine Alfredo sauce, peas and mushrooms; cook over medium heat until bubbly. Remove from heat. Gently stir in salmon and pimientos. Pour into sprayed baking dish.

2. Unroll dough into 2 long rectangles. Press edges and perforations to form 1 rectangle. Place over salmon mixture in baking dish.

3. Bake at 375°F. for 12 to 18 minutes or until crust is golden brown.

NUTRITION INFORMATION PER SERVING: **Serving Size:** ⅙ of Recipe; Calories 470; Calories from Fat 230 **% Daily Value:** Total Fat 25g 38%; Saturated Fat 10g 50%; Cholesterol 95mg 32%; Sodium 1,670mg 70%; Total Carbohydrate 27g 9%; Dietary Fiber 3g 12%; Sugars 7g; Protein 33g; Vitamin A 15%; Vitamin C 20%; Calcium 6%; Iron 15% **Dietary Exchanges:** 2 Starch, 4 Lean Meat, 2 Fat **OR** 2 Carbohydrate, 4 Lean Meat, 2 Fat **Carbohydrate Choices:** 2

doughboy tip

Dill is an herb that goes particularly well with salmon. Stir in 1 tablespoon chopped fresh dill or 1 teaspoon dried dill weed with the salmon. Garnish each serving with a sprig of feathery fresh dill. This casserole is also good made with canned tuna. Use a 12-ounce can of tuna, drained, in place of the salmon.

mini shrimp bakes

PREP TIME: 20 minutes (Ready in 45 minutes)
YIELD: 8 servings

1 (8-oz.) can Pillsbury®
Refrigerated Crescent Dinner Rolls

1 (8-oz.) pkg. cream cheese,
softened

2 tablespoons chopped onion or
1 teaspoon instant minced onion

¼ teaspoon salt

1 teaspoon prepared horseradish

1 (6-oz.) pkg. (2 cups) frozen
cooked shrimp, thawed, or
4½-oz. can shrimp,
drained, rinsed

¼ cup cooked real bacon pieces

Paprika

1. Heat oven to 375°F. Separate dough into 8 triangles. Place each triangle in ungreased muffin cup; press dough in bottom and up sides to cover.

2. In medium bowl, combine cream cheese, onion, salt and horseradish; blend well. Stir in shrimp. Spoon about ¼ cup mixture into each cup. Sprinkle with bacon and paprika.

3. Bake at 375°F. for 20 to 25 minutes or until crust is golden brown. Let stand 5 minutes before serving.

NUTRITION INFORMATION PER SERVING: Serving Size: ⅛ of Recipe; Calories 240; Calories from Fat 145 % Daily Value: Total Fat 16g 25%; Saturated Fat 8g 40%; Cholesterol 75mg 25%; Sodium 590mg 25%; Total Carbohydrate 15g 5%; Dietary Fiber 1g 4%; Sugars 5g; Protein 9g; Vitamin A 8%; Vitamin C 0%; Calcium 4%; Iron 10% Dietary Exchanges: 1 Starch, 1 Medium-Fat Meat, 2 Fat OR 1 Carbohydrate, 1 Medium-Fat Meat, 2 Fat Carbohydrate Choices: 1

doughboy tip

To make these little meals ahead of time, prepare the recipe through the end of Step 2. Cover and refrigerate for up to 2 hours, then bake as directed. If you have any left over, wrap them loosely in foil and refrigerate for the next day. Pop the wrapped mini bakes in a 375°F. oven for 12 to 15 minutes or until warmed through.

alfredo tuna over biscuits

PREP TIME: 20 minutes
YIELD: 5 servings

1 (10.2-oz.) can (5 biscuits) Pillsbury® Grands!® Refrigerated Buttermilk Biscuits

2 (9-oz.) pkg. frozen broccoli, carrots and peas in a low-fat Alfredo sauce

2 (6-oz.) cans albacore tuna, drained

1 (10-oz.) container refrigerated Alfredo sauce

1½ oz. (⅓ cup) shredded fresh Parmesan cheese

1. Heat oven to 375°F. Bake biscuits as directed on can.

2. Meanwhile, cook vegetables as directed on package. Pour into medium microwave-safe bowl. Add tuna and Alfredo sauce; mix well. Microwave on HIGH for 3 minutes or until thoroughly heated, stirring once.

3. Split warm biscuits; place bottom halves on individual serving plates. Top with half of tuna mixture. Top each serving with biscuit top and remaining tuna mixture. Sprinkle each with cheese.

NUTRITION INFORMATION PER SERVING: Serving Size: ⅕ of Recipe; Calories 570; Calories from Fat 290 % Daily Value: Total Fat 32g 49%; Saturated Fat 16g 80%; Cholesterol 90mg 30%; Sodium 1,760mg 73%; Total Carbohydrate 41g 14%; Dietary Fiber 3g 12%; Sugars 13g; Protein 33g; Vitamin A 54%; Vitamin C 14%; Calcium 36%; Iron 16% Dietary Exchanges: 1 Starch, 1 Fruit, 2 Vegetable, 3½ Very Lean Meat, 6 Fat OR 2 Carbohydrate, 2 Vegetable, 3½ Very Lean Meat, 6 Fat Carbohydrate Choices: 3

doughboy tip

Look for the new vacuum-sealed pouches of tuna and you won't need to worry about draining the can. You'll find this new product wherever you buy canned tuna. If refrigerated Alfredo sauce isn't available, use 1¼ cups sauce from a jar of Alfredo sauce.

crab and corn cobbler

PREP TIME: 15 minutes (Ready in 50 minutes)
YIELD: 4 servings

2 cups milk

⅓ cup all-purpose flour

¼ teaspoon salt

⅛ teaspoon pepper

1 (10-oz.) pkg. frozen
Southwestern-style whole kernel
corn with roasted red peppers

1 (8-oz.) pkg. chunk-style imitation
crabmeat (surimi)

3 tablespoons chopped
green onions

1 (4-oz.) can (4 rolls) Pillsbury®
Refrigerated Crescent Dinner Rolls

1. Heat oven to 350°F. Spray 1½-quart casserole with nonstick cooking spray. In medium saucepan, combine milk, flour, salt and pepper; blend well. Cook over medium-high heat until bubbly and thickened, stirring constantly.

2. Add corn with peppers, imitation crabmeat and green onions. Cook and stir until thoroughly heated. Pour into sprayed casserole.

3. Remove dough from can; do not unroll. Cut into 8 slices; cut each in half crosswise. Arrange over hot mixture.

4. Bake at 350°F. for 30 to 35 minutes or until casserole is bubbly and rolls are deep golden brown.

NUTRITION INFORMATION PER SERVING: Serving Size: ¼ of Recipe; Calories 315; Calories from Fat 65 **% Daily Value:** Total Fat 7g 11%; Saturated Fat 3g 15%; Cholesterol 25mg 8%; Sodium 1,210mg 50%; Total Carbohydrate 45g 15%; Dietary Fiber 3g 12%; Sugars 12g; Protein 18g; Vitamin A 8%; Vitamin C 8%; Calcium 16%; Iron 10% **Dietary Exchanges:** 3 Starch, 1 Very Lean Meat, 1 Fat **OR** 3 Carbohydrate, 1 Very Lean Meat, 1 Fat **Carbohydrate Choices:** 3

doughboy tip

Cobblers aren't just for fruit. This savory cobbler is packed with a creamy crab and corn mixture. Give it a blush of color by sprinkling the biscuits with a little paprika before baking. It's a perfect dish to serve for brunch or supper.

barbecued three-bean casserole

PREP TIME: 10 minutes (Ready in 45 minutes)
YIELD: 5 servings

½ cup barbecue sauce

1 teaspoon prepared mustard

1 (28-oz.) can baked beans, undrained

1 (15 or 15.5-oz.) can kidney beans, drained, rinsed

1 (15-oz.) can garbanzo beans, drained, rinsed

4 oz. (1 cup) shredded Cheddar cheese

1 (10.2-oz.) can (5 biscuits) Pillsbury® Grands!® Refrigerated Buttermilk Biscuits

2 tablespoons cornmeal

1. Heat oven to 350°F. Spray 12x8-inch (2-quart) glass baking dish with nonstick cooking spray.

2. In large saucepan, combine all ingredients except biscuits and cornmeal. Bring to a boil. Pour into sprayed casserole.

3. Separate dough into 5 biscuits; cut each into quarters. Roll biscuit pieces in cornmeal; arrange over mixture in casserole. Discard any remaining cornmeal.

4. Bake at 350°F. for 30 to 35 minutes or until biscuits are golden brown.

NUTRITION INFORMATION PER SERVING: Serving Size: ⅕ of Recipe; Calories 620; Calories from Fat 170 **% Daily Value:** Total Fat 19g 29%; Saturated Fat 8g 40%; Cholesterol 25mg 8%; Sodium 1,800mg 75%; Total Carbohydrate 85g 28%; Dietary Fiber 16g 64%; Sugars 14g; Protein 26g; Vitamin A 15%; Vitamin C 8%; Calcium 35%; Iron 20% **Dietary Exchanges:** 5 Starch, ½ Fruit, 1½ Very Lean Meat, 3 Fat **OR** 5½ Carbohydrate, 1½ Very Lean Meat, 3 Fat **Carbohydrate Choices:** 5½

doughboy tip

It's easy to prepare a quick homemade crunchy relish to accompany the casserole. In a serving bowl, combine equal amounts of chopped fresh tomato, chopped cucumber and chopped celery with a little minced onion. Toss with homemade or purchased vinaigrette, and sprinkle with chopped fresh parsley or mint.

chili casserole with cheesy crust

PREP TIME: 35 minutes (Ready in 1 hour)
YIELD: 6 servings

1 (10-oz.) can Pillsbury®
Refrigerated Pizza Crust

1 (8-oz.) pkg. string cheese

1 cup chopped onions

1 cup chopped green bell pepper

1 (15-oz.) can Southwestern chili
beans with cumin and cayenne in
chili sauce, undrained

1 (14.5-oz.) can diced tomatoes,
undrained

1 (6-oz.) can tomato paste

½ cup frozen whole kernel corn

4 oz. (1 cup) shredded
Cheddar cheese

1. Heat oven to 425°F. Grease 13x9-inch pan. Unroll dough; place in greased pan. Starting at center, press out dough over bottom and 1½ inches up sides.

2. Place string cheese, end to end, on dough around edges of pan, cutting to fit if necessary. Reserve any remaining cheese. Fold edge of dough over cheese; pinch to seal under cheese. Bake at 425°F. for 10 minutes. Remove partially baked crust from oven. Reduce oven temperature to 375°F.

3. Meanwhile, spray large skillet with nonstick cooking spray. Heat over medium-high heat until hot. Add onions and bell pepper; cook 5 to 7 minutes or until tender, stirring occasionally.

4. Add beans, tomatoes, tomato paste and corn; mix well. Bring to a boil. Reduce heat to medium; cook 6 to 8 minutes or until slightly thickened.

5. Spoon bean mixture evenly into partially baked crust. Chop any reserved string cheese. Sprinkle string cheese and Cheddar cheese over top.

6. Return to oven; bake at 375°F. for an additional 15 to 25 minutes or until crust is deep golden brown and cheese is melted. Let stand about 5 minutes before serving.

doughboy tip

Nonstick cooking spray is cooking oil in a pressurized can that allows the oil to be dispersed in a much finer layer than you could achieve by pouring oil from the bottle. If you like, you can make your own sprayer. Just purchase a spray bottle at a specialty kitchen store, fill it with your favorite oil and you're in business!

NUTRITION INFORMATION PER SERVING: **Serving Size:** ⅙ of Recipe; Calories 430; Calories from Fat 140 **% Daily Value:** Total Fat 15g 23%; Saturated Fat 9g 45%; Cholesterol 40mg 13%; Sodium 1,290mg 54%; Total Carbohydrate 50g 17%; Dietary Fiber 6g 24%; Sugars 8g; Protein 24g; Vitamin A 35%; Vitamin C 35%; Calcium 50%; Iron 20% **Dietary Exchanges:** 2½ Starch, 2 Vegetable, 1½ High-Fat Meat, ½ Fat OR 2½ Carbohydrate, 2 Vegetable, 1½ High-Fat Meat, ½ Fat **Carbohydrate Choices:** 3

Doughboy Recommends

chapter 5
Delightful Desserts and Fun Treats

FILLED COOKIE TARTLETS, page 255

fresh strawberry pie

PREP TIME: 30 minutes (Ready in 4 hours)
YIELD: 8 servings

CRUST

1 Pillsbury® Refrigerated Pie Crust (from 15-oz. pkg.), softened as directed on package

FILLING

3 pints (6 cups) fresh whole strawberries

1 cup sugar

3 tablespoons cornstarch

¼ cup water

4 to 5 drops red food color, if desired

1. Heat oven to 450°F. Prepare pie crust as directed on package for *one-crust baked shell* using 9-inch glass pie pan. Bake at 450°F. for 9 to 11 minutes or until lightly browned. Cool 30 minutes or until completely cooled.

2. Meanwhile, in small bowl, crush enough strawberries to make 1 cup. In medium saucepan, combine sugar and cornstarch; add crushed strawberries and water. Cook until mixture boils and thickens, stirring constantly. Stir in food color. Cool.

3. Arrange remaining strawberries whole or sliced, in cooled baked shell. Pour cooked strawberry mixture evenly over berries. Refrigerate 3 hours or until set. Store in refrigerator.

NUTRITION INFORMATION PER SERVING: Serving Size: ⅛ of Recipe; Calories 265; Calories from Fat 65 **% Daily Value:** Total Fat 7g 11%; Saturated Fat 3g 15%; Cholesterol 5mg 2%; Sodium 110mg 5%; Total Carbohydrate 48g 16%; Dietary Fiber 3g 12%; Sugars 32g; Protein 2g; Vitamin A 0%; Vitamin C 96%; Calcium 2%; Iron 2% **Dietary Exchanges:** 1 Starch, 2 Fruit, 1½ Fat **OR** 3 Carbohydrate, 1½ Fat **Carbohydrate Choices:** 3

doughboy tip

Shortly before serving this elegant summer berry pie, whip ½ cup whipping (heavy) cream to soft peaks. Sweeten to taste with powdered sugar and a couple drops of vanilla. Top off each slice of pie with a dollop of the cream and a sprig of fresh mint.

rosy raspberry-pear pie

PREP TIME: 15 minutes (Ready in 4 hours 5 minutes)
YIELD: 8 servings

1 (15-oz.) pkg. Pillsbury® Refrigerated Pie Crusts, softened as directed on package

3 firm ripe pears, peeled, cut into ½-inch slices

1 tablespoon lemon juice

½ teaspoon almond extract

¾ cup sugar

3 tablespoons all-purpose flour

1 cup fresh raspberries or frozen whole raspberries without syrup, partially thawed

1 tablespoon margarine or butter, melted

1 tablespoon sugar

1. Heat oven to 400°F. Place 1 pie crust in 9-inch glass pie pan as directed on package for *one-crust filled pie*. Reserve second crust for cutouts.

2. In large bowl, combine pears, lemon juice and almond extract; toss to coat. Add ¾ cup sugar and flour; mix well. Spoon about half of the pear mixture into crust-lined pan. Top with raspberries. Spoon remaining pear mixture over raspberries.

3. With floured 2½-inch round cutter, cut 9 rounds from second pie crust. Brush each with melted margarine. Place 8 rounds, margarine side up, in circle on outer edge of fruit, overlapping as necessary. Place 1 round in center. Sprinkle rounds with 1 tablespoon sugar.

4. Bake at 400°F. for 40 to 50 minutes or until crust is golden brown and filling is bubbly. If necessary, cover edge of crust with strips of foil after 15 to 20 minutes of baking to prevent excessive browning. Cool 3 hours or until completely cooled.

NUTRITION INFORMATION PER SERVING: **Serving Size:** ⅛ of Recipe; Calories 325; Calories from Fat 110 **% Daily Value:** Total Fat 12g 18%; Saturated Fat 5g 25%; Cholesterol 5mg 2%; Sodium 170mg 7%; Total Carbohydrate 52g 17%; Dietary Fiber 3g 12%; Sugars 30g; Protein 2g; Vitamin A 2%; Vitamin C 4%; Calcium 0%; Iron 2% **Dietary Exchanges:** 1 Starch, 2½ Fruit, 2 Fat **OR** 3½ Carbohydrate, 2 Fat **Carbohydrate Choices:** 3½

doughboy tip

This rosy pie is perfect for serving à la mode. Vanilla ice cream is always a hit, but other yummy possibilities include raspberry sorbet and lemon gelato. If you like, garnish each serving with a few fresh raspberries.

perfect apple pie

PREP TIME: 30 minutes (Ready in 1 hour 15 minutes)
YIELD: 8 servings

CRUST

1 (15-oz.) pkg. Pillsbury®
Refrigerated Pie Crusts, softened
as directed on package

FILLING

¾ cup sugar

2 tablespoons all-purpose flour

¾ teaspoon cinnamon

¼ teaspoon salt

⅛ teaspoon nutmeg

1 tablespoon lemon juice, if desired

6 cups (6 medium) thinly sliced,
peeled apples

1. Heat oven to 425°F. Prepare pie crusts as directed on package for *two-crust pie* using 9-inch glass pie pan.

2. In large bowl, combine all filling ingredients except lemon juice and apples; mix well. Add lemon juice and apples; toss gently to mix. Spoon into crust-lined pan. Top with second crust; seal edges and flute. Cut slits or shapes in several places in top crust.

3. Bake at 425°F. for 40 to 45 minutes or until apples are tender and crust is golden brown.

NUTRITION INFORMATION PER SERVING: Serving Size: ⅛ of Recipe; Calories 370; Calories from Fat 130 **% Daily Value:** Total Fat 14g 22%; Saturated Fat 6g 30%; Cholesterol 15mg 5%; Sodium 270mg 11%; Total Carbohydrate 59g 20%; Dietary Fiber 2g 8%; Sugars 30g; Protein 2g; Vitamin A 0%; Vitamin C 4%; Calcium 0%; Iron 4% **Dietary Exchanges:** 1 Starch, 3 Fruit, 2½ Fat **OR** 4 Carbohydrate, 2½ Fat **Carbohydrate Choices:** 4

variations

apple-cranberry pie: Use 5 cups thinly sliced, peeled apples and 1½ cups fresh or frozen cranberries, thawed. Increase sugar to 1 cup; increase flour to ¼ cup. Bake at 425°F. for 45 to 55 minutes.

caramel-pecan apple pie: Immediately after removing pie from oven, drizzle with ⅓ cup caramel ice cream topping. Sprinkle with 2 to 4 tablespoons chopped pecans.

maple-frosted apple pie: In small bowl, combine ½ cup powdered sugar and 3 tablespoons maple-flavored syrup. Drizzle over warm baked pie.

doughboy tip

With all the types of apples available, it's hard to know which ones work well for baking. In our test kitchens, we have the greatest success with apples such as Braeburn, Gala, Cortland, Granny Smith and Northern Spy that hold their shape and bake up tender and moist.

cranberry cheesecake tart

PREP TIME: 30 minutes (Ready in 5 hours 30 minutes)
YIELD: 10 servings

CRUST

1 Pillsbury® Refrigerated Pie Crust (from 15-oz. pkg.), softened as directed on package

FILLING

1 (16-oz.) can whole berry cranberry sauce

½ cup chopped pecans

6 tablespoons sugar

1 tablespoon cornstarch

12 oz. cream cheese, softened

½ cup sugar

1 tablespoon milk

2 eggs

TOPPING

1 cup sour cream

2 tablespoons sugar

½ teaspoon vanilla

1. Heat oven to 450°F. Prepare pie crust as directed on package for *one-crust baked shell* using 10-inch tart pan with removable bottom or 9-inch glass pie pan. Place prepared crust in pan; press in bottom and up sides of pan. Trim edges if necessary. Generously prick crust with fork.

2. Bake at 450°F. for 9 to 11 minutes or until light golden brown. Cool 30 minutes or until completely cooled.

3. Reduce oven temperature to 375°F. In medium bowl, combine cranberry sauce, pecans, 6 tablespoons sugar and cornstarch; mix well. Spread into cooled baked shell.

4. In another medium bowl, beat cream cheese, ½ cup sugar, milk and eggs at medium speed until smooth. Spoon evenly over cranberry mixture. Bake at 375°F. for 25 to 30 minutes or until set.

5. In small bowl, combine all topping ingredients; mix well. Spoon evenly over filling. Bake at 375°F. for an additional 5 minutes. Cool slightly. Refrigerate 3 to 4 hours or until set. Store in refrigerator.

NUTRITION INFORMATION PER SERVING: Serving Size: ¹⁄₁₀ of Recipe; Calories 480; Calories from Fat - 250 **% Daily Value:** Total Fat 28g 43%; Saturated Fat 14g 70%; Cholesterol 95mg 32%; Sodium 250mg 10%; Total Carbohydrate 52g 17%; Dietary Fiber 1g 4%; Sugars 38g; Protein 6g; Vitamin A 15%; Vitamin C 0%; Calcium 6%; Iron 6% **Dietary Exchanges:** 1½ Starch, 2 Fruit, 5½ Fat **OR** 3½ Carbohydrate, 5½ Fat **Carbohydrate Choices:** 3½

doughboy tip

To chop pecans, place them on a wooden chopping board and go to work with a sharp chef's knife. If you prefer to use a food processor, chop with short pulses to prevent the mixture from becoming pasty.

rhubarb custard tart

PREP TIME: 20 minutes (Ready in 1 hour 40 minutes)
YIELD: 12 servings

CRUST

1 Pillsbury® Refrigerated Pie Crust (from 15-oz. pkg.), softened as directed on package

TOPPING

½ cup all-purpose flour

½ cup firmly packed brown sugar

¼ cup quick-cooking rolled oats

¼ cup margarine or butter, softened

FILLING

¾ cup sugar

3 tablespoons all-purpose flour

½ cup whipping cream

2 tablespoons apricot preserves

1 egg yolk

3 cups sliced fresh rhubarb, or frozen rhubarb, thawed, drained

1. Place pie crust in 9-inch tart pan with removable bottom or 9-inch glass pie pan as directed on package for *one-crust filled pie*. Press in bottom and up sides of pan; trim edges if necessary.

2. Place cookie sheet on center rack in oven. Heat oven to 375°F. In small bowl, combine ½ cup flour, brown sugar and oats; mix well. With pastry blender or fork, cut in margarine until mixture is crumbly. Set aside.

3. In large bowl, combine sugar and 3 tablespoons flour; mix well. Add whipping cream, preserves and egg yolk; mix well. Stir in rhubarb. Pour filling into crust-lined pan. Sprinkle topping evenly over filling.

4. Place tart on cookie sheet in oven. Bake at 375°F. for 40 to 50 minutes or until filling bubbles around edges and topping is deep golden brown. Cool 30 minutes before serving.

NUTRITION INFORMATION PER SERVING: Serving Size: ¹⁄₁₂ of Recipe; Calories 260; Calories from Fat 120 % Daily Value: Total Fat 13g 20%; Saturated Fat 5g 25%; Cholesterol 35mg 12%; Sodium 120mg 5%; Total Carbohydrate 33g 11%; Dietary Fiber 1g 4%; Sugars 17g; Protein 2g; Vitamin A 8%; Vitamin C 4%; Calcium 4%; Iron 4% Dietary Exchanges: 1 Starch, 1 Fruit, 2½ Fat OR 2 Carbohydrate, 2½ Fat Carbohydrate Choices: 2

doughboy tip

Tame the rhubarb's tartness by topping each serving of this tart with a scoop of vanilla or strawberry ice cream or a dollop of sweetened whipped cream.

most requested recipe
zesty orange-pumpkin tart

PREP TIME: 20 minutes (Ready in 2 hours 15 minutes)
YIELD: 8 servings

CRUST

1 Pillsbury® Refrigerated Pie Crust (from 15-oz. pkg.), softened as directed on package

FILLING

1 (16-oz.) can (2 cups) pumpkin (not pumpkin pie filling)

1 (12-oz.) can evaporated milk

½ cup sugar

⅓ cup orange marmalade

2 eggs, slightly beaten

1 teaspoon pumpkin pie spice

½ teaspoon salt

TOPPING

1 cup whipping cream

2 tablespoons powdered sugar

½ teaspoon grated orange peel, if desired

1. Heat oven to 425°F. Place pie crust in 10-inch tart pan with removable bottom or 9-inch glass pie pan as directed on package for *one-crust filled pie.*

2. In large bowl, combine all filling ingredients; blend well. Pour into crust-lined pan.

3. Bake at 425°F. for 45 to 55 minutes or until knife inserted in center comes out clean. Cool 1 hour. Remove sides of pan.

4. Beat whipping cream in small bowl until soft peaks form. Add powdered sugar and orange peel; beat until stiff peaks form. Spoon or pipe over filling. Store in refrigerator.

NUTRITION INFORMATION PER SERVING: **Serving Size:** ⅛ of Recipe; Calories 440; Calories from Fat 210 **% Daily Value:** Total Fat 23g 35%; Saturated Fat 12g 60%; Cholesterol 115mg 38%; Sodium 360mg 15%; Total Carbohydrate 50g 17%; Dietary Fiber 2g 8%; Sugars 32g; Protein 7g; Vitamin A 260%; Vitamin C 6%; Calcium 20%; Iron 8% **Dietary Exchanges:** 2 Starch, 1½ Fruit, 4 Fat **OR** 3½ Carbohydrate, 4 Fat **Carbohydrate Choices:** 3

doughboy tip

If you're using a 9-inch pie pan for this elegant twist on the classic Thanksgiving pie, cover the edge of the pie crust with strips of foil after about 15 to 20 minutes of baking to prevent excessive browning.

cinnamon-apple crostata

PREP TIME: 20 minutes (Ready in 50 minutes)
YIELD: 8 servings

CRUST

1 Pillsbury® Refrigerated Pie Crust (from 15-oz. pkg.), softened as directed on package

FILLING

½ cup sugar

4 teaspoons cornstarch

2 teaspoons cinnamon

4 cups (4 medium) thinly sliced, peeled apples

1 teaspoon sugar

2 tablespoons chopped pecans or walnuts

1. Heat oven to 450°F. Remove pie crust from pouch. Unfold pie crust; place on ungreased cookie sheet. Press out fold lines.

2. In medium bowl, combine ½ cup sugar, cornstarch and cinnamon; mix well. Add apples; toss gently. Spoon apple mixture onto center of crust, spreading to within 2 inches of edges. Fold edges of crust over filling, ruffling decoratively. Brush crust edge with water. Sprinkle with 1 teaspoon sugar.

3. Bake at 450°F. for 15 minutes or until crust is golden brown. Sprinkle pecans over apple mixture. Bake an additional 5 to 15 minutes or until apples are tender.

NUTRITION INFORMATION PER SERVING: Serving Size: ⅛ of Recipe; Calories 210; Calories from Fat 65 **% Daily Value:** Total Fat 7g 11%; Saturated Fat 3g 15%; Cholesterol 5mg 2%; Sodium 110mg 5%; Total Carbohydrate 36g 12%; Dietary Fiber 1g 4%; Sugars 20g; Protein 1g; Vitamin A 0%; Vitamin C 2%; Calcium 0%; Iron 0% **Dietary Exchanges:** ½ Starch, 2 Fruit, 1 Fat **OR** 2½ Carbohydrate, 1 Fat **Carbohydrate Choices:** 2½

doughboy tip

A sprinkling of sugar before baking gives the crust a sparkly sweet finish. Try using coarse sugar (available in the supermarket baking aisle) instead of granulated sugar for an extra-special sugar twinkle.

ginger-lemon-blueberry pie

PREP TIME: 20 minutes (Ready in 3 hours 5 minutes)
YIELD: 8 servings

CRUST

1 (15-oz.) pkg. Pillsbury®
Refrigerated Pie Crusts, softened
as directed on package

6 teaspoons sugar

1 teaspoon half-and-half

FILLING

5 cups fresh blueberries

½ cup sugar

2 tablespoons chopped
crystallized ginger

2 tablespoons quick-cooking
tapioca

1 teaspoon grated lemon peel

1 tablespoon fresh lemon juice

1. Heat oven to 400°F. Remove 1 pie crust from pouch. Unfold crust; press out fold lines. Sprinkle top of crust with 1½ teaspoons of the sugar. With rolling pin, roll crust lightly to coat with sugar. Continue to prepare pie crust, sugared side up, as directed on package for *two-crust pie* using 9-inch glass pie pan.

2. In large bowl, combine all filling ingredients; mix well. Spoon into crust-lined pan. Top with second crust; seal edges and flute. Cut slits in several places in top crust. Brush top crust with half-and-half. Sprinkle with remaining 4½ teaspoons sugar.

3. Place foil or cookie sheet on oven rack below pie to catch any spills. Bake pie at 400°F. for 35 to 45 minutes or until crust is golden brown and filling is bubbly. If necessary, cover edge of crust with strips of foil after 15 to 20 minutes of baking to prevent excessive browning. Cool at least 2 hours before serving. Serve warm or cold.

NUTRITION INFORMATION PER SERVING: **Serving Size:** ⅛ of Recipe; Calories 370; Calories from Fat 130 **% Daily Value:** Total Fat 14g 22%; Saturated Fat 6g 30%; Cholesterol 15mg 5%; Sodium 210mg 9%; Total Carbohydrate 59g 20%; Dietary Fiber 3g 12%; Sugars 26g; Protein 2g; Vitamin A 0%; Vitamin C 15%; Calcium 0%; Iron 4% **Dietary Exchanges:** 1 Starch, 3 Fruit, 2½ Fat **OR** 4 Carbohydrate, 2½ Fat **Carbohydrate Choices:** 4

doughboy tip

Directions for this luscious pie specify cooling 2 hours before slicing, which gives the filling time to firm up a little for neater cutting. If you absolutely can't wait, serve the pie in shallow soup bowls and be ready with a large spoon to ladle up every last bit of the filling!

bananas foster tart

PREP TIME: 30 minutes (Ready in 1 hour)
YIELD: 10 servings

CRUST

1 Pillsbury® Refrigerated Pie Crust (from 15-oz. pkg.), softened as directed on package

FILLING

2 medium bananas, cut into ¼-inch-thick slices

4½ teaspoons light rum or ½ teaspoon rum extract plus 4 teaspoons water

2 teaspoons grated orange peel

⅔ cup chopped pecans

⅔ cup firmly packed brown sugar

¼ cup whipping cream

¼ cup butter

½ teaspoon vanilla

1. Heat oven to 450°F. Prepare pie crust as directed on package for *one-crust baked shell* using 9-inch tart pan with removable bottom or 9-inch glass pie pan. Press in bottom and up sides of pan; trim edges if necessary. Bake at 450°F. for 9 to 11 minutes or until lightly browned. Cool 5 minutes.

2. In small bowl, combine bananas and rum; toss to coat. Sprinkle orange peel evenly in bottom of baked shell. Arrange bananas in single layer over orange peel. Sprinkle with pecans.

3. In heavy medium saucepan, combine brown sugar, whipping cream and butter; cook and stir over medium-high heat for 2 to 3 minutes or until mixture comes to a boil. Cook an additional 2 to 4 minutes or until mixture has thickened and is deep golden brown, stirring constantly.

4. Remove saucepan from heat; stir in vanilla. Spoon warm filling over bananas and pecans. Cool 30 minutes before serving. Store in refrigerator.

NUTRITION INFORMATION PER SERVING: Serving Size: ⅒ of Recipe; Calories 300; Calories from Fat 160 **% Daily Value:** Total Fat 18g 28%; Saturated Fat 5g 25%; Cholesterol 10mg 3%; Sodium 150mg 6%; Total Carbohydrate 32g 11%; Dietary Fiber 1g 4%; Sugars 19g; Protein 2g; Vitamin A 6%; Vitamin C 2%; Calcium 2%; Iron 2% **Dietary Exchanges:** 1 Starch, 1 Fruit, 3½ Fat **OR** 2 Carbohydrate, 3½ Fat **Carbohydrate Choices:** 2

doughboy tip

The rum-spiked bananas in this nutty tart can stand up to a flavorful frozen accompaniment. Top each serving with a scoop of specialty ice cream, such as dulce de leche, cinnamon, pineapple-coconut or rum raisin.

french silk chocolate pie

PREP TIME: 50 minutes (Ready in 2 hours 50 minutes)
YIELD: 10 servings

CRUST

1 Pillsbury® Refrigerated Pie Crust (from 15-oz. pkg.), softened as directed on package

FILLING

3 oz. unsweetened chocolate, cut into pieces

1 cup butter, softened (do not use margarine)

1 cup sugar

½ teaspoon vanilla

4 pasteurized eggs or 1 cup refrigerated or frozen fat-free egg product, thawed

TOPPING

½ cup sweetened whipped cream

Chocolate curls, if desired

1. Heat oven to 450°F. Prepare pie crust as directed on package for *one-crust baked shell* using 9-inch glass pie pan. Bake at 450°F. for 9 to 11 minutes or until light golden brown. Cool 30 minutes or until completely cooled.

2. Melt chocolate in small saucepan over low heat; cool. Beat butter in small bowl until fluffy. Gradually add sugar, beating until light and fluffy. Add cooled chocolate and vanilla; blend well.

3. Add eggs 1 at a time, beating at high speed for 2 minutes after each addition. Beat until mixture is smooth and fluffy. Pour into cooled baked shell. Refrigerate at least 2 hours before serving. Top with whipped cream and chocolate curls. Store in refrigerator.

NUTRITION INFORMATION PER SERVING: Serving Size: ⅒ of Recipe; Calories 470; Calories from Fat 320 **% Daily Value:** Total Fat 35g 54%; Saturated Fat 20g 100%; Cholesterol 155mg 52%; Sodium 300mg 13%; Total Carbohydrate 34g 11%; Dietary Fiber 1g 4%; Sugars 22g; Protein 4g; Vitamin A 20%; Vitamin C 0%; Calcium 4%; Iron 6% **Dietary Exchanges:** 1 Starch, 1½ Fruit, 7 Fat **OR** 2½ Carbohydrate, 7 Fat **Carbohydrate Choices:** 2

doughboy tip

The original recipe for this ultra-rich pie used raw eggs in the uncooked filling. To ensure food safety, it now calls for either pasteurized eggs or fat-free egg product (both available in the dairy case of large supermarkets). For the smoothest, most silken texture, be sure to use butter and not margarine.

pecan pie ginger cheesecake

PREP TIME: 20 minutes (Ready in 4 hours 10 minutes)
YIELD: 12 servings

CRUST

1 Pillsbury® Refrigerated Pie Crust (from 15-oz. pkg.), softened as directed on package

FILLING

1 (8-oz.) pkg. cream cheese, softened

6 tablespoons sugar

½ teaspoon vanilla

1 egg

¼ cup finely chopped crystallized ginger

TOPPING

2 tablespoons all-purpose flour

¼ cup margarine or butter, melted

¾ cup firmly packed brown sugar

1 teaspoon vanilla

2 eggs

2 cups pecan halves or pieces

1. Heat oven to 350°F. Place pie crust in 9-inch glass pie pan or 9-inch deep-dish glass pie pan as directed on package for *one-crust filled pie.* In medium bowl, combine cream cheese, sugar, ½ teaspoon vanilla and 1 egg; beat at medium speed until smooth. Stir in ginger. Spoon and spread filling in crust-lined pan.

2. In large bowl, combine flour and margarine; mix well. Add brown sugar, 1 teaspoon vanilla and 2 eggs; mix well. Stir in pecans. Carefully spoon mixture evenly over filling.

3. Bake at 350°F. for 40 to 50 minutes or until center is set and crust is golden brown. Cool 1 hour. Refrigerate 2 hours or until thoroughly chilled. Store in refrigerator.

NUTRITION INFORMATION PER SERVING: Serving Size: ¹⁄₁₂ of Recipe; Calories 415; Calories from Fat 260 % Daily Value: Total Fat 29g 45%; Saturated Fat 8g 40%; Cholesterol 75mg 25%; Sodium 190mg 8%; Total Carbohydrate 33g 11%; Dietary Fiber 2g 8%; Sugars 22g; Protein 6g; Vitamin A 10%; Vitamin C 0%; Calcium 4%; Iron 6% Dietary Exchanges: 2 Starch, 6 Fat OR 2 Carbohydrate, 6 Fat Carbohydrate Choices: 2

doughboy tip

This decadent dessert is perfect for entertaining guests because it can be made ahead of time. Just before serving, top the pie with sweetened whipped cream and sprinkle with a little extra chopped crystallized ginger.

filled cookie tartlets **pictured on page 241**

PREP TIME: 1 hour
YIELD: 68 tartlets

TARTLET SHELLS

1 (18-oz.) pkg. Pillsbury®
Refrigerated Sugar Cookies

LEMON-PISTACHIO FILLING

1 cup lemon pie filling
(from 15.75-oz. can)

¼ cup chopped pistachios

CHOCOLATE-ORANGE FILLING

2 cups powdered sugar

¼ cup unsweetened cocoa

2 tablespoons margarine
or butter, softened

2 tablespoons grated orange peel

3 to 4 tablespoons orange juice

RASPBERRY CREAM FILLING

1 (3-oz.) pkg. cream cheese,
softened

1¼ cups powdered sugar

2 tablespoons seedless
raspberry jam

doughboy tip

To make 24 tartlets, use just
one-third of the cookie dough
and fill the baked tartlet shells
with one of the fillings. Wrap
and refrigerate the remaining
uncooked dough for later use.

1. Heat oven to 350°F. Lightly grease and sugar 24 miniature muffin cups or small tart pans. Cut ⅓ of dough into ¼-inch slices. Cut each slice in half. Roll each half into a ball; gently press in bottom and up sides of muffin cup, using floured fingers if dough is sticky. Using fork, prick dough several times.

2. Bake at 350°F. for 7 to 9 minutes or until light golden brown. Cool 5 minutes; remove from pans. Repeat with remaining dough to make 68 tartlet shells.

3. For lemon-pistachio filling, spoon or decoratively pipe 2 teaspoons pie filling into each tartlet shell. Sprinkle ½ teaspoon pistachios over top of each tart.

4. For chocolate-orange filling, in small bowl, combine powdered sugar, cocoa, margarine, orange peel and 2 tablespoons of the orange juice; beat well. Add remaining orange juice 1 tablespoon at a time, beating until filling is smooth and fluffy. Spoon or decoratively pipe 2 teaspoons filling into each tartlet shell. If desired, garnish with additional orange peel.

5. For raspberry cream filling, in small bowl, combine all raspberry cream filling ingredients; mix until light and fluffy. Spoon or decoratively pipe 2 teaspoons filling into each tartlet shell. If desired, garnish with mint leaves or chopped almonds.

6. Fill 23 tartlet shells with lemon-pistachio filling, 23 with chocolate-orange filling and 22 with raspberry cream filling. Cover loosely; store in refrigerator until serving time.

NUTRITION INFORMATION PER SERVING: Serving Size: 1 Tartlet with Lemon-Pistachio Filling; Calories 45; Calories from Fat 20 **% Daily Value:** Total Fat 2g 3%; Saturated Fat 0g 0%; Cholesterol 0mg 0%; Sodium 45mg 2%; Total Carbohydrate 6g 2%; Dietary Fiber 0g 0%; Sugars 4g; Protein 1g; Vitamin A 0%; Vitamin C 0%; Calcium 0%; Iron 0% **Dietary Exchanges:** ½ Fruit, ½ Fat **OR** ½ Carbohydrate, ½ Fat **Carbohydrate Choices:** ½

chocolate-caramel satin pie

PREP TIME: 25 minutes (Ready in 3 hours 20 minutes)
YIELD: 10 servings

CRUST

1 Pillsbury® Refrigerated Pie Crust (from 15-oz. pkg.), softened as directed on package

FILLING

24 vanilla caramels, unwrapped

⅓ cup water

⅔ cup firmly packed brown sugar

⅔ cup sour cream

1 teaspoon vanilla

2 eggs, beaten

½ cup chopped walnuts

½ oz. (⅓ cup) grated sweet cooking chocolate, reserving 2 tablespoons

TOPPING

1 cup vanilla milk chips

¼ cup milk

1 cup whipping cream

doughboy tip

Be sure to use vanilla milk chips, not almond bark or vanilla candy coating, in this recipe. The melted and cooled vanilla chip mixture will retain a creamy texture, making it easy to fold into the whipped cream; almond bark or candy coating will harden up.

1. Heat oven to 450°F. Prepare pie crust as directed on package for *one-crust baked shell* using 9-inch glass pie pan. Bake at 450°F. for 8 to 9 minutes or until lightly browned. Cool slightly.

2. Meanwhile, in heavy medium saucepan, combine caramels and water. Cook over low heat until caramels are melted and mixture is smooth, stirring occasionally. Remove from heat. Stir in brown sugar, sour cream, vanilla, eggs and walnuts; blend well.

3. Pour filling into cooled baked shell. Reduce oven temperature to 350°F. Immediately return pie to oven. Bake an additional 30 to 40 minutes or until edges of filling are set. Cool 15 minutes. Sprinkle chocolate over pie. Refrigerate about 2 hours or until firm.

4. In heavy small saucepan, combine vanilla milk chips and milk. Cook over low heat until chips are melted, stirring constantly. Remove from heat; cool. In small bowl, beat whipping cream until stiff peaks form. Fold in melted chip mixture. Spread over cooled filling. Sprinkle with 2 tablespoons reserved chocolate. Refrigerate until serving time. Store in refrigerator.

NUTRITION INFORMATION PER SERVING: **Serving Size:** ¹⁄₁₀ of Recipe; Calories 510; Calories from Fat 270 **% Daily Value:** Total Fat 30g 46%; Saturated Fat 15g 75%; Cholesterol 95mg 32%; Sodium 210mg 9%; Total Carbohydrate 53g 18%; Dietary Fiber 1g 4%; Sugars 37g; Protein 6g; Vitamin A 10%; Vitamin C 0%; Calcium 15%; Iron 4% **Dietary Exchanges:** 2 Starch, 1½ Fruit, 6 Fat OR 3½ Carbohydrate, 6 Fat **Carbohydrate Choices:** 3½

grands!® little pies

¾ cup all-purpose flour

½ cup firmly packed brown sugar

1 teaspoon cinnamon

½ cup margarine or butter

½ cup chopped nuts, if desired

1 (16.3-oz.) can Pillsbury® Grands!® Refrigerated Original Flaky Layers Biscuits

1 (21-oz.) can apple, blueberry or cherry pie filling

1 to 1½ cups whipping cream

Cinnamon-sugar blend, if desired

1. Heat oven to 350°F. In medium bowl, combine flour, brown sugar and cinnamon. With pastry blender or fork, cut in margarine until mixture resembles coarse crumbs. Stir in nuts.

2. Separate dough into 8 biscuits. Split each biscuit in half to make 16 rounds. With floured fingers, flatten each to form 4-inch round. Press each biscuit round in ungreased 2¾x1¼-inch muffin cup. Spoon 2 tablespoons pie filling into each biscuit-lined cup. Sprinkle each with about 2 tablespoons flour mixture. (Cups will be full.)

3. Bake at 350°F. for 15 to 22 minutes or until golden brown. Cool 5 minutes. Remove from muffin cups; place on wire rack. Cool 10 minutes.

4. Beat whipping cream in small bowl until stiff peaks form. Top each serving with whipped cream. Sprinkle with cinnamon-sugar blend. Store in refrigerator.

NUTRITION INFORMATION PER SERVING: Serving Size: 1/16 of Recipe; Calories 315; Calories from Fat - 155 **% Daily Value:** Total Fat 17g 26%; Saturated Fat 5g 25%; Cholesterol 15mg 5%; Sodium 440mg 18%; Total Carbohydrate 37g 12%; Dietary Fiber 1g 4%; Sugars 20g; Protein 4g; Vitamin A 10%; Vitamin C 0%; Calcium 2%; Iron 8% **Dietary Exchanges:** 1 Starch, 1½ Fruit, 3 Fat **OR** 2½ Carbohydrate, 3 Fat **Carbohydrate Choices:** 2½

doughboy tip

Did you know that you can purchase already-mixed cinnamon-sugar? You'll find it packaged in jars in the spice aisle of most supermarkets. If you prefer, you can make your own cinnamon-sugar blend by mixing ¼ cup granulated sugar with 1 to 2 teaspoons ground cinnamon.

sweet apple dumplings

PREP TIME: 20 minutes (Ready in 55 minutes)
YIELD: 8 servings

FILLING

4 cups coarsely chopped apples

½ cup sugar

½ teaspoon cinnamon

¼ teaspoon nutmeg

DUMPLINGS

1 (16.3-oz.) can Pillsbury®
Grands!® Refrigerated Original
Flaky Layers Biscuits

SYRUP

1½ cups water

2 tablespoons all-purpose flour

¾ cup firmly packed brown sugar

½ cup corn syrup

2 tablespoons margarine or butter

¼ teaspoon cinnamon

⅛ teaspoon nutmeg

1. Heat oven to 375°F. In medium bowl, combine all filling ingredients.

2. Separate dough into 8 biscuits. Press or roll each biscuit to form 6-inch round. Place ½ cup of filling on center of each biscuit; stretch dough around mixture, completely covering fruit. Pinch to seal. Place seam side down in ungreased 13x9-inch (3-quart) glass baking dish.

3. In medium saucepan, combine water and flour; blend thoroughly. Stir in all remaining syrup ingredients. Bring to a boil, stirring occasionally. Pour syrup evenly over dumplings, completely coating each.

4. Bake at 375°F. for 25 to 35 minutes or until deep golden brown. To serve, spoon warm dumplings and syrup into individual dessert dishes.

NUTRITION INFORMATION PER SERVING: **Serving Size:** ⅛ of Recipe; Calories 460; Calories from Fat 110 **% Daily Value:** Total Fat 12g 18%; Saturated Fat 3g 15%; Cholesterol 0mg 0%; Sodium 620mg 26%; Total Carbohydrate 84g 28%; Dietary Fiber 3g 12%; Sugars 51g; Protein 4g; Vitamin A 4%; Vitamin C 4%; Calcium 4%; Iron 10% **Dietary Exchanges:** 1½ Starch, 4 Fruit, 2½ Fat OR 5½ Carbohydrate, 2½ Fat **Carbohydrate Choices:** 5½

doughboy tip

Nutmeg adds a spicy touch to these sweet dumplings. For the freshest flavor, purchase whole rather than ground nutmeg. When you need ground nutmeg, grate it on a special small-holed nutmeg grater. Garnish the finished dumplings with just a tiny sprinkle of the freshly grated spice.

raspberry-sauced fresh pear dumplings

PREP TIME: 45 minutes
YIELD: 8 servings

DUMPLINGS

2 firm ripe pears, peeled, cored and coarsely chopped

¼ cup golden raisins

¼ cup firmly packed brown sugar

1 Pillsbury® Refrigerated Pie Crust (from 15-oz. pkg.), softened as directed on package

1 tablespoon milk

1 tablespoon sugar

SAUCE

1 (10-oz.) pkg. frozen raspberries in syrup, thawed

3 tablespoons sugar

1 teaspoon cornstarch

1. Heat oven to 425°F. In medium bowl, combine pears, raisins and brown sugar; mix well.

2. Remove pie crusts from pouches. Unfold crusts; cut each into quarters. Place about ⅓ cup pear mixture on each crust quarter. Brush crust edges lightly with water. Bring sides of each crust up to top of pears; press edges to seal, making 3 seams.

3. With pancake turner, carefully place dumplings seam side up in ungreased 15x10x1-inch baking pan. Brush with milk. Sprinkle with 1 tablespoon sugar.

4. Bake at 425°F. for 15 to 20 minutes or until deep golden brown. Cool on wire rack for 10 minutes.

5. Meanwhile, place raspberries in food processor bowl with metal blade or blender container; process until smooth. If desired, place strainer over small saucepan; pour raspberries into strainer. Press berries with back of spoon through strainer to remove seeds; discard seeds. Add 3 tablespoons sugar and cornstarch to raspberries in saucepan; cook over medium heat until mixture comes to a boil, stirring constantly. Place in freezer for 5 to 10 minutes to cool quickly.

6. To serve, spoon raspberry sauce evenly onto individual dessert plates. Top each with dumpling.

doughboy tip

After a taste of the raspberry sauce, you may want to double the recipe. It's absolutely delicious drizzled over ice cream, pound or angel food cake or chocolate brownies.

NUTRITION INFORMATION PER SERVING: Serving Size: ⅛ of Recipe; Calories 370; Calories from Fat 130 % Daily Value: Total Fat 14g 22%; Saturated Fat 6g 30%; Cholesterol 15mg 5%; Sodium 210mg 9%; Total Carbohydrate 59g 20%; Dietary Fiber 3g 12%; Sugars 30g; Protein 2g; Vitamin A 0%; Vitamin C 8%; Calcium 2%; Iron 6% Dietary Exchanges: ½ Starch, 3½ Fruit, 2½ Fat OR 4 Carbohydrate, 2½ Fat Carbohydrate Choices: 4

chocolate-peanut butter cookie pizza

PREP TIME: 15 minutes (Ready in 1 hour 30 minutes)
YIELD: 12 servings

CRUST

1 (18-oz.) pkg. Pillsbury®
Refrigerated Chocolate Chip
Cookies

TOPPING

1 (8-oz.) pkg. cream cheese,
softened

½ cup creamy peanut butter

1 cup powdered sugar

¼ cup milk

1 cup frozen whipped topping,
thawed

¾ cup hot fudge ice cream
topping

¼ cup chopped peanuts

1. Heat oven to 350°F. With floured fingers, press dough evenly in bottom of ungreased 12-inch pizza pan.

2. Bake at 350°F. for 15 to 20 minutes or until golden brown. Cool 30 minutes or until completely cooled.

3. Meanwhile, in medium bowl, combine cream cheese, peanut butter, powdered sugar and milk; beat until smooth. Fold in whipped topping.

4. Spread ½ cup of the fudge topping over cooled baked crust. Spread peanut butter mixture over top. Drizzle with remaining ¼ cup fudge topping. Sprinkle with peanuts. Refrigerate at least 30 minutes or until serving time. Cut into wedges or squares.

NUTRITION INFORMATION PER SERVING: **Serving Size:** ¹⁄₁₂ of Recipe; Calories 495; Calories from Fat 235 **% Daily Value:** Total Fat 26g 40%; Saturated Fat 9g 45%; Cholesterol 20mg 7%; Sodium 350mg 15%; Total Carbohydrate 55g 18%; Dietary Fiber 3g 12%; Sugars 34g; Protein 10g; Vitamin A 6%; Vitamin C 0%; Calcium 6%; Iron 10% **Dietary Exchanges:** 3 Starch, ½ Fruit, 5 Fat **OR** 3½ Carbohydrate, 5 Fat **Carbohydrate Choices:** 3½

doughboy tip

Prepare the cookie pizza crust up to a day ahead of time. After it's cooled, wrap it tightly in plastic and store at room temperature until you're ready to top it off.

rocky road cookie pizza

PREP TIME: 10 minutes (Ready in 1 hour 10 minutes)
YIELD: 12 servings

CRUST

1 (18-oz.) pkg. Pillsbury®
Refrigerated Sugar Cookies

TOPPING

½ cup salted peanuts

1 cup miniature marshmallows

1 (6-oz.) pkg. (1 cup) semisweet
chocolate chips

⅓ cup caramel ice cream topping

1. Heat oven to 350°F. Grease 12-inch pizza pan or spray with nonstick cooking spray. With floured fingers, press dough evenly in bottom of greased pan.

2. Bake at 350°F. for 15 to 20 minutes or until light golden brown.

3. Remove partially baked crust from oven. Sprinkle peanuts, marshmallows and chocolate chips evenly over crust. Drizzle with caramel topping.

4. Return to oven; bake an additional 8 to 10 minutes or until topping is melted. Cool 30 minutes or until completely cooled. Cut into wedges or squares.

NUTRITION INFORMATION PER SERVING: Serving Size: ¹⁄₁₂ of Recipe; Calories 325; Calories from Fat 115 % Daily Value: Total Fat 13g 20%; Saturated Fat 4g 20%; Cholesterol 0mg 0%; Sodium 210mg 9%; Total Carbohydrate 48g 16%; Dietary Fiber 2g 8%; Sugars 32g; Protein 4g; Vitamin A 0%; Vitamin C 0%; Calcium 2%; Iron 8% Dietary Exchanges: 1 Starch, 2 Fruit, 3 Fat OR 3 Carbohydrate, 3 Fat Carbohydrate Choices: 3

doughboy tip

Kids love this big cookie pizza. Top each serving of this chunky cookie with a scoop of vanilla or chocolate ice cream—or maybe even rocky road! Drizzle with a little chocolate syrup and you have cookie sundaes that no kid can resist!

most requested recipe
fanciful fruit pizza

PREP TIME: 20 minutes (Ready in 1 hour 50 minutes)
YIELD: 12 servings

CRUST

1 (18-oz.) pkg. Pillsbury®
Refrigerated Sugar Cookies

TOPPING

1 (8-oz.) pkg. cream cheese,
softened

⅓ cup sugar

½ teaspoon vanilla

1 cup fresh or canned peach
slices, drained,
cut into thinner slices

1 cup halved or quartered fresh
strawberries

1 cup fresh or frozen blueberries

½ cup orange marmalade, heated

1. Heat oven to 350°F. Cut cookie dough into slices as directed on package. Arrange slices in bottom of ungreased 15x10x1-inch baking pan or 14-inch pizza pan. Press dough evenly in pan, using floured fingers if necessary.

2. Bake at 350°F. for 11 to 16 minutes or until golden brown. Cool 15 minutes or until completely cooled.

3. In small bowl, combine cream cheese, sugar and vanilla; beat until fluffy. Spread mixture over cooled cookie crust. Arrange fruit over cream cheese.

4. Spoon or brush warm marmalade over fruit. Refrigerate at least 1 hour before serving. Cut into squares or wedges. Store in refrigerator.

NUTRITION INFORMATION PER SERVING: **Serving Size:** 1/12 of Recipe; Calories 320; Calories from Fat 130 **% Daily Value:** Total Fat 14g 22%; Saturated Fat 6g 30%; Cholesterol 30mg 10%; Sodium 220mg 9%; Total Carbohydrate 45g 15%; Dietary Fiber 1g 4%; Sugars 29g; Protein 4g; Vitamin A 8%; Vitamin C 15%; Calcium 2%; Iron 6% **Dietary Exchanges:** 1 Starch, 2 Fruit, 2½ Fat **OR** 3 Carbohydrate, 2½ Fat **Carbohydrate Choices:** 3

doughboy tip

For that special occasion, frame the perimeter of this picture-perfect pizza with peach slices, and arrange the strawberries in the center in a heart shape. Scatter the blueberries between the peach slices and the strawberry heart. Then go ahead and brush with the warm marmalade.

biscuit bread pudding

PREP TIME: 20 minutes (Ready in 1 hour 15 minutes)
YIELD: 6 servings

1 (16.3-oz.) can Pillsbury®
Grands!® Refrigerated
Buttermilk Biscuits

4 eggs

2¼ cups milk

⅓ cup sugar

⅓ cup raisins

1 teaspoon cinnamon

1 teaspoon vanilla

Caramel ice cream topping,
heated, if desired

1. Heat oven to 350°F. Bake biscuits as directed on can. Cool 20 minutes or until completely cooled.

2. Meanwhile, generously spray six 10-oz. custard cups or six 4½x1¼-inch disposable foil tart pans with nonstick cooking spray. Beat eggs in large bowl. Add milk, sugar, raisins, cinnamon and vanilla; mix well.

3. Cut baked biscuits into 1-inch cubes. Add to egg mixture; mix well. Let stand 5 minutes. Divide biscuit mixture evenly into greased custard cups.

4. Bake at 350°F. for 20 to 25 minutes or until set. With knife or metal spatula, loosen edges of each pudding; slide onto dessert plate. Drizzle with warm ice cream topping.

NUTRITION INFORMATION PER SERVING: **Serving Size:** ⅙ of Recipe; Calories 450; Calories from Fat 155 **% Daily Value:** Total Fat 17g 26%; Saturated Fat 5g 25%; Cholesterol 150mg 50%; Sodium 1,010mg 42%; Total Carbohydrate 60g 20%; Dietary Fiber 2g 8%; Sugars 32g; Protein 13g; Vitamin A 8%; Vitamin C 0%; Calcium 14%; Iron 14% **Dietary Exchanges:** 4 Starch, 3 Fat **OR** 4 Carbohydrate, 3 Fat **Carbohydrate Choices:** 4

doughboy tip

You can bake the biscuits up to 2 days before preparing the pudding. After they have cooled, store in a sealed plastic bag at room temperature. It won't matter if they're no longer as soft as fresh-baked—the milk and sugar mixture will work its magic either way.

strawberry-rhubarb crescent shortcakes

PREP TIME: 50 minutes
YIELD: 6 servings

TOPPING

2 cups chopped fresh or frozen rhubarb, thawed

1 cup sugar

¼ cup orange juice

2 cups sliced fresh or frozen strawberries, thawed

SHORTCAKES

4 teaspoons sugar

1 teaspoon grated orange peel

1 (8-oz.) can Pillsbury® Refrigerated Crescent Dinner Rolls

1. In medium saucepan, combine rhubarb, 1 cup sugar and orange juice; mix well. Cook over medium heat for 15 to 17 minutes or until rhubarb is very tender and mixture is thick and syrupy, stirring occasionally. Cool 25 minutes or until room temperature. Fold in strawberries.

2. Meanwhile, heat oven to 375°F. Grease cookie sheet. In small bowl, combine 3 teaspoons of the sugar and orange peel; mix well.

3. Unroll dough into 1 large rectangle. Press perforations to seal. Sprinkle dough with sugar-orange peel mixture. Starting at short side of rectangle, roll up dough; seal edges. Cut roll crosswise into 6 slices; place cut side down on greased cookie sheet. Sprinkle evenly with remaining teaspoon sugar.

4. Bake at 375°F. for 13 to 17 minutes or until golden brown. Cool 10 minutes.

5. To serve, place shortcakes in individual dessert bowls. Spoon topping over shortcakes. Store in refrigerator.

NUTRITION INFORMATION PER SERVING: **Serving Size:** ⅙ of Recipe; Calories 305; Calories from Fat 55 **% Daily Value:** Total Fat 6g 9%; Saturated Fat 1g 5%; Cholesterol 0mg 0%; Sodium 460mg 19%; Total Carbohydrate 60g 20%; Dietary Fiber 2g 8%; Sugars 46g; Protein 3g; Vitamin A 0%; Vitamin C 30%; Calcium 10%; Iron 8% **Dietary Exchanges:** 1 Starch, 3 Fruit, 1 Fat OR 4 Carbohydrate, 1 Fat **Carbohydrate Choices:** 4

doughboy tip

Garnish each shortcake with a little cloud of whipped cream topped with a juicy fresh strawberry and a sprinkle of freshly grated orange peel.

grands!® strawberry shortcakes

PREP TIME: 30 minutes
YIELD: 5 servings

SHORTCAKES

1 (10.2-oz.) can (5 biscuits)
Pillsbury® Grands!® Refrigerated
Buttermilk Biscuits

2 tablespoons margarine
or butter, melted

¼ cup sugar

STRAWBERRY MIXTURE

1½ pints (3 cups) fresh
strawberries, sliced

⅓ cup sugar

SWEETENED WHIPPED
CREAM

½ cup whipping cream

2 tablespoons sugar

¼ teaspoon vanilla, if desired

1. Heat oven to 375°F. Separate dough into 5 biscuits. Dip tops and sides of each biscuit in margarine; dip in ¼ cup sugar. Place on ungreased cookie sheet. Bake at 375°F. for 13 to 17 minutes or until golden brown. Cool 5 minutes.

2. Meanwhile, in medium bowl, combine strawberries and ⅓ cup sugar; mix well. Set aside.

3. In another small bowl, beat whipping cream and 2 tablespoons sugar until soft peaks form. Beat in vanilla.

4. To serve, split biscuits; place on individual dessert plates. Top with sweetened whipped cream and strawberry mixture.

NUTRITION INFORMATION PER SERVING: Serving Size: ⅕ of Recipe; Calories 460; Calories from Fat 200 **% Daily Value:** Total Fat 22g 34%; Saturated Fat 9g 45%; Cholesterol 35mg 12%; Sodium 660mg 28%; Total Carbohydrate 60g 20%; Dietary Fiber 3g 12%; Sugars 39g; Protein 5g; Vitamin A 10%; Vitamin C 90%; Calcium 6%; Iron 10% **Dietary Exchanges:** 2 Starch, 2 Fruit, 4 Fat **OR** 4 Carbohydrate, 4 Fat **Carbohydrate Choices:** 4

doughboy tip

Add a little extra pizzazz to the strawberry topping by tossing in a small amount of orange- or almond-flavored liqueur, or peach or apricot brandy.

pineapple upside-down biscuit cake

PREP TIME: 20 minutes (Ready in 50 minutes)
YIELD: 6 servings

3 tablespoons margarine or butter

½ cup firmly packed brown sugar

7 pineapple slices (from 20-oz. can), drained, reserving 1 tablespoon liquid

¼ cup sweetened dried cranberries

7 Pillsbury® Home Baked Classics™ Frozen Butter Tastin' Biscuits (from 25-oz. pkg.)

1 tablespoon sugar

1. Heat oven to 375°F. Place margarine in 9-inch round cake pan. Place in oven for 3 to 4 minutes or until melted. Remove pan from oven; tilt to coat with margarine. Sprinkle brown sugar over margarine. Place 1 pineapple slice in center of pan; place 6 slices around edges. Fill spaces with dried cranberries. Return to oven; bake 6 to 7 minutes or until pineapple is heated.

2. Remove pan from oven. Top each pineapple slice with 1 biscuit. Brush tops of biscuits with reserved pineapple liquid. Sprinkle with sugar.

3. Bake at 375°F. for 25 to 30 minutes or until biscuits are deep golden brown and no longer doughy in center. Immediately invert onto serving plate. Spread any topping remaining in pan over biscuits. Cut into wedges.

NUTRITION INFORMATION PER SERVING: Serving Size: ⅙ of Recipe; Calories 395; Calories from Fat 145 % Daily Value: Total Fat 16g 25%; Saturated Fat 4g 20%; Cholesterol 0mg 0%; Sodium 750mg 31%; Total Carbohydrate 59g 20%; Dietary Fiber 1g 4%; Sugars 35g; Protein 5g; Vitamin A 6%; Vitamin C 4%; Calcium 6%; Iron 10% Dietary Exchanges: 2 Starch, 2 Fruit, 3 Fat OR 4 Carbohydrate, 3 Fat Carbohydrate Choices: 4

doughboy tip
Raisins, chopped dried apricots, sweetened dried cherries or maraschino cherry halves can substitute for the sweetened dried cranberries in this recipe. Just before serving, embellish each wedge of cake with whipped cream.

blackberry-cherry cobbler

PREP TIME: 20 minutes (Ready in 50 minutes)
YIELD: 10 servings

FILLING

2 cups frozen blackberries

1 (21-oz.) can cherry fruit pie filling

¼ teaspoon cinnamon

TOPPING

1 (12-oz.) can Pillsbury®
Golden Layers™ Refrigerated
Flaky Biscuits

¼ cup sugar

½ teaspoon cinnamon

2 tablespoons margarine or butter,
melted

¼ cup sliced almonds

1 cup half-and-half, if desired

1. Heat oven to 350°F. In medium saucepan, combine all filling ingredients. Cook over medium heat until mixture is bubbly and hot, stirring occasionally. Pour into ungreased 12x8-inch (2-quart) glass baking dish.

2. Separate dough into 10 biscuits. In small bowl, combine sugar and ½ teaspoon cinnamon. Dip each biscuit in margarine; dip in sugar mixture. Arrange biscuits over hot fruit mixture around edge of baking dish. Sprinkle with almonds and any remaining sugar mixture.

3. Bake at 350°F. for 20 to 30 minutes or until biscuits are golden brown. Serve warm with half-and-half.

NUTRITION INFORMATION PER SERVING: Serving Size: ⅒ of Recipe; Calories 305; Calories from Fat 90 **% Daily Value:** Total Fat 10g 15%; Saturated Fat 0g 0%; Cholesterol 9mg 3%; Sodium 340mg 14%; Total Carbohydrate 50g 17%; Dietary Fiber 0g 0%; Sugars 0g; Protein 4g; Vitamin A 8%; Vitamin C 4%; Calcium 4%; Iron 6% **Dietary Exchanges:** 1 Starch, 2 Fruit, 2 Fat **OR** 3 Carbohydrate, 2 Fat **Carbohydrate Choices:** 3

doughboy tip

Blessed with extra berries? It's easy to freeze fresh blackberries for later. Just spread them in a single layer on a baking tray and freeze until firm. Transfer the frozen berries into a resealable food storage plastic bag for a taste of summer anytime.

crunchy coffee ice cream squares

PREP TIME: 20 minutes (Ready in 2 hours 50 minutes)
YIELD: 15 servings

½ (18-oz.) pkg. Pillsbury®
Refrigerated Sugar Cookies

¾ cup chocolate-coated toffee bits

1½ cups whipping cream

3 tablespoons powdered sugar

1 quart (4 cups) coffee ice cream,
slightly softened

1 (11.75-oz.) jar (1¼ cups) hot
fudge ice cream topping,
room temperature

1. Heat oven to 350°F. Cut cookie dough into ½-inch slices. Arrange slices in bottom of ungreased 13x9-inch pan. With floured fingers, press dough evenly in pan to form crust. Sprinkle ½ cup of the toffee bits over dough.

2. Bake at 350°F. for 10 to 15 minutes or until light golden brown. Cool 45 minutes or until completely cooled.

3. In small bowl, combine whipping cream and powdered sugar; beat until soft peaks form. Set aside.

4. Spoon ice cream over crust; spread evenly. Spoon ice cream topping by teaspoonfuls onto ice cream; carefully spread evenly. Carefully spread whipped cream over topping. Sprinkle with remaining ¼ cup toffee bits. Freeze 1½ hours or until firm. Cut into squares. Cover with foil; store in freezer.

NUTRITION INFORMATION PER SERVING: Serving Size: ⅟₁₅ of Recipe; Calories 360; Calories from Fat 170 % Daily Value: Total Fat 19g 29%; Saturated Fat 10g 50%; Cholesterol 40mg 13%; Sodium 200mg 8%; Total Carbohydrate 43g 14%; Dietary Fiber 1g 4%; Sugars 33g; Protein 4g; Vitamin A 10%; Vitamin C 0%; Calcium 10%; Iron 6% Dietary Exchanges: 1 Starch, 2 Fruit, 3¼ Fat OR 3 Carbohydrate, 3½ Fat Carbohydrate Choices: 3

doughboy tip

Instead of a quart of coffee ice cream, use a pint of coffee ice cream and then substitute a pint of another flavor. Tantalizing possibilities might include chocolate fudge, macadamia nut brittle, dulce de leche or vanilla bean.

cherry cheesecake dessert

PREP TIME: 15 minutes (Ready in 1 hour 15 minutes)
YIELD: 12 servings

FILLING

1 (8-oz.) pkg. cream cheese,
softened

¼ cup sugar

1 tablespoon all-purpose flour

½ teaspoon vanilla

1 egg

CRUST

1 (18-oz.) pkg. Pillsbury®
Refrigerated Sugar Cookies

TOPPING

2 (21-oz.) cans cherry pie filling

½ teaspoon almond extract

1. Heat oven to 375°F. In small bowl, combine all filling ingredients; beat until well blended.

2. With floured fingers, press dough evenly in bottom of ungreased 13x9-inch pan to form crust. Spoon and spread filling over crust.

3. Bake at 375°F. for 17 to 20 minutes or until edges begin to brown. Cool 40 minutes or until completely cooled.

4. Meanwhile, in medium bowl, combine topping ingredients; mix well. Spread over top. Cut into squares. Store in refrigerator.

NUTRITION INFORMATION PER SERVING: **Serving Size:** ¹⁄₁₂ of Recipe; Calories 380; Calories from Fat 130 **% Daily Value:** Total Fat 14g 22%; Saturated Fat 6g 30%; Cholesterol 45mg 15%; Sodium 240mg 10%; Total Carbohydrate 60g 20%; Dietary Fiber 1g 4%; Sugars 42g; Protein 4g; Vitamin A 10%; Vitamin C 4%; Calcium 4%; Iron 8% **Dietary Exchanges:** 1 Starch, 3 Fruit, 2½ Fat **OR** 4 Carbohydrate, 2½ Fat **Carbohydrate Choices:** 4

doughboy tip

This easy dessert is perfect for any occasion. To ensure a satiny smooth filling, make sure to start with softened cream cheese and beat the cream cheese-egg mixture with an electric mixer.

chewy chocolate-peanut butter bars

PREP TIME: 15 minutes (Ready in 2 hours 45 minutes)
YIELD: 36 bars

CRUST

1 (18-oz.) pkg. Pillsbury®
Refrigerated Sugar Cookies

FILLING

1 (14-oz.) can sweetened
condensed milk (not evaporated)

1 cup crunchy peanut butter

1 teaspoon vanilla

3 egg yolks

TOPPING

1 (12-oz.) pkg. (2 cups) semisweet
chocolate chips

1. Heat oven to 350°F. Spray 13x9-inch pan with nonstick cooking spray. With floured fingers, press dough evenly in bottom of sprayed pan to form crust. Bake at 350°F. for 10 minutes.

2. Meanwhile, in medium bowl, combine all filling ingredients; mix until smooth.

3. Remove partially baked crust from oven. Spoon and carefully spread filling evenly over crust.

4. Return to oven; bake an additional 20 to 25 minutes or until set.

5. Remove bars from oven. Sprinkle with chocolate chips; let stand 3 minutes to soften. Spread chocolate evenly over top. Cool 1½ hours or until completely cooled. Refrigerate 30 minutes to set chocolate. Cut into bars.

NUTRITION INFORMATION PER SERVING: **Serving Size:** 1 Bar; Calories 190; Calories from Fat 90 **% Daily Value:** Total Fat 10g 15%; Saturated Fat 4g 20%; Cholesterol 25mg 8%; Sodium 105mg 4%; Total Carbohydrate 22g 7%; Dietary Fiber 1g 4%; Sugars 16g; Protein 4g; Vitamin A 0%; Vitamin C 0%; Calcium 4%; Iron 4% **Dietary Exchanges:** 1 Starch, ½ Fruit, 2 Fat OR 1½ Carbohydrate, 2 Fat Carbohydrate Choices: 1½

doughboy tip

Instead of spreading the top of these chewy bars with chocolate chips, decorate with drizzles of melted chocolate chips and peanut butter chips. To do this easily, place the chocolate chips and peanut butter chips in separate resealable food storage plastic bags; seal the bags. Microwave each on HIGH for 30 to 60 seconds or until the chips are melted. Cut a tiny hole in the bottom corner of each bag and drizzle decoratively over bars.

easy caramel-pecan bars

PREP TIME: 25 minutes (Ready in 2 hours 15 minutes)
YIELD: 36 bars

1 (18-oz.) pkg. Pillsbury®
Refrigerated Sugar Cookies

¾ cup caramel ice cream topping

2 tablespoons all-purpose flour

1 cup pecan pieces

1 cup flaked coconut

1 (6-oz.) pkg. (1 cup) semisweet
chocolate chips

1. Heat oven to 350°F. Spray 13x9-inch pan with nonstick cooking spray. Cut cookie dough into ½-inch slices. Arrange slices in bottom of sprayed pan. With floured fingers, press dough evenly in pan to form crust.

2. Bake at 350°F. for 10 to 15 minutes or until light golden brown.

3. Meanwhile, in glass measuring cup, combine caramel topping and flour; blend until smooth.

4. Remove partially baked crust from oven. Sprinkle pecans, coconut and chocolate chips over crust. Drizzle with caramel mixture.

5. Return to oven; bake an additional 15 to 20 minutes or until topping is bubbly. Cool 1½ hours or until completely cooled. Cut into bars.

NUTRITION INFORMATION PER SERVING: **Serving Size:** 1 Bar; Calories 140; Calories from Fat 60 **% Daily Value:** Total Fat 7g 11%; Saturated Fat 2g 10%; Cholesterol 0mg 0%; Sodium 85mg 4%; Total Carbohydrate 18g 6%; Dietary Fiber 1g 4%; Sugars 11g; Protein 1g; Vitamin A 0%; Vitamin C 0%; Calcium 0%; Iron 4% **Dietary Exchanges:** ½ Starch, ½ Fruit, 1½ Fat **OR** 1 Carbohydrate, 1½ Fat **Carbohydrate Choices:** 1

doughboy tip

If the caramel ice cream topping is very thick and hard to pour, microwave it, uncovered, in the glass measuring cup for 10 to 15 seconds on HIGH or until it's slightly warmed and pourable.

cherry truffle bars

PREP TIME: 15 minutes (Ready in 1 hour 40 minutes)
YIELD: 48 bars

CRUST

1 (18-oz.) pkg. Pillsbury®
Refrigerated Sugar Cookies

FILLING

⅓ cup semisweet chocolate chips

¼ cup margarine or butter

¼ cup unsweetened cocoa

3 tablespoons light corn syrup

1 tablespoon milk

2 cups powdered sugar

1 (10-oz.) jar maraschino cherries,
drained, chopped
(about 30 cherries)

TOPPING

1 cup white vanilla chips

2 tablespoons shortening

doughboy tip

Garnish these decadent bars with chocolate curls or shavings. To make curls, let an unwrapped chocolate bar stand in a warm place (80 to 85°F.) for about 15 minutes to soften. With a vegetable peeler or sharp paring knife, shave the chocolate carefully across the surface to remove thin strips of chocolate. A citrus zester, available at kitchen specialty stores, can cut thin, decorative shreds of chocolate.

1. Heat oven to 350°F. With floured fingers, press dough evenly in bottom of ungreased 13x9-inch pan to form crust.

2. Bake at 350°F. for 12 to 16 minutes or until light golden brown. Cool 45 minutes or until completely cooled.

3. In medium microwave-safe bowl, combine chocolate chips and margarine. Microwave on HIGH for 1 to 2 minutes or until melted and smooth, stirring every 30 seconds. Add cocoa, corn syrup and milk; blend well. Add powdered sugar; mix until smooth. Press filling over cooled crust. Top with cherries; gently press into filling.

4. In small microwave-safe bowl, combine vanilla chips and shortening. Microwave on HIGH for 1 to 2 minutes or until melted and smooth, stirring every 30 seconds. Spoon and spread over filling. Refrigerate 20 minutes or until set. Cut into bars.

NUTRITION INFORMATION PER SERVING: **Serving Size:** 1 Bar, Calories 120; Calories from Fat 45 **% Daily Value:** Total Fat 5g 8%; Saturated Fat 2g 10%; Cholesterol 0mg 0%; Sodium 55mg 2%; Total Carbohydrate 18g 6%; Dietary Fiber 0g 0%; Sugars 15g; Protein 1g; Vitamin A 0%; Vitamin C 0%; Calcium 2%; Iron 2% **Dietary Exchanges:** 1 Fruit, 1 Fat OR 1 Carbohydrate, 1 Fat **Carbohydrate Choices:** 1

chocolate-glazed peppermint cookies

PREP TIME: 45 minutes
YIELD: 3 dozen cookies

COOKIES

1 (18-oz.) pkg. Pillsbury®
Refrigerated Sugar Cookies,
well chilled

3 tablespoons finely crushed
hard peppermint candy

GLAZE

½ cup semisweet chocolate chips

1½ teaspoons shortening

1. Heat oven to 350°F. Cut cookie dough into ¼-inch slices. Place slices 2 inches apart on ungreased cookie sheets. Sprinkle ¼ teaspoon peppermint candy in center of each slice.

2. Bake at 350°F. for 7 to 11 minutes or until light golden brown. Cool 1 minute; remove from cookie sheets. Cool 15 minutes or until completely cooled.

3. In small saucepan, melt chocolate chips and shortening over low heat, stirring constantly. Drizzle glaze over cooled cookies. Let stand until set.

NUTRITION INFORMATION PER SERVING: **Serving Size:** 1 Cookie; Calories 80; Calories from Fat 25 **% Daily Value:** Total Fat 3g 5%; Saturated Fat 1g 5%; Cholesterol 2mg 1%; Sodium 65mg 3%; Total Carbohydrate 12g 4%; Dietary Fiber 0g 0%; Sugars 0g; Protein 1g; Vitamin A 0%; Vitamin C 0%; Calcium 0%; Iron 2% **Dietary Exchanges:** ½ Starch, ½ Fat **OR** ½ Carbohydrate, ½ Fat **Carbohydrate Choices:** 1

doughboy tip

The hard peppermint candy is available in different colors such as red, green, blue and yellow. Crush a few of each color to make a colorful cookie tray.

holiday pinwheel cookies

1 (18 oz.) pkg. Pillsbury®
Refrigerated Sugar Cookies

½ cup all-purpose flour

3 tablespoons red decorator sugar

3 tablespoons green decorator
sugar

PREP TIME: 1 hour (Ready in 2 hours)
YIELD: 32 cookies

1. Divide dough in half. Sprinkle ¼ cup of the flour onto work surface. Roll out half of dough to 12x7-inch rectangle. Repeat with remaining half of dough and ¼ cup flour. Sprinkle 1 rectangle evenly with red sugar; sprinkle green sugar evenly over second rectangle.

2. Starting with short side, roll up each rectangle jelly-roll fashion. Wrap rolls in waxed paper; refrigerate at least 1 hour for easier handling.

3. Heat oven to 350°F. Cut each roll into 16 slices. Place slices 1 inch apart on ungreased cookie sheets. Bake at 350°F. for 7 to 9 minutes or until edges are light golden brown. Cool 1 minute; remove from cookie sheets.

NUTRITION INFORMATION PER SERVING: Serving Size: 1 Cookie; Calories 90; Calories from Fat 25 **% Daily Value:** Total Fat 3g 5%; Saturated Fat 1g 5%; Cholesterol 0mg 0%; Sodium 55mg 2%; Total Carbohydrate 14g 5%; Dietary Fiber 0g 0%; Sugars 7g; Protein 1g; Vitamin A 0%; Vitamin C 0%; Calcium 0%; Iron 2% **Dietary Exchanges:** ½ Starch, ½ Fruit, ½ Fat **OR** 1 Carbohydrate, ½ Fat **Carbohydrate Choices:** 1

doughboy tip

These easy cookies are great for any cookie platter or cookie exchange. They are especially nice as a gift. Layer them in a decorative tin with colored tissue paper, then include the recipe. What a welcome gift for anyone on your list!

luscious lemon bars

PREP TIME: 15 minutes (Ready in 1 hour 35 minutes)
YIELD: 36 bars

CRUST

1 (18-oz.) pkg. Pillsbury®
Refrigerated Sugar Cookies

FILLING

4 eggs, slightly beaten

1½ cups sugar

¼ cup all-purpose flour

1 teaspoon baking powder

¼ cup lemon juice

GARNISH

1 to 2 tablespoons powdered
sugar

1. Heat oven to 350°F. Cut cookie dough into slices as directed on package. Arrange slices in bottom of ungreased 13x9-inch pan. With lightly floured fingers, press dough evenly in pan to form crust.

2. Bake at 350°F. for 15 to 20 minutes or until light golden brown.

3. Meanwhile, in large bowl, combine eggs, sugar, flour and baking powder; blend well. Stir in lemon juice.

4. Remove partially baked crust from oven. Pour egg mixture over warm crust.

5. Return to oven; bake an additional 20 to 30 minutes or until top is light golden brown. Cool 30 minutes or until completely cooled. Sprinkle with powdered sugar. Cut into bars.

NUTRITION INFORMATION PER SERVING: **Serving Size:** 1 Bar; Calories 100; Calories from Fat 25 **% Daily Value:** Total Fat 3g 5%; Saturated Fat 1g 5%; Cholesterol 25mg 8%; Sodium 70mg 3%; Total Carbohydrate 18g 6%; Dietary Fiber 0g 0%; Sugars 13g; Protein 1g; Vitamin A 0%; Vitamin C 0%; Calcium 0%; Iron 2% **Dietary Exchanges:** 1 Starch, ½ Fat OR 1 Carbohydrate, ½ Fat **Carbohydrate Choices:** 1

doughboy tip

Make sure to wait until the bars have completely cooled before sprinkling them with powdered sugar. Otherwise, the sugar will simply melt into the warm lemon topping and disappear.

orangeburst cookie bars

PREP TIME: 15 minutes (Ready in 1 hour 40 minutes)
YIELD: 24 bars

CRUST

1 (18-oz.) pkg. Pillsbury®
Refrigerated Sugar Cookies

½ cup chopped hazelnuts
(filberts) or almonds

FILLING

½ cup sugar

5 teaspoons all-purpose flour

⅓ cup light corn syrup

1 tablespoon grated orange peel

¼ cup orange juice

1 tablespoon margarine
or butter, melted

1 egg

½ cup chopped hazelnuts
(filberts) or almonds

GARNISH

1 to 3 tablespoons powdered
sugar, if desired

1. Heat oven to 375°F. Cut cookie dough into ½-inch slices. Arrange slices in bottom of ungreased 13x9-inch pan. With floured fingers, press dough evenly in pan to form crust. Sprinkle with ½ cup hazelnuts; press firmly into dough. Bake at 375°F. for 10 to 12 minutes or until dough is puffed.

2. Meanwhile, in medium bowl, combine sugar and flour; mix well. Add corn syrup, orange peel, orange juice, margarine and egg; blend until smooth with wire whisk. Stir in ½ cup hazelnuts.

3. Remove partially baked crust from oven. Reduce oven temperature to 350°F. Carefully pour filling over crust.

4. Return to oven; bake at 350°F. for 18 to 23 minutes or until edges are golden brown and filling is set. Cool 10 minutes. Sprinkle with powdered sugar. Cool 50 minutes or until completely cooled. Cut into bars.

NUTRITION INFORMATION PER SERVING: **Serving Size:** 1 Bar; Calories 165; Calories from Fat 65 **% Daily Value:** Total Fat 7g 11%; Saturated Fat 1g 5%; Cholesterol 10mg 3%, Sodium 85mg 4%; Total Carbohydrate 24g 8%; Dietary Fiber 1g 4%; Sugars 16g; Protein 2g; Vitamin A 0%; Vitamin C 0%; Calcium 2%; Iron 4% **Dietary Exchanges:** 1 Starch, ½ Fruit, 1 Fat OR 1½ Carbohydrate, 1 Fat Carbohydrate Choices: 1½

doughboy tip

Instead of sprinkling the bars with powdered sugar, make a quick glaze by blending orange juice or water into a small amount of powdered sugar. Drizzle the citrus glaze over the cooled bars. Sprinkle with additional chopped hazelnuts.

chocolate chip, oats 'n caramel cookie squares

PREP TIME: 35 minutes (Ready in 2 hours 30 minutes)
YIELD: 16 squares

1 (18-oz.) pkg. Pillsbury®
Refrigerated Chocolate
Chip Cookies

1 cup quick-cooking rolled oats

Dash salt, if desired

5 tablespoons all-purpose flour

2⁄3 cup caramel ice cream topping

1 teaspoon vanilla

3⁄4 cup chopped walnuts

1 (6-oz.) pkg. (1 cup) semisweet
chocolate chips

1. Heat oven to 350°F. Break up cookie dough into large bowl. Add oats and salt; mix well. Reserve 1⁄2 cup cookie dough mixture for topping. Press remaining mixture in bottom of ungreased 9-inch square pan. Bake at 350°F. for 10 to 12 minutes or until cookie dough puffs and appears dry.

2. Meanwhile, in small bowl, combine flour, caramel topping and vanilla; blend well.

3. Remove partially baked crust from oven. Sprinkle walnuts and chocolate chips evenly over crust. Drizzle evenly with caramel mixture. Crumble reserved 1⁄2 cup cookie dough mixture over caramel.

4. Return to oven; bake an additional 20 to 25 minutes or until golden brown. Cool 10 minutes. Run knife around sides of pan to loosen. Cool 1 1⁄2 hours or until completely cooled. Cut into squares.

NUTRITION INFORMATION PER SERVING: **Serving Size:** 1 Square; Calories 320; Calories from Fat 140 **% Daily Value:** Total Fat 15g 23%; Saturated Fat 5g 25%; Cholesterol 5mg 2%; Sodium 160mg 7%; Total Carbohydrate 41g 14%; Dietary Fiber 2g 8%; Sugars 25g; Protein 4g; Vitamin A 0%; Vitamin C 0%; Calcium 2%; Iron 8% **Dietary Exchanges:** 1 Starch, 1 1⁄2 Fruit, 3 Fat OR 2 1⁄2 Carbohydrate, 3 Fat **Carbohydrate Choices:** 3

doughboy tip

We love these squares just as they are, but for a truly indulgent dessert use the cookie squares as the base for a rich sundae. Top each square with a scoop of ice cream, a generous drizzle of hot fudge or caramel ice cream topping and a dollop of whipped cream.

choco-toffee bars

PREP TIME: 20 minutes (Ready in 3 hours)
YIELD: 36 bars

CRUST

1 (18-oz.) pkg. Pillsbury®
Refrigerated Chocolate Chip
Cookies

FILLING

1 cup toffee bits

¼ cup firmly packed brown sugar

1 teaspoon vanilla

1 (3-oz.) pkg. cream cheese,
softened

1 egg

⅔ cup butterscotch chips, melted

TOPPING

½ cup miniature semisweet
chocolate chips

1. Heat oven to 350°F. Cut cookie dough into ½-inch slices. Arrange slices in bottom of ungreased 13x9-inch pan. With floured fingers, press dough evenly in pan to form crust. Sprinkle with ½ cup of the toffee bits. Bake at 350°F. for 16 to 18 minutes or until golden brown.

2. Meanwhile, in small bowl, combine brown sugar, vanilla, cream cheese and egg; beat at medium speed until blended. Add melted butterscotch chips; blend well.

3. Remove partially baked crust from oven. With spatula, gently press edges of crust down to make surface flat. Spoon and spread filling over crust. Sprinkle with remaining ½ cup toffee bits and chocolate chips.

4. Return to oven; bake an additional 20 to 25 minutes or until edges are deep golden brown and center is set. Cool 10 minutes. Run knife around sides of pan to loosen. Cool 2 hours or until completely cooled. Cut into bars. Store in refrigerator.

NUTRITION INFORMATION PER SERVING: **Serving Size:** 1 Bar; Calories 140; Calories from Fat 60 **% Daily Value:** Total Fat 7g 11%; Saturated Fat 4g 20%; Cholesterol 15mg 5%; Sodium 90mg 4%; Total Carbohydrate 17g 6%; Dietary Fiber 0g 0%; Sugars 14g; Protein 1g; Vitamin A 0%; Vitamin C 0%; Calcium 0%; Iron 2% **Dietary Exchanges:** ½ Starch, ½ Fruit, 1½ Fat **OR** 1 Carbohydrate, 1½ Fat **Carbohydrate Choices:** 1

doughboy tip

Punch up the crunch in these rich, chewy bars by sprinkling ½ cup chopped walnuts or peanuts over the top along with the chocolate chips and toffee bits.

chocolate chip-coconut cheesecake bars

PREP TIME: 10 minutes (Ready in 2 hours 20 minutes)
YIELD: 16 bars

1 (8-oz.) pkg. cream cheese, softened

½ cup sugar

1 egg

½ cup coconut

1 (18-oz.) pkg. Pillsbury® Refrigerated Chocolate Chip Cookies

1. Heat oven to 350°F. In small bowl, combine cream cheese, sugar and egg; beat until smooth. Stir in coconut.

2. Press half of dough in bottom of ungreased 9 or 8-inch square pan. Spread cream cheese mixture over dough. Crumble and sprinkle remaining half of cookie dough over cream cheese mixture.

3. Bake at 350°F. for 35 to 40 minutes or until golden brown and firm to the touch. Cool 30 minutes. Refrigerate at least 1 hour or until chilled. Cut into bars. Store in refrigerator.

NUTRITION INFORMATION PER SERVING: **Serving Size:** 1 Bar; Calories 240; Calories from Fat 120 **% Daily Value:** Total Fat 13g 20%; Saturated Fat 6g 30%; Cholesterol 35mg 12%; Sodium 150mg 6%; Total Carbohydrate 27g 9%; Dietary Fiber 1g 4%; Sugars 19g; Protein 3g; Vitamin A 4%; Vitamin C 0%; Calcium 0%; Iron 6% **Dietary Exchanges:** 1 Starch, 1 Fruit, 2½ Fat **OR** 2 Carbohydrate, 2½ Fat **Carbohydrate Choices:** 2

doughboy tip

Baking this recipe in an 8-inch pan will require slightly longer cooking and chilling times than using a 9-inch pan. In the larger pan, the dough and topping are spread slightly thinner so it bakes and cools more quickly.

mexican chocolate-filled cornmeal cookies

PREP TIME: 55 minutes
YIELD: 20 cookies

COOKIES

1 (18-oz.) pkg. Pillsbury®
Refrigerated Sugar Cookies

¼ cup yellow cornmeal

20 dark chocolate candy
miniatures (from 11-oz. pkg.),
unwrapped

GLAZE

⅓ cup cinnamon chips

1 teaspoon shortening

Dash ground red pepper
(cayenne), if desired

1. Heat oven to 375°F. Spray cookie sheets with nonstick cooking spray. Break up cookie dough into large bowl. Add cornmeal; mix well. Shape rounded tablespoon of dough around each candy, covering completely. Place 2 inches apart on sprayed cookie sheets.

2. Bake at 375°F. for 9 to 12 minutes or until edges are light golden brown. Cool 1 minute. Remove from cookie sheets; place on wire rack. Cool 10 minutes or until completely cooled.

3. In small microwave-safe bowl, combine chips and shortening. Microwave on HIGH for 30 to 45 seconds, stirring every 15 seconds until smooth. Stir in ground red pepper. Drizzle glaze over cookies.

NUTRITION INFORMATION PER SERVING: **Serving Size:** 1 Cookie; Calóries 180; Calories from Fat 70 **% Daily Value:** Total Fat 8g 12%; Saturated Fat 3g 15%; Cholesterol 5mg 2%; Sodium 100mg 4%; Total Carbohydrate 24g 8%; Dietary Fiber 1g 4%; Sugars 14g; Protein 2g; Vitamin A 0%; Vitamin C 0%; Calcium 0%; Iron 4% **Dietary Exchanges:** ½ Starch, 1 Fruit, 1½ Fat **OR** 1½ Carbohydrate, 1½ Fat **Carbohydrate Choices:** 1½

doughboy tip

These delightful cookies have a surprise in the glaze—a dash of ground red pepper! This touch of spice just brightens the flavor and hints at hotness. In a pinch, a dash of cinnamon can be substituted for the pepper.

milk chocolate-butterscotch café cookies

PREP TIME: 20 minutes (Ready in 40 minutes)
YIELD: 9 cookies

1 (18-oz.) pkg. Pillsbury®
Refrigerated Sugar Cookies

⅓ cup firmly packed brown sugar

1 teaspoon vanilla

¾ cup old-fashioned rolled oats

½ cup butterscotch chips

2 (1.55-oz.) milk chocolate candy
bars, unwrapped, finely chopped

1. Heat oven to 350°F. Spray 1 large or 2 small cookie sheets with nonstick cooking spray. Break up cookie dough into large bowl. Add brown sugar and vanilla; mix well. Add oats, chips and chocolate; mix well. (Dough will be stiff.)

2. Drop dough by rounded ¼ cupfuls 2 inches apart onto sprayed cookie sheet. Flatten to ½-inch thickness.

3. Bake at 350°F. for 13 to 18 minutes or until cookies are slightly puffed and edges are golden brown. Cool 1 minute; remove from cookie sheet.

NUTRITION INFORMATION PER SERVING: **Serving Size:** 1 Cookie; Calories 400; Calories from Fat 140 **% Daily Value:** Total Fat 16g 25%; Saturated Fat 7g 35%; Cholesterol 15mg 5%; Sodium 220mg 9%; Total Carbohydrate 59g 20%; Dietary Fiber 2g 8%; Sugars 38g; Protein 4g; Vitamin A 0%; Vitamin C 0%; Calcium 4%; Iron 10% **Dietary Exchanges:** 1½ Starch, 2½ Fruit, 3 Fat **OR** 4 Carbohydrate, 3 Fat **Carbohydrate Choices:** 4

doughboy tip

Old-fashioned rolled oats make these cookies pleasantly chewy. Although quick-cooking (not instant) oats can often be substituted in cookies, the finished cookies will have a softer texture and won't be as chewy as ones made with the old-fashioned variety.

lemon-coconut thumbprint cookies

PREP TIME: 15 minutes (Ready in 1 hour)
YIELD: 3 dozen cookies

1 (18-oz.) pkg. Pillsbury®
Refrigerated Sugar Cookies

1 cup coconut

½ cup lemon curd
(from 11¼-oz. jar)

2 oz. vanilla-flavored candy
coating, chopped, or
⅓ cup white vanilla chips

1. Heat oven to 350°F. Break up cookie dough into large bowl. Add coconut; mix well. Shape dough into 1-inch balls. Place 2 inches apart on ungreased cookie sheets.

2. With thumb or handle of wooden spoon, make indentation in center of each cookie. Spoon about ½ teaspoon lemon curd into each indentation.

3. Bake at 350°F. for 10 to 13 minutes or until edges are light golden brown. Immediately remove from cookie sheets. Cool 5 minutes.

4. Microwave candy coating in small microwave-safe bowl on MEDIUM for 2 minutes. Stir well; drizzle over cookies.

NUTRITION INFORMATION PER SERVING: Serving Size: 1 Cookie; Calories 90; Calories from Fat 35 **% Daily Value:** Total Fat 4g 6%; Saturated Fat 1g 5%; Cholesterol 0mg 0%; Sodium 65mg 3%; Total Carbohydrate 13g 4%; Dietary Fiber 0g 0%; Sugars 9g; Protein 1g; Vitamin A 0%; Vitamin C 0%; Calcium 0%; Iron 0% **Dietary Exchanges:** ½ Starch, ½ Fruit, ½ Fat **OR** 1 Carbohydrate, ½ Fat **Carbohydrate Choices:** 1

doughboy tip

Be on the lookout for lemon curd—it's a wonderful concoction of lemon, butter, sugar and eggs. You'll most likely find the citrus curd in your supermarket next to the jams and jellies. If you don't have any luck, you can substitute lemon pie filling or a favorite jam.

candy bar cookie pops

PREP TIME: 45 minutes (Ready in 1 hour 45 minutes)
YIELD: 24 cookies

24 flat wooden sticks
with round ends

24 bite-size any flavor candy
bars, unwrapped

1 (18-oz.) pkg. Pillsbury®
Refrigerated Sugar Cookies

1. Heat oven to 350°F. Insert wooden stick into each candy bar.

2. Cut cookie dough into 24 pieces. Roll each piece into ball; flatten each ball slightly in hand. Place candy bar in center of flattened dough. Wrap dough around candy, covering and sealing completely. Place 2 inches apart on ungreased cookie sheets, overlapping wooden sticks as needed.

3. Bake at 350°F. for 10 to 12 minutes or until edges are light golden brown. Cool on cookie sheets for 5 minutes. Remove from cookie sheets; place on wire racks. Cool 1 hour or until completely cooled. (Do not pick up cookie pops using stick until completely cooled.)

NUTRITION INFORMATION PER SERVING: **Serving Size:** 1 Cookie; Calories 130; Calories from Fat 45 **% Daily Value:** Total Fat 5g 8%; Saturated Fat 2g 10%; Cholesterol 5mg 2%; Sodium 95mg 4%; Total Carbohydrate 19g 6%; Dietary Fiber 0g 0%; Sugars 12g; Protein 1g; Vitamin A 0%; Vitamin C 0%; Calcium 0%; Iron 2% **Dietary Exchanges:** ½ Starch, 1 Fruit, 1 Fat **OR** 1½ Carbohydrate, 1 Fat **Carbohydrate Choices:** 1

doughboy tip

Planning a birthday party? These cookies make great party favors. Wrap the cookies individually in plastic wrap or colored cellophane, and tie with colorful, curly ribbon.

giant oatmeal-candy cookies

PREP TIME: 1 hour
YIELD: 12 cookies

1 (18-oz.) pkg. Pillsbury®
Refrigerated Sugar Cookies

1 cup miniature candy-coated
chocolate baking bits

½ cup quick-cooking rolled oats

½ cup raisins

2 teaspoons quick-cooking
rolled oats

1. Heat oven to 325°F. Break up cookie dough into large bowl. Add baking bits, ½ cups oats and raisins; mix well.

2. Shape cookie dough into 12 (2-inch) balls. Place 3 inches apart on ungreased large cookie sheets. Flatten each ball to form 3-inch round. Sprinkle with 2 teaspoons oats.

3. Bake at 325°F. for 14 to 19 minutes or until set and dry in center. Cool 2 minutes; remove from cookie sheets.

NUTRITION INFORMATION PER SERVING: **Serving Size:** 1 Cookie; Calories 300; Calories from Fat 110 **% Daily Value:** Total Fat 12g 18%; Saturated Fat 5g 25%; Cholesterol 15mg 5%; Sodium 160mg 7%; Total Carbohydrate 45g 15%; Dietary Fiber 2g 8%; Sugars 29g; Protein 3g; Vitamin A 0%; Vitamin C 0%; Calcium 4%; Iron 8% **Dietary Exchanges:** 1 Starch, 2 Fruit, 2½ Fat **OR** 3 Carbohydrate, 2½ Fat **Carbohydrate Choices:** 3

doughboy tip
These large colorful treats are great for folks who like cookies packed with plenty of good "stuff." If you wish, you can replace some or all of the baking bits or raisins with other chopped dried fruit, chocolate or peanut butter baking chips or your favorite chopped nuts.

macaroon-topped sugar cookies

PREP TIME: 45 minutes (Ready in 1 hour 15 minutes)
YIELD: 32 cookies

1 (18-oz.) pkg. Pillsbury®
Retrigerated Sugar Cookies

1½ cups coconut

⅓ cup sugar

1 tablespoon all-purpose flour

¼ teaspoon almond extract

1 egg white

16 red or green maraschino
cherries, halved, drained on
paper towel

1. Place cookie dough in freezer for 30 minutes.

2. Heat oven to 350°F. In medium bowl, combine coconut, sugar, flour, almond extract and egg white; mix well.

3. Cut chilled cookie dough into 32 slices. Place 2 inches apart on ungreased cookie sheets. Spoon 1 rounded teaspoon coconut mixture onto each slice, spreading slightly. Press 1 cherry half cut side down on each.

4. Bake at 350°F. for 12 to 15 minutes or until edges are light golden brown. Cool 1 minute; remove from cookie sheets.

NUTRITION INFORMATION PER SERVING: Serving Size: 1 Cookie; Calories 100; Calories from Fat 35 % Daily Value: Total Fat 4g 6%; Saturated Fat 2g 10%; Cholesterol 4mg 1%; Sodium 65mg 3%; Total Carbohydrate 14g 5%; Dietary Fiber 0g 0%; Sugars 9g; Protein 1g; Vitamin A 0%; Vitamin C 0%; Calcium 0%; Iron 2% Dietary Exchanges: ½ Starch, ½ Fruit, ½ Fat OR 1 Carbohydrate, ½ Fat Carbohydrate Choices: 1

doughboy tip

If the cookies seem to stick to the pan, pop the whole sheet back in the hot oven for a minute or two. The heat should soften the cookies slightly, making removal easier.

linzer bars

PREP TIME: 25 minutes (Ready in 1 hour 40 minutes)
YIELD: 16 bars

CRUST

½ (18-oz.) pkg. Pillsbury®
Refrigerated Sugar Cookies

TOPPING

½ cup seedless raspberry
preserves

1 teaspoon cornstarch

¼ cup sliced almonds

1. Heat oven to 350°F. Break up cookie dough into ungreased 8-inch square pan. With floured fingers, press dough evenly in bottom of pan to form crust.

2. Bake at 350°F. for 12 to 17 minutes or until edges are golden brown.

3. Meanwhile, in small saucepan, combine preserves and cornstarch; mix well. Cook over medium heat just until mixture comes to a boil, stirring constantly.

4. Remove partially baked crust from oven. Pour preserves mixture evenly over crust; spread to within ¼ inch of edges. Sprinkle with almonds.

5. Return to oven; bake an additional 10 minutes. Cool 1 hour or until completely cooled. Cut into bars.

NUTRITION INFORMATION PER SERVING: **Serving Size:** 1 Bar; Calories 100; Calories from Fat 25 **% Daily Value:** Total Fat 3g 5%; Saturated Fat 1g 5%; Cholesterol 4mg 1%; Sodium 60mg 3%; Total Carbohydrate 16g 5%; Dietary Fiber 0g 0%; Sugars 10g; Protein 1g; Vitamin A 0%; Vitamin C 0%; Calcium 0%; Iron 2% **Dietary Exchanges:** ½ Starch, ½ Fruit, ½ Fat **OR** 1 Carbohydrate, ½ Fat **Carbohydrate Choices:** 1

doughboy tip

These Austrian-inspired bars have a wonderful raspberry topping. Just be sure to pour the hot topping over the crust carefully, so it doesn't splash or spatter. The seedless raspberry preserves makes a pretty clear red topping. However, if you can't find seedless raspberry preserves, use raspberry jam or preserves with seeds.

Helpful Nutrition and Cooking Information

nutrition guidelines

The nutrition information can help you estimate how specific recipes contribute to your overall meal plan. The nutrition information with each recipe includes calories, fat, cholesterol, sodium, carbohydrate, dietary fiber, sugars, protein, vitamins A and C, calcium and iron.

Each recipe also lists Percent Daily Values (% DVs). The % DVs tell you how much the nutrients in one serving contribute to a 2,000-calorie diet. For example, if the % DV for total fat is 10%, this means one serving of this food contributes 10% of the total fat suggested for a person on 2,000 calories per day.

Dietary Exchanges and Carbohydrate Choices are included and are based on criteria set by the American Dietetic Association and the American Diabetes Association. If you are following a medically prescribed diet, consult your physician or registered dietitian about this nutrition information.

Recommended Intake for a Daily Diet of 2,000 Calories As Set by the Food and Drug Administration

Total Fat	Less than 65g
Saturated Fat	Less than 20g
Cholesterol	Less than 300mg
Sodium	Less than 2,400mg
Total Carbohydrate	300g
Dietary Fiber	25g

CRITERIA USED FOR CALCULATING NUTRITION

The first ingredient was used wherever a choice is given (such as ⅓ cup sour cream or plain yogurt).

The larger ingredient amount was used wherever a range is given (such as 3- to 3½-lb. cut-up broiler-fryer chicken).

The first serving number was used wherever a range is given (such as 4 to 6 servings).

"If desired" ingredients are not included, whether mentioned in the ingredient list or in the recipe directions as a suggestion (such as "Sprinkle with brown sugar, if desired").

Only the amount of a marinade or frying oil that is estimated to be absorbed by the food during preparation or cooking was calculated.

INGREDIENTS USED IN RECIPE TESTING AND NUTRITION CALCULATIONS

Ingredients used for testing represent those that the majority of consumers use in their homes: large eggs, 2% milk, 80%-lean ground beef, canned chicken broth and vegetable oil spread containing not less than 65% fat.

Fat-free, low-fat or low-sodium products were not used, unless otherwise indicated.

Solid vegetable shortening (not butter, margarine, nonstick cooking sprays or vegetable oil spread, as they can cause sticking problems) was used to grease pans, unless otherwise indicated.

EQUIPMENT USED IN RECIPE TESTING

We use equipment for testing that the majority of consumers use in their homes. If a specific piece of equipment (such as a wire whisk) is necessary for recipe success, it will be listed in the recipe.

Cookware and bakeware without nonstick coatings were used, unless otherwise indicated.

No dark-colored, black or insulated bakeware was used.

When a pan is specified in a recipe, a metal pan was used; a baking dish or glass pie pan means ovenproof glass was used.

An electric hand mixer was used for mixing only when mixer speeds are specified in the recipe directions. When a mixer speed is not given, a spoon or fork was used.

determining preparation times

The "Prep Time: minutes" at the beginning of each recipe serves as a guide for the time needed to make a recipe. The "Prep Time" is the active "hands on" preparation time. Whenever possible, active prep time is done simultaneously with other steps. The "(Ready in minutes/hours)" notation is added when a recipe requires additional time beyond the active prep time. For example, the "Ready in" time includes marinating, cooking, baking or grilling times as well as cooling, refrigerating or freezing times.

In establishing these times, the following specifics also have been used:

- The longest time in a cooking/baking range

- The shortest time for marinating ingredients

- No time is counted for heating the oven or grill

- The times listed are for the first cooking method if two methods are provided

Index

Note: Page numbers in *italics* are photographs.

Conversion Chart

volume

U.S. UNITS	CANADIAN METRIC	AUSTRALIAN METRIC
1/4 teaspoon	1 ml	1 ml
1/2 teaspoon	2 ml	2 ml
1 teaspoon	5 ml	5 ml
1 tablespoon	15 ml	20 ml
1/4 cup	50 ml	60 ml
1/3 cup	75 ml	80 ml
1/2 cup	125 ml	125 ml
2/3 cup	150 ml	170 ml
3/4 cup	175 ml	190 ml
1 cup	250 ml	250 ml
1 quart	1 liter	1 liter
1 1/2 quarts	1.5 liters	1.5 liters
2 quarts	2 liters	2 liters
2 1/2 quarts	2.5 liters	2.5 liters
3 quarts	3 liters	3 liters
4 quarts	4 liters	4 liters

weight

U.S. UNITS	CANADIAN METRIC	AUSTRALIAN METRIC
1 ounce	30 grams	30 grams
2 ounces	55 grams	60 grams
3 ounces	85 grams	90 grams
4 ounces (1/4 pound)	115 grams	125 grams
8 ounces (1/2 pound)	225 grams	225 grams
16 ounces (1 pound)	455 grams	500 grams
1 pound	455 grams	1/2 kilogram

measurements

INCHES	CENTIMETERS
1	2.5
2	5.0
3	7.5
4	10.0
5	12.5
6	15.0
7	17.5
8	20.5
9	23.0
10	25.5
11	28.0
12	30.5
13	33.0

temperatures

FAHRENHEIT	CELSIUS
32°	0°
212°	100°
250°	120°
275°	140°
300°	150°
325°	160°
350°	180°
375°	190°
400°	200°
425°	220°
450°	230°
475°	240°
500°	260°

Note: The recipes in this cookbook have not been developed or tested using metric measures. When converting recipes to metric, some variations in quality may be noted.

Pillsbury
Classic® Cookbooks

Send for a FREE Trial Issue of Pillsbury® Classic® Cookbooks

SAVE BIG DOUGH!

Past Issues

Wondering what to make for dinner? Looking for a special holiday meal? Just want a break from the routine? Get more than 40 recipes every **month from Pillsbury® Classic® Cookbooks and SAVE $32.93 off** the retail price!

Succeed in the kitchen!

Every thoroughly tested recipe includes a photo, prep time and cooking tips to make mealtime a snap. Recipes are easy to read and directions are easy to follow.

Stay healthy!

To assist you with any dietary concerns, every recipe comes with complete nutritional information, including calories, cholesterol, sodium content and more. Low-fat, easy-to-prepare recipes in every issue are clearly marked for busy, health-conscious cooks.

Subscribers benefit!

- Subscribers get their issues first—before the stores.
- Subscribers never miss an issue that is sold out.
- A subscription includes exclusive Bake-Off® Contest recipes.
- Subscribers save **68% off the regular supermarket price!**

To receive your **FREE** trial issue of Pillsbury® Classic® Cookbooks and an exclusive offer to subscribe, see order information on the back of this page.

Send in This Form to Receive a FREE Trial Issue of Pillsbury® Classic® Cookbooks

SAVE 68% OFF THE SUPERMARKET PRICE!

Past Issues

☐ **YES!** Please send me a free copy of the current issue of Pillsbury® Classic® Cookbooks and enter a subscription. If I decide to subscribe, I'll pay your invoice of only $14.95 for 11 additional issues, which is a savings of more than 68% off the supermarket price. If, after seeing the first issue, I decide not to subscribe, I'll return your invoice with "cancel" written on it. The free issue is mine to keep.

Send complete order form to:

Pillsbury® Classic® Cookbooks
P.O. Box 1908
Marion, OH 43306-8008

Name _____

Address_____Apt._____

City_____

State _____ZIP _____

Allow 6 to 8 weeks for delivery.
Offer good through 12/31/04.

APDM03

A47982

MFR COUPON **EXPIRES 12/31/04**

Save 75¢

when you buy any Pillsbury® Home Baked Classics® Dinner Rolls, Biscuits **OR** Sweet Rolls

A47982   0603

MFR COUPON **EXPIRES 12/31/04**

Save 50¢

when you buy any Pillsbury® Crusty French Loaf

A48073   0603

MFR COUPON **EXPIRES 12/31/04**

Save 50¢

when you buy Pillsbury® Refrigerated Pizza Crust

A48074   0603

MFR COUPON **EXPIRES 12/31/04**

Save 50¢

when you buy Pillsbury® Refrigerated Pie Crust (Excludes any frozen pie crust)

A48075   0603

MFR COUPON **EXPIRES 12/31/04**

Save 75¢

when you buy any Pillsbury® Crescent Dinner Rolls

A48076   0603

MFR COUPON **EXPIRES 12/31/04**

Save 75¢

when you buy any size/variety Pillsbury® Grands!® Biscuits

A48077   0603

MFR COUPON   EXPIRES 12/31/04

Save 50¢
when you buy Pillsbury®
Crusty French Loaf

Void if altered, copied, sold, purchased, transferred, exchanged or where prohibited or restricted by law. One coupon per purchase of specified product(s). Good only in USA, APOs & FPOs. **CONSUMER:** No other coupon may be used with this coupon. Consumer pays any sales tax. **RETAILER:** General Mills will reimburse you for the face value of this coupon plus 8¢ if submitted in compliance with our redemption policy. Copy available upon request. Cash value 1/100 cent. Send to GENERAL MILLS, P.O. Box 880588, El Paso, TX 88588-0588 or an authorized clearinghouse.

A48073   0603

387102

5   18000 11250   5   (8100)0 38710

MFR COUPON   EXPIRES 12/31/04

Save 75¢
when you buy any Pillsbury® Home Baked Classics® Dinner Rolls, Biscuits **OR** Sweet Rolls

Void if altered, copied, sold, purchased, transferred, exchanged or where prohibited or restricted by law. One coupon per purchase of specified product(s). Good only in USA, APOs & FPOs. **CONSUMER:** No other coupon may be used with this coupon. Consumer pays any sales tax. **RETAILER:** General Mills will reimburse you for the face value of this coupon plus 8¢ if submitted in compliance with our redemption policy. Copy available upon request. Cash value 1/100 cent. Send to GENERAL MILLS, P.O. Box 880588, El Paso, TX 88588-0588 or an authorized clearinghouse.

A47982   0603

386369

5   18000 55075   8   (8100)0 38636

MFR COUPON   EXPIRES 12/31/04

Save 50¢
when you buy Pillsbury®
Refrigerated Pie Crust
(Excludes any frozen pie crust)

Void if altered, copied, sold, purchased, transferred, exchanged or where prohibited or restricted by law. One coupon per purchase of specified product(s). Good only in USA, APOs & FPOs. **CONSUMER:** No other coupon may be used with this coupon. Consumer pays any sales tax. **RETAILER:** General Mills will reimburse you for the face value of this coupon plus 8¢ if submitted in compliance with our redemption policy. Copy available upon request. Cash value 1/100 cent. Send to GENERAL MILLS, P.O. Box 880588, El Paso, TX 88588-0588 or an authorized clearinghouse.

A48075   0603

387094

5   18000 10250   6   (8100)0 38709

MFR COUPON   EXPIRES 12/31/04

Save 50¢
when you buy Pillsbury®
Refrigerated Pizza Crust

Void if altered, copied, sold, purchased, transferred, exchanged or where prohibited or restricted by law. One coupon per purchase of specified product(s). Good only in USA, APOs & FPOs. **CONSUMER:** No other coupon may be used with this coupon. Consumer pays any sales tax. **RETAILER:** General Mills will reimburse you for the face value of this coupon plus 8¢ if submitted in compliance with our redemption policy. Copy available upon request. Cash value 1/100 cent. Send to GENERAL MILLS, P.O. Box 880588, El Paso, TX 88588-0588 or an authorized clearinghouse.

A48074   0603

387110

5   18000 10350   3   (8100)0 38711

MFR COUPON   EXPIRES 12/31/04

Save 75¢
when you buy any
size/variety Pillsbury® Grands!® Biscuits

Void if altered, copied, sold, purchased, transferred, exchanged or where prohibited or restricted by law. One coupon per purchase of specified product(s). Good only in USA, APOs & FPOs. **CONSUMER:** No other coupon may be used with this coupon. Consumer pays any sales tax. **RETAILER:** General Mills will reimburse you for the face value of this coupon plus 8¢ if submitted in compliance with our redemption policy. Copy available upon request. Cash value 1/100 cent. Send to GENERAL MILLS, P.O. Box 880588, El Paso, TX 88588-0588 or an authorized clearinghouse.

A48077   0603

387045

5   18000 15075   0   (8100)0 38704

MFR COUPON   EXPIRES 12/31/04

Save 75¢
when you buy any
Pillsbury® Crescent Dinner Rolls

Void if altered, copied, sold, purchased, transferred, exchanged or where prohibited or restricted by law. One coupon per purchase of specified product(s). Good only in USA, APOs & FPOs. **CONSUMER:** No other coupon may be used with this coupon. Consumer pays any sales tax. **RETAILER:** General Mills will reimburse you for the face value of this coupon plus 8¢ if submitted in compliance with our redemption policy. Copy available upon request. Cash value 1/100 cent. Send to GENERAL MILLS, P.O. Box 880588, El Paso, TX 88588-0588 or an authorized clearinghouse.

A48076   0603

387052

5   18000 15075   0   (8100)0 38705